The Treatment and Rehabilitation
of Offenders

The Treatment and Rehabilitation of Offenders

IAIN CROW

SAGE Publications
Los Angeles • London • New Delhi • Singapore

ISBN: 978-0-7619-6038-6 (hbk)
ISBN: 978-0-7619-6039-3 (pbk)
© Iain Crow 2001
First published 2001
Reprinted 2003, 2004, 2007

SAGE Publications Ltd
1 Oliver's Yard
55 City Road
London EC1Y 1SP

SAGE Publications Inc
2455 Teller Road
Thousand Oaks, California 91320

SAGE Publications India Pvt Ltd.
B1/I1 Mohan Cooperative Industrial Area
Mathura Road, New Delhi 110 044
India

SAGE Publications Asia-Pacific Pte Ltd
33 Pekin Street #02-01
Far East Square
Singapore 048763

British Library Cataloguing in Publication data
A catalogue record for this book is available from the British Library

Typeset by M Rules, Southwark, London

CONTENTS

ACKNOWLEDGEMENTS

Although this book reflects my own interests and concerns, because of its origins in a university course, I have drawn heavily on other publications in writing it, rather than on original research. References and quotations are duly cited, but I must acknowledge my general indebtedness to the work of others in making the book possible. I am especially grateful to those who have come as guest speakers at various times and talked to students about their work. They include Manjit Seale, Sue Hermiston, Andrew Smith, Darryl Fisher, Janice Brown and Liz Burgess (all of the South Yorkshire Probation Service), Dave Goddard, Louisa Deakin and Ian Whittaker (of the Sheffield Court Diversion Scheme), and Paul Bliss and Christine Milton of Phoenix House, Sheffield. Their contribution to the course and to this book has been invaluable.

I am also grateful to several colleagues for their helpful comments and suggestions at various times, especially Michael Cavadino, Jason Ditton and Paul Wiles. I would also like to record my appreciation of the comments received from an unknown reader to whom Sage Publications sent the book prior to final drafting. I have incorporated many of the suggestions received, which I hope have improved the text somewhat. However, the responsibility for what is in these pages is mine alone.

Finally, the book would not have been written at all were it not for the students who opted to take the course on which it is based. For their forbearance and patience (particularly those who took the course during the first couple of years), and their encouraging remarks I thank them, and dedicate this book to them and to those who may follow after them.

FOREWORD

Shortly after joining the Centre for Criminological and Legal Research at the University of Sheffield I took part in meetings with colleagues about establishing a new degree in Law and Criminology. As discussions proceeded it was put to me that I should run a course on the treatment of offenders. I think this was seen as a reasonable suggestion, since not long before I had come from heading the Research Unit at the National Association for the Care and Resettlement of Offenders (NACRO). My initial thought was to point out that neither NACRO nor I were really into treatment as such. However, I decided on further reflection that it could be rather interesting for me (and perhaps, with luck, for the students) to examine a perspective on dealing with offenders with which I was not entirely in sympathy, but one which had dominated much of my early life as a researcher. As plans for the degree and the Treatment of Offenders course proceeded, two things happened. The first was that I became more and more involved in discovering what was happening in areas that I had not paid much attention to for too long. Second, I became aware that, although there was a considerable body of literature and information, to even begin to cover some of the topics for a course of this nature involved referring to a very large number of sources. In short, there was no text to which I could direct students. I therefore set about compiling notes for the students which attempted to bring together as much material as possible in what I hoped would be a reasonably cogent and enlightening manner. Having done this, the notion of producing the book which I felt the students needed soon followed, and the idea was strengthened by the positive responses of the students concerned and of others.

But one does not write a book for a single degree course. Ideas of trying to treat and rehabilitate offenders went out of fashion for some years, with more emphasis being placed on punishment and retribution. Nonetheless, treatment and rehabilitation have continued to play a role in criminal justice in the UK and elsewhere. Furthermore, there have been important developments in treatment and its evaluation in recent years, with a resurgence of interest following indications that some things do 'work'. There is also a growing belief that a penal policy devoid of attempts to offer adequate treatment and rehabilitation opportunities will be inadequate, ineffective and unjust.

This book cannot claim to offer a comprehensive coverage of such an extensive topic as the treatment and rehabilitation of offenders. What I have tried to do is to represent the main elements of such a topic by presenting the book in four parts. The first part looks at the concepts of treatment and rehabilitation and their application. Consideration is given to the development of treatment and rehabilitation during the twentieth century, to the rise and fall of the 'treatment model', to the methods for evaluating the effectiveness of treatment and related initiatives, and recent developments in attempting to identify 'what works'. The second part of the book looks at the two main institutions that have been concerned with treatment and rehabilitation, the Prison Service and the Probation Service, with an all too limited acknowledgement of the role played by non-statutory agencies. The third part of the book tries to bring the more general issues to life by looking at treatment and rehabilitation in relation to particular groups of people and the way they are dealt with. This inevitably involved having to select groups to focus on. The three groups chosen – sex offenders, the mentally disordered, and drug misusers – were selected for various reasons. They are very much at what one might see as the 'sharp' end of treatment and rehabilitation, in that they are challenging, both to those who work with them and to society in general. As a consequence they can at times attract much public attention. These three groups also tend to be characterised by much ambivalence and ambiguity; they present dilemmas about rights and responsibilities, and about the limits of intervention. For this reason they are a good basis for student discussion. In the end, however, there is bound to be an arbitrary element to the selection of particular groups (young people and female offenders are also briefly considered in Chapter 1), and I make no claim to have necessarily chosen the 'right' ones. Finally, the book ends with a brief consideration of the social context within which treatment and rehabilitation take place.

Just as the book cannot cover all aspects of the treatment and rehabilitation of offenders, neither can it present an exhaustive discussion of the topics relevant to treatment and rehabilitation that are covered. There are, for example, various sources that can be consulted to find out about the development of criminology and criminological theory, about research methods in general, about sexual offences, mentally disordered offenders, the Probation Service and so on. Therefore, while some background to the topic under consideration is necessary, the main focus of each chapter is on treatment and rehabilitation, whether the role of the Probation and Prison Services in treatment and rehabilitation, or the treatment and rehabilitation of sex offenders and drug misusers. Nonetheless, because the book covers a lot of ground there is a danger that the coverage of topics is too general and I am painfully aware of how much I have had to leave out. I hope, however, that there is sufficient material in each chapter to provide an adequate introduction to the issues, and to point students and others towards further reading.

Then and Now: 'Old' Treatment Model and 'New' Treatment Approaches

I am conscious of the fact that while some of the issues related to the treatment and rehabilitation of offenders have developed over a long period of time – in effect over the best part of the last century or more – developments can also take place very rapidly; they have done so during the time I have been writing this book. In writing about treatment and rehabilitation one is attempting to reflect both long term and short term developments. Let me refer first to the broader, longer term development of notions of the treatment, rehabilitation and reformation of the offender. Prior to the twentieth century (as is mentioned in Chapters 2 and 5) such notions often had a moral and evangelical dimension (Garland, 1985: 8). During the twentieth century this gave way to what I would call the 'old' treatment model, also sometimes referred to as the 'rehabilitative ideal'. As Chapter 2 of the book describes, this was a paradigm of how to deal with offenders that reached its highest point during the period following the Second World War. It was characterised to a large extent by its curative nature and by its tendency to regard the offender as a passive recipient of intervention. During the mid-1970s this model collapsed in a spectacular manner, giving way to the doctrine that 'nothing works', which exerted its influence almost to the end of the century.[1] I say 'almost' because the last few years have seen a revival of the notion that treatment and rehabilitation initiatives are worthwhile. This has largely developed under the auspices of what is generally referred to as the 'what works' movement.

Just as 'nothing works' was based on the apparent ineffectiveness of interventions in reducing recidivism, the 'what works' approach justifies itself, as the phrase suggests, largely in terms of effectiveness, as measured by reducing offending. This is not unreasonable, but recent years have also witnessed a 'new' treatment approach, which has other characteristics apart from reduced reconviction rates. This new treatment approach rejects the determinist and positivist assumptions of the 'old' treatment model. There is an element of it that is 'rights based' in that it recognises the rights of both victim and offender, and the right of society at large to be protected from the impact of crime. In some ways the 'new' approach harks back to classical criminological precepts, based on the reasoning person, and therefore to the 'voluntaristic process of reform' (Garland, 1985: 15). It emphasises the exercise of choice and responsibility for one's own actions. The offender must accept the responsibility to acquire the necessary skills to control his or her behaviour. The agencies and agents of this new model are seen as facilitators and managers of change, rather than caseworkers or some kind of paramedic. It is true that, in line with what have become established 'what works' principles (See Chapter 4), much of the work of the 'new' treatment model revolves around offender reasoning and cognition, stressing risk assessment and risk management, outcomes and evaluation. But it also places the treatment of individual offenders within a wider context of social needs, recognising that rehabilitation is a two way process which has to involve offender and society, replacing social exclusion with reintegration (which is the basis for Chapter 10). We are still a long way from achieving such an ideal, but the potential for developing a 'new' treatment approach became more realisable as the end of the twentieth century approached.

In contrast, at certain times developments have been very rapid. For example, the mid-1970s constituted a period of rapid change, when the rehabilitative ideal gave way to the view that 'nothing works' and this entailed a rapid reappraisal of criminal justice policy and practice, and criminological thinking. It is always hard, and perhaps rather rash, to reflect on the time at which one is writing. However, the time when this book was written was also one of considerable change. Some changes had been in progress for some time. The responses to drug misuse, for example, seldom stay the same for very long and have not done so throughout my professional career. The 1990s saw growing media attention and public concern directed towards sex offenders and mentally disordered offenders, and this has resulted in responses from the Government of the day. The Probation Service and the nature of probation work have changed considerably in recent years, and continue to do so. Inevitably the election of a new Government in the United Kingdom in 1997 had an impact on these changes, with the new administration announcing the implementation of policies that it had promised in opposition (e.g. drug treatment and testing orders), and announcing reviews of existing policies, such as in the area of mental health. This means that, in certain respects, this book will almost certainly be out of date soon after the writing of it is completed, and the reader is cautioned to expect this to some extent. In a sense this does not matter too much; attempts to deal with offenders are always likely to change, for political reasons and because of new developments. The aim of this book is to chronicle some of these attempts in the hope that this will inspire the student to inquire further into what happens in the future. I have tried to ensure that the most recent developments at the time of writing have been recognised. If this book prompts a reader to find out more about what has happened since, then it will have achieved at least one of my ambitions for it.

Note

1   The end of the 'nothing works' doctrine could be said to have achieved official recognition in the summer of 1998 when the Home Office Research and Statistics Directorate published a major review of criminal justice policy which started by saying that, 'It was not true that "nothing works"' (Nuttall et al., 1998: 1). This is somewhat ironic since, as discussed in Chapter Two, the Home office Research Unit was instrumental in undertaking research from the 1950s onwards which led to the demise of the treatment model and the rise of the 'nothing works' doctrine.

The mood and temper of the public in regard to the treatment of crime and criminals is one of the most unfailing tests of the civilisation of any country. A calm and dispassionate recognition of the rights of the accused, and even of convicted criminals, against the state, a constant heart-searching by all charged with the duty of punishment, a desire and eagerness to rehabilitate in the world of industry all those who have paid their dues in the hard coinage of punishment, tireless efforts towards the discovery of curative and regenerating processes, and an unfaltering faith that there is a treasure, if you can only find it, in the heart of every man [sic] – these are the symbols which in the treatment of crime and criminals mark and measure the stored-up strength of a nation, and are the sign and proof of the living virtue in it.

Winston Churchill
Home Secretary
20 July 1910

PART I

THE CONCEPT OF TREATMENT

A SUITABLE CASE FOR TREATMENT?

I merely wish to suggest that we should treat the criminal as we treat a man suffering from plague. Each is a public danger, each must have his liberty curtailed until he has ceased to be a danger. But the man suffering from plague is an object of sympathy and commiseration whereas the criminal is an object of execration. This is quite irrational. And it is because of this difference of attitude that our prisons are so much less successful in curing criminal tendencies than our hospitals are in curing disease. (Bertrand Russell, 1925: 62)

This chapter looks first at various terms that are often used in dealing with offenders, and then goes on to consider the derivation of the notion of treatment in relation to crime and offenders. It looks at how the notion of treatment relates to criminological theory, and at the different forms which treatment and rehabilitation can take. Next, consideration is given to how treatment and rehabilitation may be differentially applied to different types of offender, especially how attitudes and provision may vary depending on differences of age and gender. The later part of the chapter considers some of the ambiguities and conflicting expectations that arise regarding the treatment and rehabilitation of offenders, and finally some of the important ethical issues that are raised by the treatment of offenders are covered.

Concepts of Treatment and Rehabilitation

In many ways the quotation at the beginning of this chapter encapsulates the treatment view of offenders. It highlights the belief that the offender is no more to blame for his or her condition than the patient suffering from a disease. At the time when Russell was writing it would have been regarded as a liberal and humanitarian sentiment; a statement which was progressive and even radical in its outlook. However, this view had considerable shortcomings.

It may be somewhat predictable to begin with a consideration of what is meant by treatment, but it would be a serious omission not to consider the meaning of the term, and related concepts. In the context of dealing with offenders, 'treatment' has become very much associated with medicine, and as a result has acquired a series of overtones. For example, it tends to be associated with passivity: treatment is often thought of as something done *to* someone, usually by a person who occupies a position of expertise, authority and a certain amount of power. It is also often assumed that the medical definition of treatment is a unitary concept, whereas, as Johnstone (1996: 5) points out, medicine is a diverse field in which treatment may take many forms. Probably the closest connections between criminology and medicine historically are to do with the treatment of the mentally disordered, and in this respect treatment has involved social and moral management as much as pharmaceutical, surgical or other medical techniques.

Treatment is not only a medical term. It can also be used to refer to the way we treat people. Thus, for example, Rule 2(iii) of the Prison Rules states that, 'At all times the *treatment* of prisoners shall be such as to encourage their self-respect and a sense of personal responsibility' (emphasis added). Looked at in the context of treating with people or institutions (as in making a treaty) what comes to the fore is negotiation and, while power is never far distant in negotiations, what is involved in such a situation is two parties working from positions of mutual recognition of each other's position. So treatment not only has specific meanings, but carries with it diverse connotations.

In criminology, treatment has traditionally been linked with ideas about the nature of criminality (about which more later), and with an approach to dealing with crime which has usually been contrasted with retribution and punishment. Those in favour of treatment have tended to be seen as of a liberal persuasion, perhaps even as 'do-gooders'. Like many stereotypes this is an oversimplification, but because of these associations treatment is often linked to other terms, notably 'reform', 'rehabilitation' and 'resettlement'. What these terms have in common is the notion of change, even if the change is a restorative one returning someone to a position in society which they formerly held. A dictionary definition of rehabilitation refers to restoring 'former privileges or reputation or proper condition' (*Concise Oxford Dictionary*). The title of this book refers to rehabilitation as well as treatment, and this is because I see them as two parts of a connected process; without rehabilitation the process is incomplete. In the archetypal popular crime thriller the dénouement is followed by the villain getting his or her just deserts and being hauled off for chastisement. In the real world that is not the end of the story. The criminal completes his or her sentence, and then what? A wise parent knows that, however they deal with an erring child, if the family is to flourish some restorative process is necessary. Hence in Greek drama and mythology punishment is followed by expiation, and in a more recent criminological theory shame needs to be accompanied by re-integration (Braithwaite, 1989). We neglect the second part of the process at our peril.

There has a been a distinct shift in the ways in which terms such as treatment and rehabilitation have been used in criminology and criminal justice over the years. Indeed there have also been changes in the *extent* to which they have been used. Reading Government White Papers, texts and articles about crime and offenders produced between the end of the Second World War and the early 1970s one finds frequent allusions to the treatment of offenders, with the term 'treatment' being used to cover almost any way of dealing with offenders.[1] Treatment and rehabilitation were widely regarded at that time as desirable and worthwhile objectives, and initiatives that hoped to attract political and financial backing sought to espouse these objectives. After the 1970s criminal justice discourse changed significantly. Other considerations came to the fore, and the application of the term 'treatment' to offenders became more likely to be reserved for certain specific forms of intervention, usually with a clear diagnostic or clinical purpose. These other considerations have been described elsewhere (Cavadino et al., 1999: Ch. 1) and have reflected a concern with prevention, retribution, efficiency (managerialism), and restoration. During much of the 1990s, for example, the language of discourse became that of penalties and punishment (even when these were non-custodial in nature), of just deserts and making amends. In part this book is about how and why this happened, and the implications that follow from it. In general, however, I intend to adopt a broad, but not limitless, definition of treatment as any form of intervention that is designed to alter the way that offenders think, feel or behave. Within this broadly based conception, the rights and responsibilities of the parties involved are an important component, and I regard the processes of treatment and rehabilitation as requiring the active participation of all parties, rather than a relationship between an active donor and a passive recipient.

The Treatment Paradigm

In order to understand the origins of the treatment paradigm in criminology it is necessary to refer to its basis in sociology, where it is linked with positivism, and in particular with an organic view of society. This view is most closely associated with the early sociologist Herbert Spencer (1820–1903), and from his organicism developed social Darwinism, which transferred Darwin's notions of the survival of the fittest to the social and economic sphere. The sociologist Emile Durkheim also employed the organic analogy, in which the whole organism was described as constituting a unity greater than the sum of its constituent parts (as in *The Elementary Forms of the Religious Life*, 1912, and to some extent in his earlier work *Suicide*, 1897), although Durkheim was more circumspect than Spencer in his application of the organic analogy. Durkheim propounded a functionalist approach which suggested that we can best understand social structures by comparing them with biological organisms in which the organs need to work together.

This means that all the parts are *essential*, they are *interdependent*, they perform a *function* for the whole, and work as an *integrated* whole. Any part of the whole that does not fulfil these criteria is dysfunctional, and therefore in need of treatment. This fitted well with societies that believed that everything was ordered and that everything and everyone had their place in this order. This conception of society is, however, a very limited one. For one thing it is a largely static conception which is constrained in its ability to explain social change and conflict. It is also a determinist view in that individuals' capacities for independent action and interpretation are restricted, and it follows from this that since people cannot help what is wrong with them and have limited choice for action the scope for blame is also limited. The solution, where something or someone is dysfunctional, is to rectify or cure the malfunctioning part.

It is easy to see how crime and criminals are defined as dysfunctional for a healthy society and in need of treatment, hence the medical analogy. Such an approach also tends to focus on the individual as the element that needs to be dealt with and cured. The implication is that the way to solve the crime problem is to discover effective ways of treating offenders: the need to deal with social problems is thereby avoided. However, this is not to say that it is not worth making a distinction between the treatment *of* individuals and treating people *as* individuals: although the treatment approach focuses on the treatment of the individual, it is all too easy to treat offenders as if they were a homogeneous group and neglect their individuality.

Within criminology the development of a treatment approach has its roots in the Lombrosian school of positivism. This stands in contrast to what is generally referred to as the 'classical' school of criminology, commonly associated with the writings of Beccaria (1963). The classical school tended to see the offender in strictly legal terms as a rational actor, and consequently to focus on deterrence and retribution as the twin objectives of criminal justice (Garland, 1985: 16). The idea of reform only developed later as a result of attempts to apply scientific principles to ever more fields of human endeavour. This resulted in greater attention being given to the offender. Increasingly,

> Criminals are presented as individuals to be pitied, cared for and, if possible, reclaimed. . . . since what was being presented was not just a more civilised or liberal penality, but also a more preventative, reformative and efficacious form of control. (Garland, 1985: 27)

But this was not a simple and clear cut line of development. For one thing an extreme determinism, based on physiologically predisposed criminal types, would suggest that there is little possibility of change, and therefore little point in treatment. As Garland makes clear, the form of positivism initiated by Lombroso and his followers only developed into the treatment model of the twentieth century after much modification (Garland, 1997: 31–34).

Although the ideal of seeing the treatment and rehabilitation of offenders as a major part of the answer to crime has its roots in an organic model and a certain stream of criminological thinking, the organic model has given rise to some specific theories about crime and offending. For example, the work of Cloward and Ohlin (1960) on delinquency as a response to the lack of legitimate opportunity stems in part from the organic school, by way of the functionalism of Robert Merton. At the same time, while some theories about crime and criminality are concerned with the nature of society, others are biological or psychological (Hollin, 1996b: Chapter 2). Theories about what causes crime and offending give rise to hypotheses about what might be done to reduce them. Consequently there are many ideas about what kinds of intervention are needed. Some of these forms of intervention are referred to as treatment. In a later chapter we will encounter what are termed cognitive behavioural programmes for offenders, which are based on psychological theories of social learning. Some forms of intervention are not concerned with individual offenders at all, but more concerned with social change. What follows from this is that when we encounter an attempt to do something about crime and offending, whether it be directed at the individual offender, his or her community, or the wider society, we need to ask what theory lies behind the intervention. Although this may sound obvious, it is often overlooked when various forms of intervention are being evaluated. I shall return to this theme in Chapter 3, where more consideration is given to the evaluation of treatment and rehabilitation.

Types of Treatment and Rehabilitation

The adoption of a treatment paradigm in dealing with offenders means that some forms of intervention have been literally medical or quasi-medical in nature, involving various forms of therapy. But many other forms of intervention have gone under the broad heading of treatment and rehabilitation. In order to give some idea of the range of possible interventions which can be encompassed by this heading, I will briefly mention some of the most common types, although not all are clearly and easily defined. Similar types of intervention may go under different titles at different times, depending on the latest thinking in criminal justice policy.

The first form of intervention is that which is **medical** in nature. This is a wide ranging category, although the use of surgical attempts to alter behaviour through such procedures as lobotomy has now largely (but not entirely) disappeared. Medical treatment has also included the use of drugs, such as Antabuse for alcoholism, and what is referred to as 'chemical castration' for sex offenders. More commonly, drugs are used in conjunction with some other form of treatment. In the context of offenders medical interventions most commonly take the form of **psychiatric** treatment, such as psychotherapy. Johnstone (1996) outlines two main forms of psychiatric approach, the medical-somatic approach, which tends to be modelled on treatment in physical medicine, and the social-psychological approach, consisting of 'the use of environmental, organisational and personal influences' (Johnstone, 1996: 21). According to Johnstone, psychotherapy falls somewhere between these two approaches, and consists 'not of physical tinkering, but of talk – albeit a special type of talk – which the therapist uses as an instrument of personal influence' (Johnstone, 1996: 20). Closely related to the medical profession are clinical psychologists, and various psychological approaches to the treatment of offenders have been used for many years and are currently attracting much interest.[2]

Less medical in nature, but nonetheless based on a treatment paradigm are **casework**, which has been used by social workers and probation officers for many years, and **counselling** techniques. These are usually based on a one-to-one relationship. Other forms of intervention involve **group work**, including role play and encounter groups – especially likely to be found in therapeutic communities – which will be referred to again later. Some forms of intervention focus on the development of **skills**, such as cognitive skills, social skills, parenting skills and anger management, while others centre on promoting certain **activities**. Examples of the latter include motor projects, arts projects and projects featuring sports and other forms of physical activity. Other types of treatment are directed at **offences** and **offending**, either general offending behaviour or specific offences, such as sex offences, driving offences or offences of violence. Last, but by no means finally, there is a wide variety of interventions directed towards the **social re-integration** of offenders. These include schemes which aim to provide offenders with accommodation, education, training and employment. They are more concerned with rehabilitation and resettlement than with what is traditionally regarded as treatment, but they are included here partly because of the linkage between treatment and rehabilitation made earlier, and also because such schemes are usually concerned with the needs of individuals rather than with the underlying problems of high unemployment, inadequate housing and poor educational or training provision *per se*.

This is by no means a complete list or a full description of the efforts made at treating and rehabilitating offenders. More will be encountered as the book proceeds. Nor are the various approaches to offenders mentioned above mutually exclusive. For example, schemes directed at enhancing skills may use group work as a means of achieving their ends. Indeed, many programmes use more than one technique or approach and are therefore **multi-modal**. This can lead to complications regarding the aims, delivery and evaluation of such programmes, but it is often thought that using a combination of approaches may be more successful than using a single form of intervention on its own, and there is some evidence to support this (McGuire and Priestley, 1995: 18). The various forms of treatment and rehabilitation could be characterised in several ways, depending on whether they are individual or group centred, offence or offender directed, and so on. It is tempting to develop a typology of offender treatment and rehabilitation. But it is not particularly useful to try to cram such a wide diversity of activity into an ill-fitting and inadequate straitjacket, perhaps resulting merely in stereotyping different approaches.

This book does not intend to adopt a narrow, purely medical, approach to the treatment of offenders, but the wide variety of activities that are sometimes covered by the term needs to be constantly borne in mind. It is useful to define some limits if the term is to retain meaning. For example, this book will not, by and large, consider crime prevention initiatives and community safety measures. These may incorporate elements of treatment, and one way of preventing crime is the reduction of re-offending by treating and rehabilitating offenders, but clearly there are limits to what can be meaningfully covered by the terms 'treatment' and 'rehabilitation'. It is also useful to distinguish between the sentences that offenders are given and particular types of treatment that those sentences may involve; more will be said about this in the next chapter.

Types of Offender

Given that treatment and rehabilitation cover many diverse forms of intervention, are these directed at all offenders, or are they associated with certain groups of offenders? There has been a change in the answer to this question over the years, but two important distinctions have held for many years, based on age and gender.

Age

The first is the distinction between young people and adults. Although treatment has been applied to offenders of all ages, where young offenders are concerned there has tended to be more emphasis on treatment than on punishment – at least until recent years. This has happened for a variety of reasons. One is that the young are regarded as less culpable,

and therefore more deserving of treatment than punishment. Because
young people are regarded as being at a formative stage they are also
likely to be seen as more amenable to change, and treatment as more
likely to produce results. However, treatment has only been one strand
in the distinction between the way young people and adults are dealt
with. There has also been more emphasis on training for young offenders, most clearly epitomised by the borstal system, abolished by the
Criminal Justice Act 1982, which brought an almost public-school
approach to the way young offenders were dealt with. This too was
phrased in treatment terminology, borstal training being described as
suitable for young offenders 'who need a longer period of remedial
treatment than that available in detention centres' and as 'designed to
achieve recovery from established criminal habits' (Home Office, 1971:
para. 108). The treatment of young offenders also tended to be couched
in terms of 'welfare'. Welfare in this context usually meant a social work
response to young people which regarded their welfare and well-being
as having priority over a judicial response. This was based on the argument that offending is only one aspect of some young people's
underlying personal, family and social problems. But treatment, training and welfare have been intermingled components of responses to
young offenders, and there has often been fierce debate between the
courts on the one hand, and social workers and child psychiatrists on
the other, about who should have responsibility for dealing with young
offenders.[3] It is also worth recalling that corporal punishment in borstals
was only abolished in 1967. On the whole, however, while views have
differed as to the means to be employed when dealing with young
offenders, for much of the twentieth century the concern of policy
makers and practitioners has been with how best to influence the development of the young and move them away from crime and criminal
influences.

   During the 1980s the use of treatment for young offenders took on a
new lease of life and a new meaning. A major plank of policy was the
introduction of Intermediate Treatment (IT). This was developed as a
more intensive form of intervention than ordinary supervision orders,
which could be made for up to three years, with the young person being
supervised by a local authority social worker or a probation officer.
Intermediate Treatment could be included as part of a supervision order
with a requirement that the young person take part in quite intensive
programmes of activities. IT was introduced by the Children and Young
Persons Act 1969, and was at first used for a wide variety of young
people. But in 1983 the Department of Health and Social Security (as it
was then), which had overall responsibility for matters relating to young
people, issued a circular (LAC 3/83) that made funding available for
schemes which used IT as a means of diverting young people from local
authority care and custodial institutions. Thus IT became targeted on

what were known as 'heavy end' young offenders at risk of a custodial sentence. As a consequence of this, and a general concern to reduce the use of custody for young people, the number of juveniles receiving custodial sentences in 1988 was less than 42 per cent of the number in 1981 (Newburn, 1997: 643), although other factors, such as a decline in the number of young males, also played a part in this reduction (Farrington, 1992). During the 1990s, however, there was a marked change, fanned by media coverage of certain high profile cases, and a shift in Government thinking during 1993. This was the year when the then Home Secretary, Michael Howard announced a major change in Government policy which led, amongst other things, to more emphasis being placed on young offenders receiving their 'just deserts'.[4]

One indication of this shift in attitudes is the law on *doli incapax*. The age of criminal responsibility is fixed at different ages in different countries. In England and Wales it has been the age of ten since the Children and Young Persons Act 1963, but there has been a presumption that young people between the ages of 10 and 13 cannot be held fully responsible for their actions, unless it can be proved otherwise. This is the principle known as *doli incapax*: incapable of criminal intent. Shortly after coming to power in May 1997 the Labour Government announced its intention of abolishing this presumption, which it did under the provisions of the Crime and Disorder Act 1998. Although the principle did not attract as much attention as some of the more lurid stories about supposedly out-of-control youngsters, its abolition was a signal that henceforth the treatment of children would be more akin to that of their older counterparts.

Gender

Another important distinction in the treatment of offenders is that which exists between male and female offenders. This is in part related to the fact that there are far fewer female offenders in the criminal justice system than male offenders. One consequence of this is that the women who are dealt with by the criminal justice system tend to be seen as unusual and more deviant than other women. In their work *The Female Offender*, Lombroso and Ferrero studied the 'criminal type in women and its atavistic origin' (Chapter 8), and concluded that women were less predisposed to criminality than men, but that this in itself made them distinctive, and that more criminality would be found amongst women as civilisation progressed:

> We have now got to the reason why criminality increases among women with the march of civilisation. The female criminal is a kind of occasional delinquent, presenting few characteristics of degeneration, little dulness,

&c., but tending to multiply in proportion to her opportunities for evil-doing; . . . In short, the female criminal is of less typical aspect than the male because she is less essentially criminal. But it cannot be denied that when depravity in woman is profound, then the law by which the type bears the brand of criminality asserts itself in spite of all restraint. (Lombroso and Ferrero, 1895: 111–112)

Although women are to be found working in the criminal justice agencies as lawyers, magistrates, clerks, judges, police officers, probation officers and prison officers, the system as a whole is still very much male dominated, and tends to be coloured by male perceptions of women and how they should, or should not, behave. There is also much ambivalence about how female offenders are viewed, and consequently how they should be dealt with (Heidensohn, 1996; Cavadino and Dignan, 1997: 280). On the one hand there may be a tendency to see women as less threatening than male offenders, and because of this and their nurturing role a 'chivalrous' attitude may be adopted. On the other hand, because society may be more shocked by women who step out-side the conventional stereotypes of what women should be like, the ones who do get into trouble are liable to be regarded as particularly 'bad', and as more deserving of reprobation. There has been some debate about whether female offenders are dealt with more harshly or more leniently than male offenders (Walker, 1994). Comparing like cases as far as possible, it is at least clear that there are differences in what happens to male and female offenders. Females are more likely to be cautioned (Hedderman and Hough, 1994; Home Office, 1999), less likely to be fined (Hedderman and Gelsthorpe, 1997: Part 1), more likely to get probation, but less likely to get a community service order and less likely to get a custodial sentence (Moxon, 1988; Hedderman, 1991; Home Office, 1999). There are also particular areas of concern, such as the disproportionate number of women who are fined for TV licence evasion (Walker and Wall, 1997; Pantazis and Gordon, 1997), and sub-sequently default on payment of the fine, resulting in some cases in a prison sentence. Furthermore, although women are on the whole less likely to get a prison sentence it is often pointed out that conditions in prison can be more difficult for female prisoners. For one thing there are fewer establishments catering for women, so they have a greater chance of being further from home, a matter of concern given that an estimated 55 per cent of the women in prison have a child under the age of 16 (Home Office, 1999). In addition, educational and training provision has in the past favoured those things which enhance the traditional female domestic role (cooking and sewing) rather than skills that equip women for careers where they can be independent (Heidensohn, 1989: 103–104; Hamlyn, 2000: 2).

Of particular relevance for the topic of this book is the tendency for women offenders to be regarded as mentally disturbed rather than bad, and therefore in need of psychiatric treatment (Cavadino and Dignan, 1997: 286). In an in-depth study of 129 male and female offenders Allen concluded that

> A woman appearing before the criminal court is about twice as likely as a man to be dealt with by psychiatric rather than penal means. In the first place, psychiatric considerations are more likely to influence the verdict of the court . . . . In the second place, if convicted of a crime, she is also more likely than a man to be ordered to receive psychiatric treatment instead of a normal penalty. (Allen, 1987: xi)

Heidensohn explains the discrepancy in terms of the treatment model's focus on the individual offender:

> The individualisation approach, which tends to locate the causes of crime within each offender and then 'treat' or 'cure' them for their own good, seems, more likely to be applied to women than men. This is because women are deemed to be twice deviant, having flouted two sets of social rules, and thus peculiarly suitable and susceptible to such approaches. (Heidensohn, 1996: 51)

This is especially likely if the women in question seem not to be conforming to traditional norms. Thus, Pearson (1976) found that single mothers were more likely to be remanded for psychiatric reports than other female offenders, even though their offences were mainly trivial thefts and forgeries.

Perhaps the most striking example of the medicalisation of female offenders was the planned conversion of Holloway, the main prison for women in Britain, into a secure psychiatric establishment during the 1960s. Paul Rock describes how it was intended to convert a 'grim Victorian fortress' into a new establishment 'to be arrayed as a therapeutic continuum, a string of small, linked, flexible spaces that would plot a moral career for the inmate' (Rock, 1996: 9). Central to these plans was the notion that 'women prisoners were special' because they were less of a security threat (ibid.: 86). As a result of numerous delays the project was not completed until 1985, by which time a change in the penological climate meant that 'a collection of special therapeutic spaces' was used instead for the purposes of control, containment and discipline. In her book on work and training in prison Frances Simon described Holloway as 'a large modern five-storey building *designed very like a hospital*, enclosed by a high perimeter wall and with lawns and ornamental garden beds' (Simon, 1999: 42; emphasis added). Heidensohn also comments on Holloway's perceived role:

> Women offenders were, it was argued, mentally and physically sick, or possibly both. Few (and declining) in numbers, they were to be offered

> therapeutic regimes ranging from psychotropic drugs to deep analyses and
> counselling. Legal and justice models were to be abandoned for treatment.
> (Heidensohn, 1996: 73)

Although the plan was subsequently modified, Holloway has continued, like other establishments catering for women, to be criticised for its
poor environment, and to have a high incidence of self-harm among its
inmates. In the early 1980s another female establishment, Bullwood
Hall in Essex, gained notoriety for a while for its high incidence of self-
mutilation amongst young women, until the regime was altered
(Cullen, 1981).

The treatment of female offenders has tended to be associated with
the roles that women have traditionally filled in society, and, as with
young offenders, women have been regarded as less culpable, less in
control, and less responsible for their actions than men. This has been
accompanied by a medical approach to dealing with female offenders.
Whether this will continue and what its consequences will be is a
matter for conjecture. Two things may change what has happened in
the past. One is increasing awareness of the issues highlighted above,
and the need for a change of approach. The other is the perception on
the part of sentencers that the offences women commit are more serious
than in the past,[5] and the rising number of women in penal institutions.[6] This may indicate that a less condescending attitude is being
taken to female offenders and also that female offenders are held more
responsible for their actions and should therefore receive their 'just
deserts'.

Other groups

Apart from these primary distinctions of age and gender, treatment as a
part of criminal justice has also (even at a time when the treatment
model prevailed throughout the criminal justice system) tended to be
associated with certain groups of people, such as mentally disordered
offenders, drug addicts, habitual drunken offenders and petty persistent
offenders. Some of these groups are discussed further in Part III of this
book. It is noticeable that these are groups of people who can be characterised as being on the fringes of society, and who have sometimes
been referred to as 'social inadequates'. In the distinctions I have mentioned we can discern a common thread. This has to do with
responsibility for one's actions and the fact that all of these groups – the
young, women, those with mental health, drug or alcohol problems –
have often been presented as in some way having diminished responsibility for their actions. Consequently we find that the treatment model
is associated with a determinist outlook on human behaviour, one in

which people are seen as controlled by their nature or external forces, rather than in control.

Issues in Treatment and Rehabilitation

This brings me to the fact that certain issues tend to be encountered whenever the treatment and rehabilitation of offenders are considered. Society's responses to offenders are often characterised by ambiguity. Are they villains or the victims of their circumstances? Are they bad or mad? Behind such ambiguities lie questions about the existence of evil and free will. Are offenders rational beings wholly responsible for their actions, or are they affected by circumstances over which they themselves have limited control? What rights do offenders have, or have they forfeited certain rights?

From such ambiguities arise further questions about whether to treat or punish and the relationship between the two. For example, are some treatments more onerous than punishments? Which system is more appropriate, the medical system or the criminal justice system? If the criminal justice system, what is the relationship between treatment and sentencing? Is the point of sentencing to exact retribution for a morally culpable act which is the fault of the offender, or is it to cure the offender of whatever it is that has caused him/her to offend, or both? For how long should one continue the treatment or the retribution? Thus, a consideration of the treatment of offenders inevitably raises questions concerning rationality and responsibility, free will and determinism, rights, and the exercising of power. One view is that presented by John Patten, a former Minister at the Home Office, who had responsibility for promoting the changes which led to the Criminal Justice Act 1991:

> Any general theory of punishment would have to start with the recognition that people sometimes freely choose to be bad, by quite deliberately harming other people or their property. There may be explanations, or mitigations, for it but badness is at the root. (Patten, 1991)

This is quite a different view from that taken by the philosopher Bertrand Russell:

> One other respect in which our society suffers from the theological conception of 'sin' is the treatment of criminals. The view that criminals are 'wicked' and 'deserve' punishment is not one which a rational morality can support. (Russell, 1925: 60)

Clearly, behind the questions posed above lie some very different conceptions of crime, and indeed of human behaviour. These are themes that have featured in criminological debate since its emergence as a distinctive area of study in the eighteenth century. The positivist approach sees offenders as, if not exactly determined by their background and circumstances, then as influenced by them to such an extent that the probability of offending is significantly increased. In contrast to this is the view that people are fully responsible for their actions, irrespective of their circumstances, and therefore to be held accountable for them. The contrast here is somewhat oversimplified, but such divergent views of the nature of offending inevitably result in different approaches towards dealing with offenders. The former approach has favoured attempts to reform the offender and ameliorate his or her circumstances, while the latter view has favoured an approach based on the application of justice regardless of the circumstances of the offender.

In this context it is worth bearing in mind that law breaking is not the preserve of a small group of people within society. Official records of offending and studies of the general population have consistently indicated that quite a high proportion of the population commit offences. This is especially true of younger age groups (Belson, 1968; Graham and Bowling, 1995). It also tends to be more true of males than females: about a third of males born in 1953 had been convicted of an offence by their 31st birthday (Tarling, 1993: 22). Nonetheless, a much smaller proportion of offenders are responsible for a larger proportion of known offending (Barclay, 1995: 20). So views of offending and how to deal with it need to take account of widely varying patterns of behaviour.

Ethical Issues in Treatment and Rehabilitation

Medical treatment is guided by certain ethical principles. Similar principles apply to a wide range of activities, and most professions and learned societies have ethical guidelines or rules. In medicine new forms of treatment or research have to be approved by an Ethics Committee. It is not intended to consider the ethics of treatment at length here, but an awareness of ethical principles is important because they raise a number of issues regarding the treatment of offenders.[7]

We need ethical guidelines because the activities engaged in by doctors, social workers, researchers, lawyers, and other professional groups involve exercising power and control over others. This use of power has to be constrained to ensure that the fundamental human rights of others are respected. This means observing certain ethical principles:

Autonomy – respecting the right to freedom and self-determination;
Beneficence – furthering others' legitimate interests and well-being;
Non-maleficence – not inflicting harm on others;
Justice – ensuring fair entitlements and duties, benefits and burdens.

In order to observe these principles it is necessary to respect a number of rules that follow from them:

Veracity – telling people the truth;
Fidelity – keeping promises and undertakings;
Confidentiality – respecting people's right to control information about themselves;
Privacy – respecting people's right to control access to themselves.

It has been proposed that these principles form a sound basis for moral behaviour (Kent, 2000) and so any breach of them needs to be justified. However, even if such moral principles are not intentionally breached, situations can occur where one principle comes into conflict with another, giving rise to an ethical dilemma. For example, avoiding harm to one person might mean breaching the confidentiality of another. Safeguarding the rights of one person or group may, in some circumstances, infringe the rights of others. It is sometimes argued that the rights of the few have to be sacrificed for the good of the many, and that applied ethics is about achieving a balance of good and harm. Alternatively it may be that observing one ethical principle would involve a breach of another. Ethical guidelines can help to resolve such dilemmas, but ethical judgements have to be made by professional workers in many situations.

Central to any form of treatment or research is the principle of informed consent. A participant should be able to choose freely whether or not to take part in an experiment, survey, operation, etc. This is an integral part of the principle of autonomy, and in medicine it is important in order to ensure that patients enter treatment voluntarily, knowing what they are freely choosing. Hence informed consent requires:

- *information* about what will or may happen;
- *understanding* of what is involved;
- *competence* to make a judgement about what is involved;
- *voluntariness* and freedom from any pressure;
- *consent*, which should be explicit and not assumed.

Having set out some of the ethical principles that govern medical treatment and other forms of intervention, the obvious question is how far these apply when it comes to the treatment of offenders. The first point that is made by many is that since offenders have usually breached the rights of others they have forfeited their own right to be treated on the same basis as others. Indeed, it may be argued that, by definition, offending is an offence against the very moral precepts that are the basis for the ethical principles outlined above and that, assuming the offender to be a rational being, he or she has knowingly and wilfully put their own rights at risk. Does this mean that an offender has therefore relinquished *all* his or her rights? Clearly not, since the commission of a morally wrong act (or offence) does not necessarily imply total relinquishment of what is right. The offender is dealt with for a specific act, not for being a particular person, (although some might dispute this distinction). In their report on the prison disturbances which occurred in April 1990 Lord Justice Woolf and Judge Stephen Tumim say that, 'in spite of his imprisonment a convicted prisoner retains all his civil rights which are not taken away expressly or by necessary implication' (Woolf and Tumim, 1991: para. 10.22). Ashworth bases the moral argument on the principle of proportionality:

> Surely there should be a right not to be punished more than is proportionate to the seriousness of the offence: . . . since this shows respect for the offender as a rational and autonomous being. . . . Thus, convicted offenders should not forfeit all their rights: their essential humanity ought to be recognised. (Ashworth, 1994: 52–53)

Nonetheless Ashworth recognises that there may be exceptional circumstances and that where an offender presents a continuing 'vivid danger' to the public, detention beyond the proportionate sentence may be justified although, he adds, 'the fallibility of such predictions is well documented'. Hence there remains a grey area and this has become a source of concern as far as dealing with some particularly dangerous offenders is concerned.

When dealing with offenders the principle that is affected most explicitly is that of autonomy: the offender is denied a measure of freedom and self-determination. This happens most clearly when someone is sent to prison. However, most other forms of disposal also involve a measure of restriction of freedom. This has been spelled out most explicitly in the Home Office guidelines for the Criminal Justice Act 1991, where it is stated that:

> Most penalties restrict the offender's liberty in some way. It is that restriction of liberty which is the punishment for the offence.
>
> Although fines and other financial penalties do not restrict the offender's liberty in quite the same way as a community or custodial sentence, they deprive the offender of money and therefore of the ability to spend that money in other ways. . . .
>
> Community sentences . . . restrict the offender's liberty, though to a lesser degree than custody. . . .
>
> The severest restriction of liberty is imprisonment. It is right that this penalty should be reserved for the most serious offences. (Home Office, 1991: paras 2.2–2.5)

Although the Act was subsequently amended by the Criminal Justice

Act 1993, only certain specific provisions were changed and the sentencing framework, incorporating a graduated scale of restriction of liberty, remains in force.

But while the withdrawal of autonomy may be justified by the state in dealing with offenders, it does not follow that offenders' other rights are curtailed, and hence all other ethical principles should be observed as much in dealing with offenders as with anyone else. It is these principles that often form the basis of the arguments of those who seek to safeguard the rights of prisoners in this country and elsewhere. What causes those involved with the treatment of offenders most difficulty is the principle of informed consent, since this is an integral part of the principle of autonomy. Even so, until recently an offender's consent was required before most community sentences could be imposed (a probation order, a community service order, a combination order, and a curfew order), although it may be doubted how free and well informed this consent was. This requirement was abolished, despite protests from some quarters, by Section 38 of the Crime (Sentences) Act 1997, which came into effect on 1 October 1997. Nonetheless, it is arguable that, unless the law states otherwise, the principle of informed consent applies as much to offenders involved in specific treatment programmes, schemes and projects, as to any other individual.

Further Reading

A useful starting point for background reading is Chapter 2 of *The Penal System: an Introduction* (1997), by Michael Cavadino and James Dignan. A consideration of the application of the medical approach to criminal justice can be found in Gerry Johnstone's *Medical Concepts and Penal Policy* (1996), which as well as considering the medical model looks at policies on dealing with drunken offenders and mentally disordered offenders. *The Oxford Handbook of Criminology* (1997) contains several chapters relevant to the subject matter of this book. One such is the chapter by Tim Newburn on 'Youth, Crime, and Justice', which looks at young people and youth justice. For those interested in reading further about the treatment of female offenders, a good introduction is Frances Heidensohn's *Women and Crime* (1996).

Questions to Consider

- What is meant by treatment?
- What forms does the treatment of offenders take?
- Are some offenders treated differently to others?
- Is there a theory about how best to treat offenders?

- To what extent are offenders themselves responsible for the success or otherwise of any treatment?
- What rights do offenders have to, and during, treatment and rehabilitation?

Notes

1   The 1959 White Paper, *Penal Practice in a Changing Society*, for example, referred to the desirability of undertaking 'research into the use of various forms of treatment and the measurement of their results' (Home Office, 1959: 5).

2   There are a number of texts edited by Clive Hollin and Kevin Howells covering clinical approaches to various types of offender and criminal behaviour, which are cited elsewhere in this book (e.g. Howells and Hollin, 1989; Hollin and Howells, 1996).

3   In 1965, for example, a White Paper, *The Child, the Family and the Young Offender* proposed the abolition of the juvenile court, but was successfully opposed by lawyers and magistrates (Home Office, 1965).

4   In contrast to the treatment model, this stresses the importance of due process in proceedings against offenders, determinate (rather than indeterminate) sentencing, and sentences where the penalty is proportionate to the gravity of the offence.

5   In research involving interviews with magistrates, judges, court clerks and social workers in recent years when asked about female offenders the response has been that the number of female offenders appearing in court has been increasing, that they are appearing at a younger age, and that their offences are more serious than formerly, with violence on the part of young women becoming more common (Crow et al., 1996; Crow, 1996a). However, this is not borne out by the available evidence (Home Office, 1999: Chapter 2).

6   Between 1993 and 1998 the average population of women in prison almost doubled (Home Office, 1999), and in November 1998 the female prison population in England and Wales was 3,213; its highest level since 1905.

7   A fuller consideration of ethical principles as they apply to social research can be found in Part Two of *Research Training for Social Scientists: a Handbook for Postgraduate Researchers*, edited by Dawn Burton (2000). This is based on a course for social science research students that I and others have been involved in teaching, and I acknowledge my indebtedness in particular to Dr Gerry Kent's contribution to this course.

2

NOTHING WORKS!

In this chapter the historical background to the treatment model is explored, leading up to the period of its highest influence around the middle of the twentieth century. The reasons for its decline are explained, along with a brief review of some of the key studies that led to the belief that 'nothing works'. The chapter ends by considering what followed the decline of the rehabilitative ideal.

A Historical Perspective

This chapter does not set out to provide a history of criminal justice or criminology in general, since there are already several sources which present historical perspectives (for example, Cavadino and Dignan, 1997: Ch. 2; Fattah, 1997, Part 3; Foucault, 1977; Garland, 1985, 1988, 1997; Ignatieff, 1978; Rock, 1988). However, in order to understand the place that treatment and rehabilitation occupy in current criminological thinking and criminal justice policy it is necessary to have an appreciation of how they have developed. The first part of this chapter looks at this development, but a word of caution is necessary. Because this book is about treatment and rehabilitation there is a danger of seeing these as the most significant features of the way that criminal justice policy has developed over the last two hundred years or so. In fact, at almost any point during that period several strands of thinking have existed along-side, and competed with, each other. The main competition has been between a retributive approach, which mainly looks back towards the crime that has occurred, and approaches which concern themselves with what can be done for the future. In general, treatment and rehabilitation can be said to be forward looking. Some can be said to combine the two: for example the restorative model of justice recognises that a past event has to be dealt with, but also tries to look at how those involved can move forward. Thus, whilst at a certain time the 'treatment model', or the 'rehabilitative ideal', was in the ascendancy, even during its most dominant period other forces were at work.

The line of development associated with attempts to reform the offender is most commonly traced back to the work of Cesare Lombroso. However, Garland (1997: 31) points out that, although Lombroso's work gave rise to a scientific approach to criminality, it required much shaping and refashioning before it could form the basis for a realistic policy. The positivist school of Lombroso stood in contrast to the classicism of Beccaria and Bentham that had preceded it. Whereas 'classical' criminology emphasised dealing with the offence, the positivists focused more on the offender. Classical thinkers stressed the importance of reasoning, justice and uniformity of sentencing. The positivists saw offenders as fundamentally different from non-offenders (Fattah, 1997: 214), and as people who could not help being who they were. Hence, 'criminal justice was to cease being a punitive reactive system and was to become instead a scientifically informed apparatus for the prevention, treatment and elimination of criminality' (Garland, 1997: 32). As Bottoms has pointed out, by denying the intentional content of human action, positivism tends to regard offenders as being innately 'crime-prone'; it treats crime as a naturally occurring phenomenon and sees the role of the organs of the state as unproblematic, and it relies on the ability of behavioural science 'experts' to accurately predict and treat the problem behaviour (Bottoms, 1977: 81–82).

As important as the emergence of the Lombrosian School of scientific inquiry was the growth during the eighteenth and nineteenth centuries of new institutions and forms of administration, not only of justice and punishment, but of health and manufacture. The development of the prison, the factory and the lunatic asylum had much in common (Melossi and Pavarini, 1981), and this nexus was related to ideas about spiritual and moral well-being which had to do with health in its broadest sense. Ignatieff points out that the penal reformers, such as John Howard, were supported by physicians like the Quaker John Fothergill who worked in penitentiaries:

> These doctors regarded the hygienic reform of institutions as a moral, no less than a medical crusade. The sicknesses of the poor were interpreted as the outward sign of their inward want of discipline, morality and honour. (Ignatieff, 1978: 60)

Reformers were also aided by the nonconformist industrialists and manufacturers of the time. One such was Jedediah Strutt who helped Richard Arkwright set up a model cotton spinning factory at Cromford, near Matlock, in 1771. Strutt claimed that the establishment of the factory with its regular work and wages, together with the stabilising influence of a closely supervised village community, had transformed the behaviour of the local inhabitants, which had previously been characterised by vice and immorality (Fisk, 1998). 'In that first generation of industrialisation, factories could still be justified not simply as technical achievements, but as moral ones as well' (Ignatieff, 1978: 63) and, 'It was no accident that penitentiaries, asylums, workhouses, monitorial schools, night refuges, and reformatories looked alike, or that their charges marched to the same disciplinary cadence' (Ignatieff, 1978:

214–215). Behind this similarity of institutional structures was the idea
that 'science', whether in medicine or the new forms of 'scientific management', could answer all society's needs. The penal reformers of the
nineteenth century have usually been seen as enlightened and well-
meaning individuals, concerned with the rights and welfare of people
who were victims of an unjust and oppressive society as much as they
were offenders. But, as Ignatieff, Foucault and others have pointed out
with the benefit of hindsight, their reforms often led, unwittingly, to
new forms of repression, including extended periods of solitary confinement. Cruel physical punishments, such as whippings and beatings,
continued within the new institutions, usually without any due legal
process as to their administration, but the institutions themselves introduced a new form of social and moral control over the poorer classes of
society, whether they were criminals, lunatics or just impoverished:

> The new martyrs do not die a slow death in the torture chamber but instead
> waste away spiritually as invisible victims in the great prison buildings
> which differ in little but name from madhouses. (Horkheimer and Adorno,
> 1973: 228)

In Britain in particular, early criminology in the nineteenth century was
shaped as much by doctors and prison governors as by scholars, if not
more so (Garland, 1988). The psychiatrist Henry Maudsley, for example,
made a study of the criminals who constituted the patients under his
care. British criminology had its basis in an applied medico-legal culture
derived from the penal and psychiatric establishments, and was dominated by figures who were involved in running prisons and hospitals.
Their academic interests tended to run alongside dealing with individual offenders. Apart from Maudsley in the late nineteenth century, these
included, in the twentieth century, Hamblin Smith (a prison doctor
whose interest was in the psychiatric assessment of inmates), Norwood
East (who undertook an experiment in psychological therapy at
Wormwood Scrubs prison in the 1930s), and Trevor Gibbens (who had
a particular interest in the psychology of young delinquents).

Garland has suggested that the development of British criminology
can be seen as having several 'streams'. Norwood East represented the
mainstream of medico-psychiatric criminology. A more radical offshoot
of this was the clinical psychoanalytic school centred on the Institute for
the Scientific Treatment of Delinquency (ISTD, later to become the
Institute for the Study and Treatment of Delinquency) set up in 1932,
which had close links with the Tavistock Institute. A rather different
stream was that initiated in 1913 when Charles Goring published *The
English Convict: A Statistical Study*. This was the first work to put forward a conception of criminality as normal rather than pathological, but
it did not initially have much influence. Its detractors, such as W. C.

Sullivan, medical superintendent at Broadmoor, argued that clinical rather than statistical methods were the only reliable basis for policy. It was Goring, however, who laid the foundations for the kind of statistical prediction studies which later underlay the work of the Home Office Research Unit, whose studies in the 1970s contributed significantly to the decline of the treatment approach as a dominant force in British criminology. A third stream of development was what Garland describes as 'the "eclectic", multifactorial, social-psychological' research exemplified by Sir Cyril Burt in his 1925 study, *The Young Delinquent*.

The 1950s saw the founding of the *British Journal of Delinquency* (now the *British Journal of Criminology*), which at first had a predominantly medical emphasis. In 1955 a special number of the journal contained papers presented at a Symposium on Predictive Methods in the Treatment of Delinquency, held at the Medical Society of London. An article in this issue by Edward Glover, one of the leading criminologists of the time and an editor of the journal, shows how firmly crime had been associated with pathology. He explained that to people like him notions of recidivism and the prediction of recidivism were 'redundant, misleading and tendentious', and that they were more used to thinking in terms of relapse. Glover went on to say,

> There is no more reason to describe the symptoms of pathological delinquency as recidivism than to say that tubercular symptoms which persist beyond the average time range in spite of various measures of treatment are signs of recidivism. It would be equally absurd to describe the victim of a skin disease as a recidivist because his rash continued after tentative steps had been taken to control it. (Glover, 1955: 121)

The Symposium papers clearly reflect a difference between those with a psychiatric background, such as Glover, and those like Leslie Wilkins, who brought a more sociological perspective to bear on criminological inquiry. In the same year (1955) publication of *Prediction Methods in Relation to Borstal Training* (Mannheim and Wilkins) by the Home Office Research Unit saw the beginning of the process of evaluating the effects of training and treatment. This raised questions about whether the results achieved by borstal training were anything more than a reflection of the selection procedure. It was this kind of analysis which in due course undermined the treatment ideology. The late 1950s also saw the formation of the British Society of Criminology as a breakaway from the ISTD's dominance by psychiatry and psycho-analysis. Garland has described the scientific criminology that developed in Britain between the 1890s and the Second World War as 'heavily dominated by a medico-psychological approach, focused upon the individual offender and tied into a correctionalist penal-welfare policy' (1997: 44). This approach flourished during the 1920s and 1930s and was at its height in the period following the Second World War. It had always had its competitors, and at the time of its greatest success during the 1950s the seeds of its downfall were already being sown. The opening of Grendon Underwood, a therapeutic prison, in 1962 could be regarded as one of the high points of the rehabilitative ideal, but it was also one of the last fruits of the traditional treatment approach in British penal policy.

The Decline of Treatment

The latter part of the 1960s and the 1970s saw the treatment model coming under attack at three levels: theoretically, ethically and empirically. Most attention has focused (and will do here) on the last of these, particularly on certain well-known and frequently cited studies. But this empirical work took place against the background of a wider disenchantment with the treatment approach. A criminology dominated by those running the system was being challenged at a theoretical level, by Becker (1963) and other labelling theorists (e.g. Matza, 1969), and by the 'new' criminologists (Taylor et al., 1973, 1975). Apart from critiques of the disease analogy, a frequent theme of this era was that, because the treatment approach focused on changing the individual, a criminology associated with it effectively operated in the service of the state and neglected the need for change in society.

Alongside this was a growing disquiet about the implications of a treatment-based approach for the institutions of justice. While formal sentencing was in the hands of the courts, the logic of a treatment approach was that people should be 'treated' until they got 'better'. As a consequence much discretion regarding the nature and extent of a particular penal disposition lay in the hands of the executive arm of criminal justice, rather than those of the judiciary. In the early 1970s the American Friends Service Committee (1971) challenged the treatment ideology on the basis of its frequent association with injustice and neglect of the rights of the individual. They concentrated in particular on indeterminate sentencing, which often led to people being detained for longer periods than their offences warranted, on the grounds that they were undergoing a form of treatment. The rationale was that the length of treatment should be decided by individual needs and individual responsiveness to it, and this could not be determined in advance. However, whereas a sentence was announced in a public forum where all the information was available for scrutiny and according to due legal process, subsequent decisions which prolonged incarceration and other forms of 'treatment' were often taken without such public scrutiny: a prisoner who did not co-operate could be portrayed as not responding to treatment. This was more of an issue in the United States, where indeterminate sentencing was more common, than elsewhere. But even as the effectiveness of treatment was coming under attack in the 1970s, the Butler Committee (1975) was proposing a new form of indeterminate, 'reviewable' sentence for England and Wales for 'dangerous' offenders, and an important element of the parole system still centres around whether the prisoner has demonstrated change or willingness to change, even if the phraseology of treatment has altered.[1]

In the UK the main custodial sentence affected by indeterminacy was that of borstal training, although the indeterminate element of the sentence was limited, so that young offenders aged between 15 and 21 served a minimum of six months and up to two years, the actual date of release being determined by the Home Secretary 'as soon as he is satisfied that the objects of the training have been achieved' (Home Office, 1971: para. 107). Nonetheless, the consequence of the concerns raised by the American Friends Service Committee report and others (von Hirsch, 1976) was to draw attention to numerous instances where doctors, social workers and other professionals took executive decisions which directly or indirectly affected people's freedom and autonomy without being able to be effectively challenged. This happened because the treatment approach was imbued with notions of paternalism and authority; of 'doctor knows best'. The challenge to the treatment approach was part of the breakdown of such assumptions. It is worth noting that the medical world itself was not immune to such movements: in psychiatry traditional approaches were being challenged by R.D. Laing (1965), among others. However, it was the interpretation of the results of a number of empirical studies that proved most conclusive in dislodging the treatment model from its position of pre-eminence, and it is to some of these that we now turn.

Martinson (1974)

During the 1960s a team of researchers undertook a review for the New York State Governor's Committee on Criminal Offenses to assist the planning of rehabilitative programmes. It looked at 231 studies reported between 1945 and 1967. The conclusions the review came to were more uncomfortable than the Committee had anticipated; so much so that publication was delayed for some time. Eventually one of the research team published a journal article (Martinson, 1974) that proved to be a watershed for the treatment approach. Its broad conclusion that 'nothing works' became synonymous with a way of characterising the treatment and rehabilitation approach for a generation. The article looked first at various types of intervention in custodial institutions, including education and training, individual and group counselling, medical treatment (drugs and surgery), the 'therapeutic' environment, and the length and security of imprisonment. Martinson also considered non-institutional programmes, including psychotherapy, probation and parole, and intensive supervision. He concluded that, while programmes in the community did not 'work' in terms of reducing offending, at least most did not make things worse,[2] and they cost less than prison.

If nothing works, what are the implications? Martinson suggested that there were three possible considerations:

1   flawed methodology – some treatment programmes may be working to some extent, but research was not capable of identifying this;
2   flawed treatment – the programmes were not yet good enough;
3   flawed theory – this would be the case if crime was a social phenomenon rather than a disease.

Martinson concluded that a deterrent strategy was apparently the best option, but that since relatively little was known about the efficacy of deterrent effects more studies were needed.

Martinson's article has been criticised over the years on a number of grounds. One of the main ones is that the study used a very limited measure of recidivism as the criterion of effectiveness, looking simply at whether or not reconviction had occurred, rather than at the nature of any reconviction. Arguably if someone was reconvicted of a lesser crime than previously, or the treatment intervention was followed by a longer period of non-offending than was the case prior to intervention, it could be said to have had some effect. The study has also been criticised on the grounds that by the time it was published the studies on which it was based were so out of date as to be irrelevant to the mid-1970s. It has also been suggested that Martinson quite simply overstated the case and failed to distinguish that there were promising programmes that were worth considering further. Related to this is the further point that some things may have worked for some offenders, and that the work by Martinson and others failed to distinguish this differential effectiveness (Palmer, 1975).

The IMPACT Study (1976)

In the UK there had also been some investment in evaluating the effectiveness of measures for dealing with offenders. The Home Office Research Unit had begun to consider questions related to treatment effectiveness. With growing attention to 'alternatives to custody', a key question was whether certain kinds of intensive community-based treatment, of the kind needed for those who might otherwise go to prison, would work. At about the time that Martinson's work was published the results of the Home Office Research Unit's Intensive Matched

Probation After-Care and Treatment (IMPACT) study were becoming available (Folkard, Smith and Smith, 1976).

The programme was quite an intrusive one, providing intensive practical intervention in the family, work and leisure situations of 'high-risk' probationers. Such a high degree of intervention in itself raises questions about whether there are limits to the extent to which intrusion in various aspects of a person's life in the name of treatment can be justified, but this was accepted at the time as part of the prevailing positivist orthodoxy. The study was conducted in four areas – Dorset, Inner London, Staffordshire and Sheffield – on males aged 17 and over, randomly allocated to experimental and control groups during 1971–72. There were approximately 500 young males overall in each of the experimental and control groups. The findings were consistent with Martinson's conclusion that no general treatment effect could be demonstrated, but not inconsistent with Palmer's (1975) view that some pointers could be provided to suggest differential effects for different types of offender. The researchers looked for interaction effects, i.e. whether things such as social background and personality variables interacted with treatment effects. A personality inventory (the Mooney inventory) and pre-trial assessment of criminal tendencies did show a tendency to discriminate: there was some indication (though not statistically significant) that offenders assessed as having low criminal tendencies and more personal problems did better in intensive treatment.

Brody (1976)

In some ways Brody's work could be regarded as the British version of Martinson in that it was a review of existing work, and covered many of the same studies. However, the focus was more broadly on *sentencing* policy than specific forms of treatment, and the report contains useful reviews of the purposes of sentencing and methodological problems. Despite reinforcing the general 'nothing works' conclusion, Brody also said that some kinds of treatment seemed to work for certain offenders: intensive counselling and supervision were mentioned, for example (Brody, 1976: 40). This again underlines the importance of interaction effects – 'the matching of appropriate treatment to different types of offender' (Brody, 1976: 41). It also raises the question of whether we know that treatment is really taking place. Perhaps the 'treated' see it differently. Some might say that it does not matter whether the recipients of treatment are aware that they are recipients, or how they perceive that treatment. But others may argue that in a social context the perceptions and motivations of those who participate in some form of intervention are crucial to its impact.

The Relationship between Treatment and Sentencing

Treatment takes many forms. Treatment has often been closely related to the sentencing of offenders. It may be possible to conclude, as the Brody review does, that in terms of reconviction rates, no one type of sentence will reduce the level of re-offending better than any other. But this is not the same as establishing that *'nothing* works'. Treatment and sentences should not be equated or confused. For one thing sentences fulfil functions other than treatment and rehabilitation, including restriction of liberty and retribution. Furthermore, sentences may incorporate various forms of treatment. For example, several different kinds of treatment have been and still are undertaken in prison establishments. Similarly probation can involve various types of work with offenders, some of which may be successful in reducing re-offending, while others are not. The successful and unsuccessful activities may cancel each other out in terms of the overall reconviction success of probation as a sentence. This point has also been made by Moxon in a review of the role of sentencing in reducing offending. Having repeated the well-established conclusion that there is little difference between sentences in terms of their impact on reconviction rates, Moxon says, 'These findings are at a general level, and it would be wrong to conclude that individual programmes within prisons or run by the Probation Service may not have an effect' (Moxon, 1998: 98).

Sentences reflect the dominant penal thinking of the time. So when the treatment model was in the ascendant, sentences would be likely to be thought of in treatment terms. Hence reviews of sentencing, such as that of Brody, were considered to be a critique of treatment. More recently the degree of punishment has been the prime concern. Therefore sentences tend to be equated with, and thought of predominantly in terms of, their punitive potential.

Treatment has moved from being a central feature of sentencing to occupying a more marginal role, perhaps valid only for certain offenders with specific characteristics, rather than for most. Consequently the history of sentencing policy is a reflection of the battles that have taken place about how offenders should be dealt with. As penal thinking and policy have changed, so the sentence of the court may reflect the extent to which criminal justice policy seeks to punish, rehabilitate or, more recently, seek restoration (as in the Crime and Disorder Act 1998, with the introduction of restoration orders). The main point here is that one needs to ask what a particular sentence involves. Is it primarily punitive or primarily rehabilitative, or a mixture? Community service orders, for example, may be seen as having a mixture of objectives, including elements of punishment, reparation and the potential for rehabilitation (Advisory Council on the Penal System, 1970: para. 33).

What Replaced the Treatment Model?

> It is abundantly clear that there is no adequate overarching penal theory to replace the collapsed rehabilitative consensus of fifteen years ago. (Bottoms, 1977: 91)

The decline of treatment and rehabilitation as the central focus of penal policy had a considerable impact on criminal justice. A vacuum appeared that was not only intellectual, but was experienced in practice and policy. This had an impact on the institutions of criminal justice, including (as will be seen in Chapters 5 and 6) the Prison and Probation Services. What would a non-treatment approach look like? Discussions took place about the nature of a 'non-treatment paradigm'. Kuhn (1970) describes how, in certain conditions, a prevailing paradigm can be replaced by another paradigm, with far reaching consequences. But in the case of the treatment model there was no alternative paradigm waiting to assume its place.[3] The paradigm shift had been largely negative in nature: there was no single school of thought or initiative that was ready to move unequivocally into the gap left by the virtual demise of the treatment model. Instead, several developments occurred, although not necessarily as direct and explicit responses to 'nothing works'. Some of these involved a shift of emphasis towards other functions of sentencing, while others centred more on what needed to be done regarding crime control if measures to reduce offending amongst known offenders could not be relied upon. Amongst the former were attempts to focus on the incapacitative potential of sentences, especially imprisonment, and to look more closely at the costs of different measures. Amongst the latter were such things as an increasing emphasis on different kinds of crime prevention measures.

Incapacitation   One response was that 'even if imprisonment does not provide any effective treatment at least it prevents the offender from committing further crimes during the period of his incarceration. This is known as "containment" or "incapacitation"' (Tarling, 1979: 6). Although this view has had a certain popular appeal, it has been pointed out that 'incapacitation is impossibly open-ended as a general principle of criminal punishment' (Zimring and Hawkins, 1995: ix). Furthermore, much depends on incarcerating the right group of people. Incapacitation assumes that a high proportion of the crimes that would otherwise be committed are prevented by being able to lock up those who would have committed them. It is at least possible that a high proportion of offences are committed by people who never get caught or who, if caught, would be unlikely to offend again. For example, Van Dine, Dinitz and Conrad (1977) found in a study that they conducted that over two-thirds of their sample were first offenders, and therefore many offences could not have been prevented by imposing incapacitating sentences at a previous conviction. Pease and Wolfson (1979) point out that the assumptions on which studies of incapacitation are based are critical.

The appeal of incapacitation has also been restrained by the realisation that massive amounts of money have to be spent on locking people up to gain even a modest impact on offending rates. Tarling pointed out in 1979 that 'One fact, however, is clear. Mandatory sentences of three to five years, whether preventing many or only a few crimes, would enormously increase the size of the prison population' (Tarling, 1979: 7). After undertaking further research he estimated that to achieve a 1 per cent reduction in recorded crime would require a 25 per cent increase in the prison population, and commented that, 'Increasing the general use of imprisonment to counter crime does not appear to be a cost effective option' (Tarling, 1993: 162). Nonetheless, incapacitation attracted some support in the United States (Shinnar and Shinnar, 1975) where it has played a part in criminal justice policy (Currie, 1996: 11). It was felt to have had some impact there because the United States already had a larger prison population than the United Kingdom, so an increase in imprisonment has a larger effect on crime rates than would the same percentage increase in the United Kingdom (Moxon, 1998: 95). But even in the United States the impact has been limited, as research on incarceration in California has found (Zimring and Hawkins, 1995), and an American commentator has highlighted the shortsighted nature of the policy:

> To say that we are winning the war on crime because we've had to put everyone in prison, in short, is like saying that we're winning the war on disease because we've had to put everyone in hospital. (Currie, 1996: 10)

As this quotation indicates, the medical analogy did not die out altogether.

Alternatives to Custody   Another response to 'nothing works' was to argue for a greater development of non-custodial sentences for certain offenders, on the grounds that if everything was equally ineffective, then at least non-custodial methods had the advantage of being much cheaper (Shaw, 1980).[4] However, this view was not fully appreciated until shortly after the 1987 General Election when a reappraisal of penal policy was confronted with the increasing cost of a rising prison population (Windlesham, 1993). Although the promotion of 'alternatives to custody' was very much favoured as a liberal approach to penal policy, it had its dangers in, first of all, elevating custody to the presumed sentence with which all others appeared to be in competition (NACRO, 1989: para. 5.2). Second, if non-custodial options were used more, then there was the possibility that they would also be used to a greater extent for those who might not have been sent to prison anyway but who could have been given a less severe sentence. For example, a Home Office study estimated that only about 45–50 per cent of those given community service orders were displaced from custody (Pease et al., 1977).[5] It was not until the Criminal Justice Act 1991 brought in a sentencing framework that clearly established the relationship between custodial and community-based penalties that the misleading notion of 'alternatives to custody' began to disappear.

Bifurcation   Although no more a replacement for the treatment paradigm than any other development, another policy which was pursued in the wake of 'nothing works' was to combine different approaches to dealing with offenders by, on the one hand punishing and incapacitating very serious offenders as much as possible, while developing more limited forms of non-custodial measures for the less serious offenders: a bifurcated approach. In 1977 Tony Bottoms explained what he referred to as 'the renaissance of dangerousness' in the context of the 'decline of the rehabilitative ethic' (Bottoms, 1977). In such a climate, he suggested, it was not surprising that there should be a 'switch of attention from treatment to prevention and containment', (Ibid.: 87) with a particular emphasis on the notion of dangerous offenders. This prompted the emergence of a bifurcation in penal policy 'between, on the one hand, the so-called "really serious offender" for whom very tough measures are typically advocated, and on the other hand, the "ordinary" offender for whom, it is felt, we can afford to take a much more lenient line' (Bottoms, 1977: 88). The consequence, Bottoms suggested, would be a penal policy in which there were the 'mad' and the 'bad', against whom we wish to take serious action, and the 'rest', for whom 'situational' theories of crime, relating to poverty and bad housing and so on are appropriate, for whom we are prepared to reduce penalties. This prediction proved to be well founded. In 1984 the Government introduced changes to the parole system which had the effect of lowering the threshold of eligibility for parole from twelve months to six months, while extending the period of imprisonment that would be served for certain types of murder and for offences of violence and drug trafficking. Further bifurcatory measures were introduced in the Criminal Justice Act 1991, which gave effect to a framework of proportionality for sentencing, so that a custodial sentence would be commensurate with the seriousness of the offence, but made an exception in the case of violent and sexual offenders, who could be sentenced 'for such longer term (not exceeding the maximum) as in the opinion of the court is necessary to protect the public from serious harm from the offender' (Criminal Justice Act 1991, s. 2(2)(b)).

Reparation   Another development that began to gain ground in the 1970s was that more attention started to be given to the victims of crime (Shapland et al., 1985). If little could be done to reform offenders, then perhaps more could be done for their victims. This happened in several ways. One was the development of victim support schemes, the first one being established in Bristol, leading eventually to the setting up of a national body, Victim Support, to co-ordinate their efforts. Another aspect of the concern for victims introduces the notion of reparation, which can take various forms. It can be in the form of general reparation to society, as in the case of community service orders, which increased in use during the 1970s and 1980s, or it can be financial. The Criminal Justice Act 1982, s. 67(b) provided that where financial penalties were imposed on an offender, 'courts shall give preference to compensation'. Reparation can also take a more direct form whereby the offender performs a service for, or on behalf of, the victim. The Home Office funded four experimental victim–offender mediation pilot schemes during the mid-1980s, but they produced mixed results. Although there were some benefits for those involved, the schemes encountered difficulties in securing the interests of victims and offenders simultaneously (Marshall and Merry, 1990). Thus, while reparation can be seen as having an element of just deserts, as well as being a cheaper and more positive response to offending than custody, development following the pilot schemes proceeded more cautiously and slowly. It was only with a change of government following the 1997 General Election that serious consideration was given to how reparation could be incorporated in a framework of sentencing, which happened with the introduction of reparation orders in the Crime and Disorder Act 1998.

The Justice Model and Just Deserts   This was the approach that was best placed to move into the space left by the collapse of the treatment model, because it had a coherent theoretical rationale that was rights based rather than utilitarian. Indeed it was partly responsible for that collapse. The justice model received a lot of support in the United States in the late 1970s and early 1980s, where a number of states moved away from sentencing on the basis of the individual offender and towards a sentencing policy in which the offender received a specific sentence for a specific crime, with limited leeway to take account of individual circumstances. Several of these regimes were later modified when they resulted in rapidly spiralling prison populations and expenditure. The British system, being more cautious and slower to espouse new causes, did not embrace the justice model so warmly. Indeed the justice model was seen as depriving sentencers of discretion and the Criminal Justice Act 1982 was concerned to enhance sentencers' ability to sentence as they felt appropriate in individual cases. But 'just deserts' did eventually find expression in the Criminal Justice Act 1991, although subsequently the Government attempted to shift the emphasis towards a more punitive approach, especially when Michael Howard became Home Secretary in 1993.

Crime Prevention   The development of various forms of crime prevention was already taking shape in the 1970s, with planners like Oscar Newman (1973) talking about 'defensible space' and the role of architecture and the environment in crime. One consequence of the waning of the rehabilitative ideal was that crime prevention began to receive more attention and was given greater priority (Tilley, 1993: 53), especially 'situational' crime prevention. The Chief Constable of the Metropolitan Police in the mid-1970s, Sir Robert Mark, gave crime prevention a boost when he declared that the police and courts alone could not provide the answer to crime; they needed the active involvement of the community. This novel idea caused a bit of a stir at the time, and was probably the first time that a Chief Constable had acknowledged the limitations of policing.

Continued Efforts at Treatment and Rehabilitation   Finally, though not necessarily exhaustively, attention did continue to be given to the prospects for rehabilitation and treatment style interventions with offenders. However, the climate following the collapse of the treatment model was such that for many years treatment regimes *per se* would be a fringe activity. More attention focused on socially oriented efforts to rehabilitate offenders. For example, during the later part of the 1970s and into the 1980s the National Association for the Care and Resettlement of Offenders (NACRO) established a number of schemes that concentrated on developing educational provision, accommodation, training and employment for offenders, and underwent rapid growth as an organisation as a result. Continuing efforts at individualised treatment were largely based on the suggestion in the IMPACT study that what was needed was to consider, 'which methods work best for which types of offender under what conditions and in what types of setting?' (Folkard et al., 1976: 2). Further consideration will be given to the fruits of some of this work in Chapter 4.

End of an Era?

In this chapter we have seen that the belief that the main response to crime should be to treat and rehabilitate individual offenders emerged in the latter part of the nineteenth century, and reached its peak around the middle of the twentieth century. It was then challenged theoretically, ethically and empirically, leading to the simplistic conclusion that 'nothing works'. This created a vacuum that led to various other avenues of criminal policy being explored.

Before leaving the era of 'nothing works' it is relevant to refer briefly to the political context of the time. The studies mentioned earlier came out in the mid-1970s, at a time when a Labour Government with a small majority was encountering economic and other difficulties, unemployment was rising (and even exceeded one million!), and the trade unions were proving to be a problem. Those on the political right characterised this as part of a wider social malaise affecting the United Kingdom and Western society in general. The treatment model was part of a broader liberal ideology, and its failure could be seen as a weakness in the social fabric of the time (Cavadino et al., 1999). Echoes of this persisted for many years, with allusions to an era of permissiveness that, it has been alleged, continued to have effects many years later.[6] Consequently by 1979 the Conservative Party was making an issue of law and order, something that had not happened to any great extent previously. There was a call for a return to a stricter, more authoritarian approach, epitomised by the Shadow Home Secretary, William Whitelaw's promise to re-introduce tougher regimes in detention centres for young offenders, generally referred to as the 'short, sharp, shock'.

Although some of the developments that took place following the waning of the rehabilitative approach have been mentioned, nothing quite occupied the central role in criminal justice policy that the treatment model had achieved. Nor did consideration of different types of intervention disappear, even if the term 'treatment' was not used as much. A concern with effectiveness continued, especially amongst sentencers. In putting forward proposals for sentencing or for new projects there is still a wish to know whether a particular measure 'works', and initiatives are still evaluated in terms of reconviction rates. We are therefore concerned with the relative status of treatment within criminology and criminal justice. There was a period when it was the dominant paradigm. It then became more marginal, but the treatment and rehabilitation of offenders never disappeared from the agenda, and their partial resurgence is the subject of a later chapter.

Further Reading

Several sources relating to a history of the development of criminology and criminal justice were referred to at the beginning of the chapter. Useful introductions can be found in Chapter 2 of Michael Cavadino and James Dignan's *The Penal System: An Introduction* (1997), and the first chapter of *The Oxford Handbook of Criminology* by David Garland (1997). A brief review of post-war developments in criminal justice policy can also be found in Chapter One of *Criminal Justice 2000: Strategies for a New Century* (1999) by Michael Cavadino, Iain Crow and James Dignan. An issue of the *British Journal of Criminology* (28, 2, 1988) was devoted to a history of British criminology, and Paul Rock has also published a book of the same name in 1988. For the material on 'nothing works' I would encourage readers to refer to the original sources if at all possible. The article by Martinson can be found in a book of readings edited by Francis Cullen and Brandon Applegate, *Offender Rehabilitation* (1997), which is also worth looking at for several other articles that it contains. Another important reference, for this and later chapters, is the article by Tony Bottoms, 'Reflections on the Renaissance of Dangerousness', in the *Howard Journal of Criminal Justice* (1977).

Questions to Consider

- Why did medical thinking and practice become so closely associated with the development of criminology and criminal justice?
- Why did the rehabilitative ideal collapse during the 1970s, and what are its prospects in the current climate?
- Do we still 'treat' offenders?
- Is the criminal justice system better off without the dominance of the treatment model?
- Many would argue, on ethical and effectiveness grounds, that treatment requires consent; can people therefore be sentenced to treatment?

Notes

1   When Reginald Kray, the former East London gangster, was told in April 1998, after 30 years of a life sentence, that his parole application had been turned down it was reported that one of the factors in the decision was that he had not 'addressed his offending behaviour', as required (*Guardian*, 2 April 1998, 1).
2   Although he also cited several programmes that did (Martinson, 1974: 39–40).
3   In retrospect it is possible to see that the justice model, referred to later, was probably the best-placed alternative paradigm, but this was not immediately apparent at the

time, and nor was it waiting in the wings ready to move into the place occupied by the treatment model.

4   As with other developments, the decline of the rehabilitative ideal was not the only factor involved; prison overcrowding and unrest within prisons also played their part.

5   For a fuller review of alternatives to prison see Stanley and Baginsky, 1984.

6   For example, in 1993 former Home Secretary, Michael Howard, was reported as saying that he believed that those who became parents in the 1960s exerted less discipline and authority over their children than previous generations ('Howard's War Babies Theory Under Fire', *Guardian*, 11 November 1993).

3

DETERMINING WHAT WORKS: METHODOLOGICAL ISSUES

Having said at the close of the last chapter that the decline of the reha-bilitative ideal was followed by a later resurgence of interest in finding out what works best with particular offenders, it would seem logical to go on to consider these developments. However, before looking at how the treatment and rehabilitation of offenders has progressed since the arrival of the 'nothing works' doctrine, some consideration needs to be given to the methods used in evaluating the effectiveness of treatment. It is important to understand these in order to appreciate how conclu-sions are reached about whether or not something 'works'. This book is not primarily concerned with research methods, but evaluation methodology is crucial to an understanding of the treatment and reha-bilitation of offenders for several reasons:

1 It is possible that failure to demonstrate treatment effects in the past has been due to flawed research rather than to flawed treatment.
2 Methodological considerations are related to theories about the treatment of offenders.
3 The development of approaches towards the treatment of offenders has been influenced by changes in thinking about, and techniques for, evaluating treatment.

This chapter will therefore consider, first, what may be termed the 'tra-ditional' approach to evaluation. A development called meta-analysis is then described and reviewed. The chapter ends by outlining the main features of a debate about approaches to evaluation which developed during the 1990s, which has been referred to by some of those involved as the 'paradigm wars'.

The 'Traditional' Model of Evaluation

The traditional model for evaluating most types of intervention is based on the methods of natural science. In a clinical controlled trial some patients, the 'experimental' group, are given the treatment under inves-tigation, such as a new drug, while others, the 'control' group, are not;

their conditions before and after treatment are then compared. Three types of variable are involved:

1   the dependent variable, which is the outcome that the researcher is interested in, such as whether someone gets better;
2   the independent variable, which is the input into the experiment, the new drug or other form of treatment;
3   intervening, or extraneous variables, which might influence the effect of the independent variable upon the dependent variable; for example, something else creeps into the experiment such as the way the drug is administered, which might affect the impact of the drug itself, or whether the subjects involved in the experiment have a predisposition to be affected one way or the other.

Essentially, in the classic scientific paradigm the researcher is attempting to establish whether there is a direct causal relationship between the independent variable and the dependent variable by holding all extraneous variables constant, so that the independent variable, whether or not someone receives the treatment, is the only thing that varies (Figure 3.1).

Figure 3.1

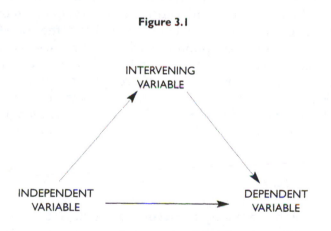

When measuring treatment effects it is essential to ensure that like is compared with like, so the experimental and control groups must differ *only* by one being given the treatment and the other not. Consequently, once it has been established who is eligible for treatment, patients are assigned to the experimental and control groups on a random basis. It is also important to ensure that the dosage and administration of the drug (or whatever) is standardised and is the same for both groups.

An approximation to this model is adopted in the social sciences for evaluating interventions; this is usually referred to as the quasi-experimental method, because rather than using random allocation it attempts to match 'treated' participants with a comparison group. However, this raises a series of issues of some significance. I will characterise these as being of three kinds: *epistemological*, *theoretical* and *technical*. The three types of issue are intertwined, since once a particular perspective on evaluation is adopted this affects other issues.

Epistemology

Epistemology is about how we know what we know. It is about the theory of knowledge itself, and hence is at a higher level of analysis than specific theories about, for example, criminal behaviour. What I have termed the 'traditional' model of evaluation, described above, comes within a particular school of thought (usually termed empiricist because it relies on observation or experimentation) about how knowledge is acquired. Many researchers would argue that any evaluation that does not wholeheartedly embrace the kind of methodology described above is lacking in rigour, the implication being that the results of any such research are to be disregarded. Indeed reviews of the literature regarding the evaluation of particular forms of intervention frequently do reject studies on such grounds.[1] On the other hand, there are those who would argue that the adoption of such a natural science paradigm, which effectively sees society as a kind of laboratory, is naïvely positivistic, viewing the subjects as passive recipients with no capacity for interpretation of, and reaction to, what is happening to them. Although I am not going to consider epistemological matters at length, they are important and I shall refer to them again towards the end of the chapter.

The Role of Theory

The outline of the traditional model of evaluation given above is a fairly standard textbook description, and it comes across as a rather mechanical procedure in which behaviour before intervention is compared with behaviour afterwards, without much consideration of the ideas that form the basis for the intervention. This omits a key component of the whole research process: the part played by theory. A more adequate outline of the research process would describe it as starting with a theory, from which are derived hypotheses about what one may expect to find as a result of empirical inquiry. Data are collected and analysed to test whether these hypotheses are true or false and, depending on the results, the theory is rejected or modified. In the classic scientific paradigm an experiment may be set up to collect the data necessary to test the hypothesis, and in the sphere of medicine this frequently involves some form of treatment. So the experiment or treatment is performed on the basis of a theory about what is likely to work: new drugs are not just concocted at random, but on the basis of much investigation into the nature of the disease and a hypothesis about the likely impact of specific steps that are taken to deal with it.

When it comes to social intervention, what is being expressed is a theory about the nature of the problem being addressed. Treatment is essentially the empirical test of a theoretical proposition, and programmes for offenders may be seen as the basis for testing a hypothesis.[2] The process is illustrated in Figure 3.2.

Figure 3.2

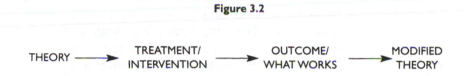

THEORY ⟶ TREATMENT/ INTERVENTION ⟶ OUTCOME/ WHAT WORKS ⟶ MODIFIED THEORY

When evaluating the impact of a programme intended to influence such things as crime or drug addiction it is important to consider the 'programme theory' that underlies it. For example, if a new project is set up with the stated intention of rehabilitating drug addicts, then inherent in this project is a theory about the nature of drug addiction and what should be done to 'cure' it. Similarly, a new crime prevention initiative is likely to contain a theory (or theories) about the causes of crime. Alternatively, programmes that offer education or employment training for offenders contain ideas about the rehabilitative potential of education, or the relationship between crime and unemployment. As a last example, developing programmes of sporting activities for young offenders may involve a variety of ideas about what such programmes seek to do, and why they might be expected to have some relevance for young offenders (whether or not one actually expects them to reduce offending). A study of a sports counselling scheme for offenders offers a good illustration of this because if one is studying what effect such a scheme has on young offenders it may be relevant to consider *why* it is thought it might have an impact. Is it because (a) the scheme occupies their free time, (b) brings them into contact with non-delinquent peers, (c) increases their self-esteem, (d) increases their social and physical skills, and consequently (e) improves their prospects of employment, or (f) because the activity leader presents them with a good role model (Nichols and Taylor, 1996: iii), or is it a mixture of several of these things?

This is very simply expressed, but in reality the relationship between a particular phenomenon and a specific form of intervention may be quite complicated. Nonetheless, whenever one reads or hears about a programme for dealing with offenders it is important to ask what theoretical assumptions are contained within that form of treatment or intervention. It is one thing to say this, but it is a precept that is not always easy to apply. There are instances of intervention programmes that have a definite and clearly articulated theoretical rationale. During the 1960s, for example, a poverty programme was established in the United States that incorporated a project called Mobilization for Youth, which was based on the theories of Cloward and Ohlin about delinquency and opportunity, its aim being to extend the non-delinquent options for young people (Marris and Rein, 1974, Ch. 1). More recently a programme has been developed called Communities That Care (which originated in the United States and has been introduced into certain areas in the United Kingdom). This long term programme attempts to build safer neighbourhoods for children by establishing a working partnership between local people, agencies and organisations to support and strengthen families, promote school commitment and success, encourage responsible sexual behaviour and achieve a safer, more cohesive community. It starts by assessing the levels of various risk factors in a community, such as family conflict, low school achievement and community disorganisation and neglect, and measures outcomes in relation to drug abuse, youth crime, school-age pregnancy and school failure. The approach is grounded in studies of empirical associations between risk factors and problem behaviour amongst young people, and hence can be seen to be based on previous scientific inquiry.

However, there are many more initiatives where the rationale underlying a programme of intervention is implicit, unclear and may be quite confused. There may even be several different theories within the same programme, which are not even consistent with each other. This happens especially where a programme of treatment or intervention involves several different organisations and a range of people, each with their own 'theories' about what needs to be done. In order to achieve a politically acceptable compromise the ideas underlying a programme may be left vague in order not to alienate one party or another. Hence one should not be too surprised to find that in many social projects theory is at quite a low level, and may not be explicitly stated.

'Technical' Issues

The third set of issues that are raised by the traditional model of evaluation are what I would term 'technical' issues. The word 'technical' in this context does not indicate that they are trivial: far from it. If one is undertaking the kind of evaluation reported in many studies of attempts to treat and rehabilitate offenders, then they are of much consequence. These technical concerns stem in large part from the fact that when evaluating social programmes, and some psychological methods of treatment, it is often impossible to match the conditions of a laboratory experiment or a clinical trial. Consequently various techniques are employed to ensure that like is compared with like, and that all variables except the experimental, or independent, variable are controlled in some way. There are problems with this as far as the treatment of offenders is concerned, the most obvious being that offenders are seldom dealt with by being randomly assigned to treatment and control groups.

There have been exceptions to this. Some years ago a juvenile court in the north of England adopted a system whereby not all delinquents who had been truanting from school were dealt with by the court immediately, but had their cases adjourned for a number of months, during which time their school attendance was monitored. What happened to them subsequently depended on their behaviour during the period of adjournment. This was nicknamed the Damocles experiment, and in order to test its efficacy juveniles were randomly allocated either to be given the Damocles treatment, or to be dealt with in the normal way (Hullin, 1978, 1985). The procedure was controversial and was eventually discontinued.

It is more common for efforts to evaluate the treatment of offenders to attempt to approximate the clinical approach by matching 'treated' and 'untreated' offenders, and by using statistical techniques to control for the effects of intervening variables. This can become problematic because, as explained earlier, what is referred to as treatment can take a wide variety of forms, often being more in the nature of complex social intervention than a carefully controlled clinical situation. Far more needs to be done to satisfy the conditions necessary to conduct a rigorous evaluation. Even when this is done, several matters need to be examined when evaluating programmes for the treatment and rehabilitation of offenders; some of the most important are considered below.

Programme Aims   The first consideration is what the stated aims of an intervention are. An appreciation of aims and objectives is needed because they are likely to indicate, among other things, the programme's theoretical underpinnings: what assumptions it is making about the nature of crime, drug addiction, or whatever is being addressed. The aims of a project are, however, liable to vary in the degree of clarity with which they are set out. Some projects may articulate their aims very precisely, while others refer in rather general terms to things like 'improving community safety' or enabling offenders to lead 'a worthwhile and productive life'. Where statements are of a general nature careful pre-evaluation probing of the perceptions of the parties involved in the intervention is necessary, using semi-structured interviews or other qualitative methods. These inquiries should include the perspectives of as many different people as possible, not forgetting the participants themselves. It is not uncommon for senior staff and officials to have one idea of what a programme is about, while those who actually deliver it on the ground interpret the aims rather differently. There always is a theory of some kind, even if it is not set out as such by those who have initiated the programme of intervention. Attempting to clarify what the aims of a programme are will also indicate the appropriate criteria for assessing its effectiveness.

Confusion in specifying aims may be due to a failure on the part of those responsible for the initiative to articulate the aims clearly, or it could be that they are fudged and deliberately vague because they have to meet the needs and objectives of different groups. Indeed, it is not uncommon to find that initiatives set up to do one thing (e.g. youth work, involving young people in drama workshops, promoting social or educational skills), claim to be reducing crime amongst young people because that is how they can best get funding. On closer examination it may be found that the project is not necessarily doing things aimed at crime reduction, or if it is, the connection is an indirect one.

An initiative may have several components (such as individual therapy, group sessions, vocational training and social skills training), or may be addressing several aims. This makes the task of evaluation more complex since it can be difficult to establish which component, if any, is having an impact on which participants. Projects may also accord different priorities to their activities and aims. Consequently it is essential to look for hierarchies of objectives, with organisations perhaps having primary and secondary (and even tertiary) goals. For example, a project set up to work with drug addicts may have as its stated aim, 'enabling people to lead a drug free and meaningful life as productive members of society'. But the reality may be that most of the people they deal with lead very chaotic lives, and simply turning up to an appointment is a major achievement. This is progress and needs to be recognised as such, but it reveals the gap that sometimes exists between stated aims and reality. A good evaluation should do more than tell the project that it has not rehabilitated anyone recently; it should look at what is happening or not happening in the intervention as a whole. It is, however, a good idea to be wary of organisations that have bland aims, or whose expressed aims amount to little more than trying to change the world.

Programme Integrity   Another key element of any evaluation is to establish whether a programme is actually doing what it claims to be doing. This is known as 'programme integrity'. It may sound rather obvious, but it is easy even for treatment programmes set up in institutional settings to drift and be drawn off course. In this context it is relevant to consider how long the programme has been running. An evaluation may be set up at the outset of a new form of treatment or social initiative, but it may be some while before the programme 'settles down' and is running in the way intended. On the other hand, a programme that has been going for some time may have lost its original impetus and sense of direction, perhaps because of changes in staff, or through changes in the outside world as one type of treatment goes out of fashion and another becomes more attractive. Programme integrity will be referred to again in the next chapter.

Relevant Criteria   A programme's aims will also indicate the criteria by which it is appropriate to measure its success, and several criteria may be relevant. However, the researcher must always check whether the criteria that s/he thinks are appropriate are seen as such by all the parties involved in an initiative. It is all too easy, where offenders are concerned, to assume that reconviction is the relevant outcome measure. But this may not necessarily be the case. For example, a number of schemes have been established which were concerned with training offenders, and had as their *main* objective the obtaining of a qualification or a job, or going on to further training. It would be inappropriate to evaluate such schemes on the basis of whether or not participants are reconvicted if this was never explicitly acknowledged as one of their main objectives (see Crow et al., 1989: 77–84, for a fuller discussion of this example). Similarly, in recent years a number of victim–offender mediation schemes have been started. Before assuming that such schemes should be evaluated on the basis of the reconviction rates of the offenders it is necessary to consider whether they are in fact designed to achieve such an objective. It may reasonably be argued that such schemes are about mediation, not rehabilitation, and should therefore be judged by other criteria, such as the satisfaction of the parties concerned with the mediation process, and any agreements reached during mediation.[3] However, be on the lookout for projects that redefine their criteria so that they are easier to achieve. Having failed to reduce recidivism there may be a temptation to revert to such things as increasing offenders' self-confidence or social skills as a fallback to a 'softer' outcome measure.

As long as this is not the case, it is reasonable to consider criteria other than reconviction as legitimate measures. One may be the cost of the programme. If the programme has a high unit cost and the impact on reconviction rates is marginal, it may be worth considering whether the same effect might be achieved by alternative means. This criterion became more significant when the aspirations of treatment and rehabilitation to reduce reconviction rates received a setback during the 1970s (Shaw, 1980). Other criteria of success may include whether the programme diverts people from custody, and whether there is some change in the attitudes of the offender. A word of warning is necessary when it comes to attitudinal measures, since it should not be assumed that these are related to changes in behaviour. It has also been common in recent years to judge projects, not just by whether they reduce crime and offending, but by whether they reduce the fear of crime amongst potential victims and the public at large. Recent research has indicated that 'fear of crime' may not be such a significant and reliable measure after all (Farrall et al., 1997). Finally, it may be appropriate to use several criteria of success, some of them being defined as primary outcome criteria and some as secondary; or to consider whether a programme has adverse or unintended consequences, such as 'net-widening' – bringing into contact with the criminal justice process and its agencies people who might not otherwise have been so.

Studying Reconviction   Although it should not be assumed that reconviction is always an appropriate criterion of the success of a programme, it will be relevant for many programmes, if only because it is the question that is most likely to be asked of any form of intervention involving offenders. If reconviction is to be used as a measure of success, then a number of factors need to be considered:

- Reconviction is not the same as re-offending. As a measure of outcome reconviction is affected by detection rates and enforcement policies.
- The length of the follow-up period used has to reflect the need to make comparisons with other studies (a two-year follow-up period is most often used), the nature of the offence (where sex offenders are concerned, for example, long follow-up periods are necessary), and the nature of the offenders (young people in their teens change quite rapidly in their behaviour and a shorter follow-up period may be appropriate).
- The presence or absence of reconviction may be too crude a measure on its own. For example, some offenders, especially young ones, commit a number of offences within a short period of time. An indication that some form of intervention is having an impact on the *rate*

of reconviction over a given period may be relevant. It may also be worth considering whether the nature of offences has changed; moving from more serious to less serious offences may be considered an improvement. In other words, success and failure can be relative.

- Care also needs to be taken to avoid false positives. These arise when someone, after becoming involved in a programme, is convicted by a court for an offence that occurred prior to that involvement. And, of course, when calculating the reconviction rate any time spent in custody needs to be discounted, since obviously the offender is not at liberty to commit offences in the community.[4]

Apart from random allocation and quasi-experimental methods, reconviction studies can also be carried out by calculating the *expected* rate of reconviction for a given group of offenders using the Offender Group Reconviction Scale (OGRS). This uses known predictors of re-offending to produce a predicted probability of reconviction, which is then compared with actual reconviction. The method has been used in several studies in recent years, including the study by Lloyd, Mair and Hough (1994) comparing reconviction rates of community and custodial penalties, and Sugg (1998) in looking at the impact of motor projects on reconviction rates. Use of the OGRS for evaluating reconviction outcomes does, however, have drawbacks, including the fact that it is no better than the original data on which the prediction variables are based, and the possibility that variables other than those used influence outcome. Kershaw (1998: 14) says that 'the difference between actual and predicted reconviction rates for a group of offenders does not provide an absolute measure of effectiveness. For this reason any evaluation should include a similar control group for comparison'.

Meta-analysis

What is meta-analysis?

Following the rise of the 'nothing works' doctrine during the 1970s the studies that had given rise to the doctrine (especially Martinson's) were subjected to a certain amount of critical scrutiny. Several points were made about the satisfactoriness or otherwise of the studies, but one line of questioning was whether existing research methodology was adequate to detect treatment effects. It has been suggested that looking at studies of treatment programmes on a one by one basis obscures the overall impact that they are having. It is possible for positive and negative findings to cancel each other out, or to overlook the significance of positive findings amongst the negative ones (as probably happened in the case of Martinson), thus giving a negative impression of the state of knowledge. Many reviews of research literature are 'narrative' in nature: the reviewer attempts a synthesis of the results of a number of studies using their own words. This was essentially the approach used by Martinson and others. Meta-analysis is an attempt to produce a more powerful means of analysing outcome research by bringing together the results of different studies. It is a statistical technique for combining the results of sometimes quite large numbers of studies, taking account of the different methods used to evaluate the effects of intervention. It is claimed that meta-analyses are more scientific than the narrative method. Furthermore, by combining studies, it is claimed, the positive and negative findings of individual studies are less likely to cancel each other out, because one is able to examine aggregated statistical data.

Meta-analysis has been around since at least the 1930s, and has been used in clinical and educational settings to combine data and evaluate treatment and intervention programmes. The method has been described and advocated for social science research by Glass, McGaw and Smith (1981), who stress its quantitative nature, in contrast to the narrative reviews and integrative studies from which it evolved. 'The essential character of meta-analysis is that it is the statistical analysis of the summary findings of many empirical studies' (Glass et al., 1981: 21). Meta-analysis, they say, seeks general conclusions and does not prejudge the quality of research findings

---

Other authors have also given definitions of the technique:

Wolf (1986: 5) – 'the application of statistical procedures to collections of empirical findings from individual studies for the purpose of integrating, synthesizing, and making sense of them'.

McIvor (1990: 11) – 'the pooling of data across a number of studies to compute the overall size of the effect achieved by a given method of intervention. Advocates argue that measuring size of effect, and not just whether it has occurred, is more accurate and realistic'.

Izzo and Ross (1990: 135) – 'The procedure of meta-analysis involves collecting relevant studies, using the summary statistics from each study as units of analysis, and then analysing the aggregated data in a quantitative manner using statistical tests'.

McGuire (1995: 7–8) – '[Meta-analysis] involves the aggregation and side-by-side analysis of large numbers of experimental studies.... Essentially, the procedure of meta-analysis requires recalculation of the data from different experiments in a new all-encompassing statistical analysis'.

Wolf (1986) identifies two types of meta-analytic approach:

> *Combined results* – which focus on testing the statistical significance of the combined results across primary research studies;
> *Treatment effects* – which focus on the estimation of the magnitude of the experimental, i.e. treatment, effect across studies.

The *effect size* of the latter is what is most commonly used as the statistical basis for meta-analyses. Different researchers use different formulae for estimating the effect size of various studies, but they all involve deriving a standardised measure of the magnitude of treatment effect that can be used across all the studies that comprise the meta-analysis. One method, for example, is to measure the mean difference in outcome between 'experimental' and 'control' cases in standard deviation units.[5]

Over the years there have been a number of large-scale meta-analytic reviews of the treatment of offenders, and it is claimed that these have on the whole shown positive results, confounding the 'nothing works' doctrine. In one review McGuire says,

> Taking all of these meta-analyses together, it can be demonstrated that the net effect of 'treatment' in the many studies surveyed is, on average, a reduction in recidivism rates of between 10 per cent and 12 per cent. (McGuire, 1995: 9)

Criticisms of Meta-Analysis

There are a number of concerns about the technique of meta-analysis. These are acknowledged by Glass, McGaw and Smith (1981: 218), and summarised as being of four main kinds:

1. What Glass, McGaw and Smith call the 'apples and oranges' problem. This is the obvious objection that it is dangerous to mix and attempt to integrate the findings of different studies. As outlined earlier, evaluation studies can have widely differing aims and samples, and take place in very different circumstances. Aggregating the data from them may not be valid.
2. In attempting to incorporate the findings of diverse studies, there is a likelihood that badly designed, poor quality research will be included. It has been suggested that meta-analysis advocates low standards of research quality (Eysenck, 1978).
3. Meta-analysis depends on using the findings that researchers report and publish. There are various reasons why the results of evaluations may not be incorporated in a meta-analysis. Much grant-aided research results in a final report submitted to the funding body. It

may then be up to the funding body whether that report is ever published. For example, the Home Office in the UK is under no obligation to publish the results of research that it commissions. Also many small community-based projects involving offenders may result in reports that only appear in what is generally termed the 'grey' literature; that is, reports produced internally for an organisation. Thus, a probation service may get its research officer to evaluate one of its schemes, the results of which are produced as an internal report. The meta-analyst may simply miss some studies that are relevant to the area of interest. Consequently there is likely to be selection bias in the results that are incorporated into a meta-analysis. There may well be systematic differences between the results of research that appear in journals, books and reports. It is quite probable that successful interventions are more likely to be published than unsuccessful ones, and the results of any meta-analysis will therefore be biased.

4. Meta-analyses are conducted on large data sets in which multiple results are derived from the same study. This means that different sets of results may not be independent of each other, giving a mistaken impression of the reliability of the results. The main consequence of this non-independence is a reduction in the reliability of the estimation of averages and equations.

Mair and Copas (1996)[6] express several reservations about meta-analysis. They distinguish between *Level I* meta-analysis, a descriptive technique for reviewing a body of literature in a systematic and consistent way, which they believe is valid, and *Level II* meta-analysis, which draws inferences from the results using formal statistical procedures, about which they are much more dubious. In addition to the criticisms relating to publication bias, and the variable quality of design referred to above, Mair and Copas point out that meta-analyses quite often cover varying forms of treatment and a variety of outcome measures. In particular, they emphasise that what meta-analysis has *not* done is to establish precisely what works, to what extent, with whom, and in what settings and circumstances. As a cautionary note they cite the instance of a medical meta-analysis of small scale studies of the use of magnesium in the treatment of heart disease, which concluded that intravenous magnesium was a safe, simple and effective form of intervention. However, when the opportunity arose to undertake a single large-scale study involving 58,000 people, it was found that magnesium had virtually no effect. Mair and Copas's conclusion is that although meta-analysis has successfully demolished the proposition that 'nothing works', it only takes a moment's thought to realise that this is a fairly meaningless formulation anyway. They end by recommending that probation managements be cautious, and encourage a critical approach to programme development, setting up carefully monitored programmes and being prepared to find that some of them don't work.

In the light of these criticisms the kind of claim made above by McGuire needs to be viewed with caution. Meta-analyses have indeed helped us to put the 'nothing works' nostrum behind us, but much still needs to be done to understand how and why, what works with whom, and recent debates have indicated that there is a need to move towards a more interpretive, and less positivist approach to treatment evaluation.

Other Approaches to Treatment Evaluation

Although it seeks to refine and advance the evaluation of treatment programmes for offenders, meta-analysis is an extension of the traditional model of evaluation, combining a number of outcome evaluations. The traditional approach to evaluation in social research has been criticised on the basis that, although it may be an appropriate way of evaluating outcomes, it is deficient in other respects. The traditional approach is sometimes referred to as 'black box' research: we can measure what went in before treatment and what came out afterwards, but understand little about what went on during the intervention itself. So, whatever the results were, do we know *what* happened, and why something did or did not work?

This is especially relevant where there are several strands to an intervention – something that happens quite often where offending is concerned. As a result, other approaches to evaluation research have developed, some complementing the traditional model, others at variance with it. One approach has been the development of 'process evaluation', placing more emphasis on studying what happened and why. Others have engaged in 'action research' a form of research in which there is a dialogue between researchers and researched, so that the results of research feed into developments, contributing to interventions rather than simply pronouncing on their success or failure. Everitt and Hardiker describe several types of evaluation that stem from the interpretivist tradition in social research, including illuminative evaluation, stakeholder evaluation, and pluralist evaluation. These have in common an attempt to understand the processes that are taking place in the implementation of an initiative, and the perspectives of the various parties involved. Everitt and Hardiker themselves favour a critical evaluation approach, which they characterise as incorporating some of the features of interpretivist evaluation, but with a critical awareness of the power relationships which operate in any form of intervention (Everitt and Hardiker, 1996).

'Paradigm Wars': 'What Works in Evaluation Research?'

Other researchers have raised more fundamental objections to the 'standard' model of outcome evaluation, objecting to what they regard as its positivist underpinning. In an article in the *British Journal of Criminology* Ray Pawson and Nick Tilley (1994) argued that the quasi-experimental paradigm had resulted in moribund evaluation, and had been 'itself a contributing factor to the "nothing works" lament' (Pawson and Tilley, 1994: 291). They refer to the traditional quasi-experimental paradigm as the OXO model (Figure 3.3).

Figure 3.3

	Pre-test	Treatment applied	Post-test
Experimental group	O_1	X	O_2
Control group	O_1		O_2

Ironically, although they claimed to be raising fundamental objections to the traditional model, their main criticism is not novel. It is essentially the familiar criticism that such an approach fails to comprehend *how* a programme works (Pawson and Tilley, 1994: 294), and they submitted to critical scrutiny an evaluation by Trevor Bennett of a police initiative for reducing fear of crime (Bennett, 1991). Pawson and Tilley recognised this to be a well-executed study in OXO terms, but say that it failed to explain how police activities might bring about change in a community (Pawson and Tilley, 1994: 297). It was suggested that what is needed is to understand a programme's *mechanisms* and the *context* in which it takes place. Pawson and Tilley then put forward their solution, citing a study by Nick Tilley of the operation of closed circuit television in car parks as a model of such an approach. This approach is what they term a 'scientific realist' evaluation. It is explained that for a realist evaluator,

> Outcomes (O) are understood and investigated by bringing to the centre of investigation certain hypotheses about the mechanisms (M) through which the programme seeks to bring about change, as well as considering the contextual conditions (C), which are most conducive to that change. (Pawson and Tilley, 1994: 300)

The original article was the subject of subsequent exchanges in the *British Journal of Criminology* between Pawson and Tilley and Trevor Bennett (Bennett, 1996; Pawson and Tilley, 1996). Bennett did not think that researchers who use quasi-experimental designs 'overlook . . . mechanisms and contexts' (Bennett, 1996: 568), citing Cook and Campbell's seminal work (1979) on quasi-experimentation in support. He also denied that competent evaluators merely seek associations between treatments and outcomes. In defence of his own work Bennett said that he did consider causal mechanisms and the areas in which the research took place. He suggested that, although there is a need to refine evaluation methods, Pawson and Tilley offer 'little that is new and nothing that is useful in moving towards this goal' (Bennett, 1996: 572).

The debate continued in the pages of the journal *Evaluation* where it focused on the Communities That Care (CTC) programme referred to earlier. David Farrington who was, like Trevor Bennett, at the Institute of Criminology in Cambridge, has for a number of years been involved with the Institute's study of a cohort of young people, looking at the factors associated with some young people becoming offenders. He has been interested in the role that parenting, families, schools and communities play in young people growing up in a non-delinquent manner. In 1996 he published a report for the Joseph Rowntree Foundation about these matters (Farrington, 1996) and was subsequently involved with the Foundation in looking at the possibility of trying out in the United Kingdom the Communities That Care programme, which had been running in a number of areas in the United States. In 1997 he wrote an article about how such a programme might be evaluated (Farrington, 1997), recommending the comparison of experimental and control communities, and taking measures of key outcome variables (crime, delinquency, substance abuse and adolescent problem behaviour) before and after the intervention package. This amounts to a particular application of what I have referred to as the 'standard', or quasi-experimental, model of evaluation. In this article Farrington mentions the possibility that not all criminologists would accept such a design and refers to Pawson and Tilley's 1994 *British Journal of Criminology* article, but stresses the importance of internal validity (i.e. being able to unambiguously attribute any change in the outcome variable to the effects of the intervention) in any evaluation.

Pawson and Tilley responded with a further article (Pawson and Tilley, 1998a) in which they criticised Farrington's design for taking insufficient account of the complexity of the Communities That Care programmes. They suggest that the design favoured by Farrington would miss the opportunity to look at 'what works for whom in what circumstances' (Pawson and Tilley, 1998a: 83). Instead they stress the importance of studying the theories that underlie a programme such as CTC, and suggest that a 'scientific realist' study would transform the evaluation 'so that the test of the program becomes a test of whether its theories come to pass' (Pawson and Tilley, 1998a: 85). Accompanying Pawson and Tilley's article was a response from Farrington in the same issue of the journal, which argued that the main difference was that whereas he had seen CTC as a 'well-developed technology waiting to be tested', Pawson and Tilley assumed it to be an 'iterative, evolving, ill-defined, highly variable procedure that essentially required further exploratory and developmental work'. The last word, for this issue of the journal exchange anyway, went to Pawson and Tilley, who made a brief rejoinder to Farrington regarding mechanisms and meaning, contextual contingency and programmes and methodologies (Pawson and Tilley, 1998b).

One of the reasons why the debate between Pawson and Tilley on the one hand, and Bennett and Farrington on the other, became such a prolonged, and indeed heated, one is because it concerns different philosophical approaches to evaluation, hence the reference in one of the articles to the 'paradigm wars' (Pawson and Tilley, 1998a: 73). Pawson and Tilley make a distinction between two modes of causative explanation:

(a) 'successionist' causal thinking (more frequently referred to as deterministic causality), which describes a constant conjunction between events ('the action of billiard balls is archetypally describable in these terms' Pawson and Tilley, 1994: 293). This is the approach, they say, of quasi-experimentation.
(b) the 'generative' conception of causation, which they explain as describing the transformative potential of phenomena, rather like gunpowder whose potential to explode inheres in its chemical composition. This is the approach of the school of thought that they espouse: 'scientific realism' .

In his response to the original Pawson and Tilley article Bennett denied that quasi-experimentation is necessarily deterministic, and said that in the social sciences probabilistic causality is generally accepted to be more appropriate. In their response to Bennett's criticism of their article Pawson and Tilley said that Bennett had failed to grasp the basic difference between the principles of successionist and generative causation (Pawson and Tilley, 1996: 574), and that while Bennett's own research may have incorporated some attempts to describe what was happening alongside his outcome evaluation, these do not constitute a realist approach to evaluation:

> He seeks to steal our realist clothes in claiming that all along his inquiry *was* attentive to the contexts and mechanisms of (police) contact patrols. We still beg to differ. Instead of understanding *mechanisms*, he deals with *mechanics*.

Rather than considering the salience of *context*, he provides a touch of local *colour*. (Pawson and Tilley, 1996: 576; emphases in original)

A key passage in the exchanges which have taken place occurs when David Farrington refers to Pawson and Tilley's contention that mechanisms provide the 'reasons and resources' to change behaviour. Farrington's comment is that it is not clear how reasons could be investigated:

Many psychologists are reluctant to ask people to give reasons for their behaviour, because of the widespread belief that people have little or no introspective access to their complex mental processes. . . . Hence, it is not clear that reasons in particular and verbal reports in general have any validity, which is why psychologists emphasise observation, experiments, validity checks, causes, and the scientific study of behaviour. (Farrington, 1998: 207)

This passage epitomises the difference between the positivist, and in this instance specifically behavioural, approach to inquiry, and the interpretive approach. It is not surprising to find that Pawson and Tilley take issue with this in their rejoinder:

Suppose a woman locks a door and is asked why she is doing so. If she says that it is a precaution against intruders, there seems no reason to us not to take her reply seriously. To be sure, and as we have argued repeatedly, such reasoning may have unacknowledged conditions and unintended consequences, but these do not place the ideas beyond investigation. (Pawson and Tilley, 1998b: 211)

Pawson and Tilley's approach has been set out in more detail in their book *Realistic Evaluation* (1997). The exchange in *Evaluation* ended with Pawson and Tilley concluding their rejoinder to Farrington by saying, 'The UK evaluation of CTC will be under way by the time this exchange is published. Let us see what happens!' (Pawson and Tilley, 1998b: 213).

Although this is not a book about research methodology, the debate between different schools of thought on how initiatives should be evaluated is relevant to what has been said in Chapter 1, and earlier in this chapter, about the relationship between theories of crime and offending and initiatives designed to do something about crime and offending, and the methods for seeing whether those interventions work. We need to know whether or not a particular way of dealing with offenders does result in a reduced likelihood of reconviction, whatever the practical difficulties involved in achieving this. For this reason any evaluation needs to be able to tell us in what circumstances and with whom such an intervention, *if sufficiently well replicated*, would work in future. This means that it has to be concerned, first and foremost, with looking at measurable outcomes. At the same time the pure quasi-experimental model has deficiencies when applied in areas of social research such as criminology, and I am sympathetic to the criticisms of the technique made by Pawson and Tilley. However, my own view is that these criticisms are based on the fact that much evaluation research has been overly concerned with the mechanics of programme evaluation, and insufficiently concerned with the theories that underlie them. Good scientific method has at its heart the interaction of theory and practice. I do not see that it is necessary to invoke an entirely new paradigm, such as scientific realism, in order to get round the fact that some evaluation research does not do this. What is needed, as I have suggested elsewhere (Crow, 1998), is first to employ good, theoretically informed methods of inquiry. To do this it is necessary to examine the theoretical basis of any intervention. This theoretical basis may not be a unitary framework defined by a single person (the social equivalent of the laboratory researcher). It is more likely to be a mixture of the different theoretical approaches of the various parties who take part in an intervention; an emergent property of the actors, sometimes referred to as 'practitioner theories'. What is usually termed process research needs to investigate what these different theoretical perspectives are and what impact they have on the implementation of a programme. Finally, little mention has been made in all this of the offenders themselves who, in the 'traditional' model at least, are seen as largely passive – to be acted upon rather than to act and react. The interpretive criminologist would want to consider rather more than has happened in the past the possibility that the delinquent might himself or herself affect the intervention process. I have covered the recent debate about evaluation at some length because we need to understand that in a field such as criminology it is impossible to separate 'what works' from how we know what works.

Further Reading

You will now be aware that it is possible to approach methods of evaluation from different perspectives. Although Pawson and Tilley put forward a specific view of evaluation their book *Realistic Evaluation* (1997) is worth reading not only for learning about their approach at first hand, but because it contains an entertaining first chapter on the history of evaluation. The more traditional approach is exemplified by Cook and Campbell's *Quasi-Experimentation* (1979). Another very useful text is the book by Everitt and Hardiker (1996), which is written with social work professionals in mind, and like Pawson and Tilley's book also adopts a critical approach towards methods of evaluation. *Evaluating the Effectiveness of Community Penalties* (1997a), edited by George Mair, is a useful compilation of several people's approaches to evaluating criminal justice initiatives.

Questions to Consider

- How might you set about studying a project working with offenders, such as a motor project, a sporting activities project or an arts workshop? What things might be considered?
- Who do you agree with – Pawson and Tilley or Bennett and Farrington?

Notes

1 Furby, Weinrott and Blackshaw (1989), for example, in their review of sex offender recidivism studies, consider several methodological criteria for the acceptability of a study.

2 Karl Popper argues that a hypothesis can be falsified, but not verified (Popper, 1968: 40–42). When a hypothesis is falsified an alternative hypothesis is developed, which may in turn be refuted, and so on. This can lead to better theories, but not to certainty.

3 This particular example is discussed further in Crow, 1998.

4 The factors referred to here are reservations that have been expressed by researchers on numerous occasions, and are explained at greater length by George Mair, Charles Lloyd and Mike Hough in 'The limits of reconviction rates', in a book edited by George Mair (1997a).

5 This can be expressed as $\quad ES = \dfrac{\bar{X}\,\text{exptl} - \bar{X}\,\text{control}}{SD}$

6 Although it is unpublished, Vennard, Hedderman and Sugg (1997: 4, 10) make use of this paper in their review of cognitive behavioural approaches.

4

WHAT WORKS?

Treatment and Rehabilitation after 'Nothing Works'

Chapter 2 ended by saying that following the rise of the 'nothing works' doctrine the focus of criminal justice policy and of criminological inquiry shifted towards other developments, but that treatment and rehabilitation in various forms did continue, even if the terminology changed. A concern with treatment and rehabilitation may not have altogether disappeared, but it became more marginal within criminal justice policy and thinking, and more broadly conceived in terms of different types of intervention with offenders. It also became more sophisticated in trying to identify what works for particular offenders.

This chapter looks at what has happened regarding the treatment of offenders since Martinson. It starts with critiques of Martinson (including his own), and then goes on to look at what has become known as the 'what works' movement and the related literature. The next section gives some consideration to cognitive intervention, which became one of the key components in attempts to work with offenders, and then various sources of material are drawn on in order to decide whether we do now know 'what works'. The chapter ends on a cautionary note, suggesting that perhaps effectiveness may not be everything.

Martinson Recants

Although it had considerable impact, Martinson's article had several shortcomings and was subject to criticism. Palmer (1975) noted that 18 of the studies reviewed by Martinson in fact reported some degree of success. Palmer also remarked that Martinson's findings on the effectiveness of intensive forms of supervision were quite favourable. In addition, because he was concerned with the efficacy of each treatment method as a whole, Martinson tended to overlook indications that some programmes seemed to be effective in certain circumstances (Palmer, 1975: 137–138). Although the twelve main kinds of intervention considered by Martinson had produced positive as well as negative findings, they did not achieve what Martinson was looking for: a guaranteed way of reducing recidivism. Having subjected Martinson's work to detailed scrutiny Palmer suggested, first, that 'Various methods of intervention . . . are more likely to be associated with positive behavioural outcome (i.e. less "recidivism") in relation to some offenders as compared with others', and second, that certain 'middle risk' offenders who have 'relatively strong personal controls' are more suited to certain forms of treatment than others. Methods of treatment that had been of value to only some offenders were counted as unsuccessful. Palmer concluded that,

> Rather than ask, 'What works – for offenders as a whole?' we must increasingly ask 'Which methods work best for *which* types of offenders, and under *what* conditions or in what types of setting?' (Palmer, 1975: 150; emphasis in original)

Martinson himself retracted what he had said in his 1974 article in a little-known journal (Martinson, 1979).[1] In this later article Martinson discussed the potential for sentencing reform in the United States, arguing first that, 'Contrary to common belief, the rate of recidivism in this country is not high, it is quite low' and, second, that

> Contrary to my previous position, some treatment programs do have an appreciable effect on recidivism. Some programs are indeed beneficial; of equal or greater significance, some programs are harmful. . . . Indeed, it was misleading to judge criminal justice on the basis of these evaluation studies. (Martinson, 1979: 244)

He cited data from a survey of 555 research studies undertaken after the earlier review (called the *Effectiveness of Correctional Treatment* (ECT) review which led to the 'nothing works' article) to show that recidivism was not especially high in the United States, and then went on to criticise the earlier research saying,

> However, new evidence from our current study leads me to reject my original conclusions and suggest an alternative more adequate to the facts at hand. (Martinson, 1979: 252)

Martinson pointed out that the earlier review was based purely on evaluation studies and 'excluded about ninety per cent of the research it had available because it was not evaluation research. . . . In comparison to *ECT*, our (current) sample is much more representative of criminal justice nationally' (Martinson, 1979: 253). He explained that in his earlier article he was looking to see whether treatment added to existing criminal justice patterns had an appreciable effect, but

> The very evidence presented in the article indicates that it would have been incorrect to say that treatment had *no* effect. . . . More precisely, treatments will be found to be 'impotent' under certain conditions, beneficial under others, and detrimental under still others. (Martinson, 1979: 253–254)

Martinson went on to point out that, as others were also finding, 'The critical fact seems to be the *conditions* under which the program is delivered'. Thus a treatment given to juvenile offenders in a group home may have different results to the same programme delivered in a prison institution. One of the main thrusts of Martinson's article was to argue that sentencing reforms needed to be implemented with care, and he specifically 'warns against confining juvenile offenders without some kind of treatment' (Martinson, 1979: 256), stating that post-release parole supervision is of particular value and that it would be inadvisable to dispense with it (Martinson, 1979: 257).

Martinson's retraction attracted little attention compared to the original article, and in any case by then the fate of the treatment model in its traditional form was sealed so Martinson's later article had little policy impact. Reviewing developments eight years later, Walker (1987: 82) makes the point that, 'if it is the case that nothing works better than anything else, then another way of looking at this is to say that nearly everything works to more or less the same extent'.

The 'What Works' Movement

Others have not been happy to accept such an undiscriminating state of affairs, pointing out that the conclusion that 'nothing works' was unjustified, and setting out to promote a body of evidence about what can be shown to work. This developed into a substantial literature, drawing on hundreds of original studies. There have also been academic 'what works' conferences, and conferences for probation managers and staff wanting to apply what can be learned from research. Several key figures have become prominent in this enterprise and their work has been noted by practitioners and policy makers. The body of work has become quite extensive and beyond the capacity of this book to review in detail. But to an extent the 'what works' literature has acquired an almost hierarchical structure, which means that it can be accessed through certain key references. At the lowest level (in terms of structure; not necessarily quality) are the many hundreds of primary research evaluations of particular treatments and projects dealing with offenders of various kinds. At the next level up are works that have attempted to synthesise the results of these studies, often (though not invariably) using meta-analysis as a way of doing so (see the previous chapter). The syntheses most commonly cited include Garrett (1985), Whitehead and Lab (1989), Izzo and Ross (1990), Andrews et al. (1990), and Lipsey (1992). In addition to these syntheses of the treatment of adult and juvenile offenders in general, there are also syntheses in particular areas, such as the meta-analysis of evaluations of the treatment of sex offenders by Furby et al. (1989). Finally, at the top of this literature hierarchy, are more wide ranging reviews which have sought to bring together or scrutinise the 'what works' literature as a whole, such as McGuire (1995), Mair and Copas (1996), and Vennard et al. (1997). Consideration of the treatment and rehabilitation of offenders must include an awareness of the work that has been done in this area.

The 'What Works' Literature

Foremost amongst those who have figured in the 'what works' movement, are Paul Gendreau and Robert Ross, who wrote one of the earliest post-Martinson reviews. Gendreau and Ross (1979) argued that social research is young compared to other scientific disciplines, and that it is too early to say nothing works just because so far we have failed to discern treatment effects, especially given the inadequacies of much evaluation research. They also suggested that part of the problem was that treatment programmes often didn't do what they should be doing, and that much of the 'nothing works' conclusion was based on inadequately designed projects published before 1967 (Gendreau and Ross, 1979: 468). Gendreau and Ross reviewed 95 programmes from 1973 to 1978, a period after that covered by Martinson's review, which met criteria of good design, statistical analysis and at least a six-month follow-up. The programmes were considered under several headings:

Family and community intervention – This involved attempts to improve family functioning in such a way as to reduce the kinds of behaviour that result in delinquency.

Contingency management – a form of behaviour modification in which approved behaviour is reinforced by a token economy system, and individuals are rewarded for demonstrating such things as 'appropriate verbal interaction, completion of assigned chores, and promptness in schoolwork'. Other approaches included behavioural contracts, such as the study by Doctor and Polakow (1973), where the targeted behaviour was employment. In this instance the time worked increased between 45 and 77 per cent, and re-arrests decreased from 2.0 to 0.15 per year.

Counselling – This included social learning, modelling, and transactional analysis.

Diversion – This covered interventions that sought to avoid bringing people into the correctional system, using a variety of intervention strategies. One concentrated on family communication, another on vocational counselling and training. However, interventions using a single technique were found to be less successful than those employing a variety of techniques. This raises the question of which of several techniques is the effective one, or whether the use of multiple techniques *per se* is more effective. It is also relevant to consider the role and impact of diversion from criminal justice in itself as a form of intervention.

Biomedical – These interventions included remedying nutritional and other chemical deficiencies, with claims of success rates of 80 per cent and more having been made for vitamin therapy and nutritional regimes.

Miscellaneous treatment – Several studies that were difficult to classify were covered here, including probation, work leave programmes, a pre-release programme for incarcerated drug offenders offering academic education and counselling, the treatment of alcoholic offenders with Antabuse, financial assistance and job finding services, and related programmes addressing alcoholism, drug abuse and sexual deviation.

One of the reasons for itemising Gendreau and Ross's categories is to illustrate the very wide range of interventions involved. Several of these included economic and work related programmes, and it is interesting to note that, despite such clearly socio-economic interventions, Gendreau and Ross talked throughout their paper about effective correctional *treatment*.

On the basis of their review Gendreau and Ross came to several conclusions:

- Studies that used a combination of techniques were more successful than a single treatment method.
- Recidivism is only one outcome, and others need to be considered.
- Treatment settings interact and there are individual differences.
- Compared to the resources put into dealing with crime, relatively few resources were devoted to treatment.
- There was a lack of co-ordination amongst agencies.

Garrett (1985) conducted a meta-analysis of 111 studies completed between 1960 and 1983 of offenders less than 21 years of age in an institutional or community residential setting, which had some form of control procedure. Over all the studies there was an average effect size (see the section on meta-analysis in Chapter 3) of + 0.37, meaning that treated young offenders performed, on average, at + 0.37 standard deviations better than a comparable group of untreated offenders. However, while Garrett concludes that 'treatment of adjudicated delinquents in residential settings does work' (Garrett, 1985: 303), the studies covered a range of treatments, and varied in the degree of rigour with which the evaluation was conducted, and in the outcome measures used. So the results are not as clear as they may at first appear. Garrett distinguished four main types of treatment: psychodynamic counselling or therapy, treatments based on behavioural theory (discussed further below), treatments designed to enhance life skills, such as academic and vocational experience and leisure pursuits, and an 'other' category, including music therapy, and vitamin treatment. Although initially treatments in the behavioural category resulted in the greatest amount of change (with an effect size of + 0.63), when the degree of rigour with which the studies were conducted was taken into consideration the picture changed somewhat. The more methodologically rigorous studies in this category had an effect size of + 0.30, compared with + 0.86 for studies conducted with less rigour. Nonetheless, Garrett found that treatments using a cognitive behavioural approach seemed to be more successful, even in the more rigorous studies. So the broad indications were that some things work, even if it is not always easy to discern precisely which, and in what conditions.

Whitehead and Lab (1989) carried out a meta-analysis on evaluations of juvenile correctional treatment (defined as 'any intervention aimed at reducing subsequent recidivism') appearing in professional journals from 1975 to 1984 inclusive. After a thorough reading of some 200 professional journal articles, all but 50 were eliminated from the analysis on the grounds of lack of adequate data, absence of a control group, lack of a clear treatment method, focus on adult behaviour, or duplication of results in more than one journal. Five main kinds of treatment category were identified: programmes diverting youths from the formal justice system; programmes which operated as an extension of the formal justice system; community corrections, such as probation and parole; institutional or residential treatments; and 'speciality' interventions such as Scared Straight (where young offenders are confronted by what might happen to them if they continue to offend) and Outward Bound (physical activities). Chi square and the phi coefficient were computed for the studies used, but because chi square is affected by sample size most reliance was placed on the phi coefficient, which ranges from zero to one. A phi coefficient of + 0.2 was regarded as the minimum indication of treatment effectiveness, and the authors claimed that this was a very generous criterion and 'could be criticised for being too low'.

Considering the studies in their meta-analysis Whitehead and Lab found that relatively few in any treatment category demonstrated much impact on recidivism, and 'many appear to exacerbate the problem'. They concluded that,

> This reanalysis of juvenile correctional treatment provides little encouragement for advocates of correctional intervention. No single type of intervention displays overwhelmingly positive results on recidivism. (Whitehead and Lab, 1989: 285)

The treatment categories initially used by Whitehead and Lab did not specifically cover behavioural interventions. Given that previous studies had suggested that this was a promising approach, Whitehead and Lab did a further analysis comparing studies involving a behavioural approach of some kind with those that did not. Although a greater proportion of the behavioural interventions (44 per cent) had a phi coefficient of 0.2 or greater compared with non-behavioural interventions (35 per cent), the behavioural interventions also had more negative phi coefficients, indicating that juveniles subjected to behavioural interventions had done worse than their controls. Consequently Whitehead and Lab concluded that 'The results of this comparison of behavioral and nonbehavioral interventions does not provide the strong support reported by other reviews' (Whitehead and Lab, 1989: 286). Whitehead and Lab's judgement, based on their findings, was that 'The results are far from encouraging for advocates of correctional intervention'.

Whitehead and Lab's meta-analysis was criticised on several grounds. One was that the phi coefficient criterion of 0.2 was too stringent (McGuire, 1995; Vennard et al., 1997). Another was that they used the phi coefficient as the measure of effect size, and that when the mean effect size is computed directly it is found to be positive (Lösel, 1993). It is also apparent that the treatment categories used by Whitehead and Lab are rather broad and that at least one of them, diversion from justice, was hardly an intervention at all and did not address offending behaviour (Vennard et al., 1997). Moreover, despite their pessimistic conclusions overall, their results indicated that some things were working.

Andrews, Zinger, Hodge, Bonta, Gendreau and Cullen (1990) suggested that there was a need to move forward on this basis, and find out what works for whom in particular settings. They argued that effective treatment has to be based on clinically relevant and psychologically informed principles, which include risk (delivering higher levels of intervention to higher risk offenders), targeting criminogenic needs, and responsivity (matching treatment to the learning styles of offenders). Andrews et al. applied these principles in a re-analysis of 45 of the 50 studies used by Whitehead and Lab, and also to a second, non-representative sample of 35 studies dating from the 1950s to 1989 which they had on file, in order to gauge how well the conclusions based on the Whitehead and Lab sample might generalise to adult samples. They also used the phi coefficient as the estimate of effect size. Andrews et al. hypothesised that type of treatment, which incorporated their principles regarding appropriateness of intervention, would be the main determinant of effect size. The analysis supported their hypotheses that type of treatment 'was clearly the strongest of the correlates of effect size sampled in this study' and that 'appropriate and unspecified correctional services were significantly more effective in reducing recidivism than were criminal sanctions and inappropriate service' (Andrews et al., 1990: 382–383). They also found that treatment in institutions and residential settings appeared to dampen the positive effects of 'appropriate service' while augmenting the negative impact of 'inappropriate service'. Thus they concluded that,

> As predicted, the major source of variation in effects on recidivism was the extent to which service was appropriate according to the principles of risk, need and responsivity. Appropriate correctional service appears to work better than criminal sanctions not involving rehabilitative service and better than services less consistent with our a priori principles of effective rehabilitation. (Andrews et al., 1990: 384)

Like Whitehead and Lab, Andrews et al. looked in particular at the impact of behavioural techniques. Whilst initially behavioural intervention yielded a greater mean phi coefficient than non-behavioural treatment, this difference became non-significant when the 'Type of Treatment' principles were controlled for. Consequently Andrews et al. concluded that 'use of behavioral methods contributes to the reduction of recidivism, but those contributions are subsumed by the broader implications of risk, criminogenic need and responsivity as represented in our Type of Treatment variable'. Finally, Andrews et al. made the point that although there is not a perfect correlation between treatment and reduced recidivism, other perspectives concerned with the impact of social class, incapacitation and crime prevention appeared to offer nothing better.

Izzo and Ross (1990) carried out a meta-analysis of 46 studies of intervention programmes for young offenders aged between 11 and 18 years. This specifically looked at whether programmes that included a cognitive component were more effective than those that did not, in terms of recidivism. Programmes were classified as having a cognitive element if they addressed problem solving, negotiating skills, interpersonal skills, rational-emotive therapy, role playing and modelling or cognitive behaviour modification. It was found that cognitive programmes were more than twice as effective as non-cognitive programmes.

Lipsey (1992) summarised a meta-analysis based on 'over 400' treatment studies of juvenile delinquents with control or comparison groups, published and unpublished. He looked first at whether there was evidence of positive treatment effects on delinquency, arguing that if there was no effect, then one would expect a 50–50 split, with half the studies showing results which favoured the treatment group and half favouring the control group. In fact he found a modest 10 per cent decrease in recidivism with treatment (Lipsey, 1992: 134–135). He then went on to look at the fact that there was wide variability in the range of the effect size amongst the studies and found that, 'to a considerable extent the effects found in a delinquency intervention study are a function of the research methods used and not the nature of the intervention being studied' (Lipsey, 1992: 137). Looking in more detail at the treatment effects (using regression analysis), Lipsey found that the characteristics of the subjects treated bore little relationship to the magnitude of treatment effect, and the largest factor related to effect size differences was the nature of the treatment itself (Lipsey, 1992: 137–138 and Table 4). In particular, 'we find larger effects for skill-oriented, behavioural and multi-modal treatment than for traditional counselling, casework and the like'.

Lipsey then went on to consider what Pawson and Tilley would call the 'mechanisms' of treatment effect and found that 'reduced delinquency in a sample of juveniles is most regularly accompanied by increased school participation' (Lipsey, 1992: 143). School participation, in turn, was most regularly associated with positive effects on psychological and interpersonal variables (such as self-esteem, attitudes towards authority, and self-control). Lipsey concluded that, 'apparently the important issue is whether or not the juveniles attend school, not how well they do academically' (Lipsey, 1992: 141).

The 'what works' literature has been reviewed by others. Gill McIvor (1990) concluded her review by supporting the 'risk principle': that more intensive interventions are more suitable for higher risk offenders, and that there is little justification for intensive intervention with low risk offenders. She also endorsed a multi-faceted approach which uses more than one form of treatment, and stressed the importance of programmes which involve community integration, suggesting that an investment in work training and work experience is especially worthwhile. For adults in particular McIvor supported the provision of concrete services aimed at the provision of non-criminal opportunities and highlighted the importance of addressing the problems and needs of offenders. James McGuire has been involved with the 'what works' movement for a number of years, and the review by himself and Philip Priestley (1995) has a distinctly optimistic tone, claiming that, 'Taking all of these meta-analyses together, it can be demonstrated that the net effect of "treatment" in the many studies surveyed is, on average, a reduction in recidivism rates of between 10% and 12%', although it was acknowledged that this was not a striking achievement. A rather more distanced piece of work is that by Vennard et al. (1997) in the Home Office Research Studies series, which specifically reviewed the use of cognitive behavioural approaches with offenders. This concluded that cognitive behavioural methods had been more successful than traditional counselling and therapy in changing offenders' patterns of thinking and behaviour. But while these methods, combined with training in social skills and problem solving, achieved the most promising results with juvenile and adult offenders, even these approaches did not achieve large reductions in re-offending for *mixed* (my emphasis) groups of offenders, with reconviction levels being on average 10–15 per cent lower than for matched comparison groups.

Some publications have attempted to compile reviews of 'what works' in reducing crime generally, considering programmes dealing with individual offenders alongside crime prevention initiatives, and work involving families and schools. In the United States researchers were commissioned to provide an independent review of the effectiveness of state and local crime prevention programmes. This produced an extensive list of initiatives divided into four categories of what works, what doesn't work, what's promising and what's unknown. In the first category were frequent home visits by nurses and other professionals to infants, improvements in schools' organisational development, communication and teaching of social competency skills, ex-offender job training, and rehabilitation programmes with risk-focused treatments. However, the researchers' central conclusion was that, 'Many more impact evaluations using stronger scientific methods are needed before even minimally valid conclusions can be reached about the impact on crime of programs costing billions each year' (Sherman et al., 1998: 12). In the United Kingdom the Home Office Research and Statistics Directorate produced a somewhat similar review in an attempt to develop an effective crime reduction strategy. Again the consideration of effective interventions with offenders formed part of this, largely summarising the previous review by Vennard et al., and concluded that 'None of the initiatives identified as promising will reduce crime on its own. An effective crime reduction strategy is one in which an integrated package of best practice is developed and delivered consistently over time' (Nuttall et al., 1998: 135).

Cognition and Crime

Several of the studies of effectiveness have featured cognitive behavioural methods of treatment as holding out some promise. It is therefore worth looking at this approach a little more closely. This takes us into the field of psychology. In an earlier chapter it was said that what is done to respond to crime depends on one's theories about the causes of crime (whether explicit or implicit). One of the main theories of crime causation that has emerged from psychology is that criminal behaviour, like other behaviour, is a learned activity. This is clearly expressed by Gendreau and Ross in their challenge to the 'nothing works' doctrine:

Most behavioural scientists have agreed that criminal behaviour is learned. The 'nothing works' belief reduced to its most elementary level suggests that criminal offenders are incapable of re-learning or of acquiring new behaviours. (Gendreau and Ross, 1979: 465–466)

Such linkage underlines the importance of being aware of how a programme of treatment and its evaluation are related to a theory of the cause of the problem. The original form of learning theory (operant learning) is based on learning through receiving positive or negative reinforcements of one's actions. It is therefore a *behavioural* theory since behaviour is seen to be determined to a large extent by the external environment, and in this sense it is within the positivist tradition. However, from the basic model, different branches of learning theory have developed. In particular *social* learning theory has sought to understand how the process of learning occurs at a cognitive level, by looking at what other people do and what the consequences are. In other words we don't just learn by what happens to us directly, but by reasoning from what happens to others. As Hollin (1996b: 46) points out, the term 'cognition' is used to cover a variety of processes, but in general it simply means the process of thinking. Thus delinquency represents a failure in learning or alternatively, as Sutherland (1947) has suggested, it can mean learning the wrong kinds of behaviour through differential association with people who hold favourable definitions of crime.

An element of social learning theory is the suggestion that offenders are deficient in cognitive skills and reasoning, and in particular that they have poorer social skills than non-delinquents (see Hollin, 1996b: 46–51). Essentially the cognitive behavioural theory suggests that many offenders have poor problem solving skills, and that much offending is compulsive and ill considered. Some psychological studies have also found that offenders tend to have an external *locus of control*, which means that they believe they are controlled by external factors, rather than being able to take responsibility for their own actions. In her meta-analytic review of the effects of residential treatment on young offenders, Garrett (1985) summed up why she thought that treatments using a cognitive behavioural approach seemed to be more successful. She suggested that such treatments give the offender 'the ability to control his or her own behavior, an internal rather than an external control system' (Garrett, 1985: 304). Having found that the Outward Bound (adventure training) experience also seemed to offer promising results in terms of lower reconviction rates, she argued that Outward Bound and cognitive behavioural treatment, 'both emphasize the juvenile's own control over his or her environment – the first an external, the second an internal environment' (Garrett, 1985: 304). In recent years there has been much emphasis by the media and politicians on imposing controls on young people (for example, the provision for curfews on young people in the Crime and Disorder Act 1998), and this has perhaps caused us to neglect the prospect that the most successful and desirable form of control is that which people exert themselves. This is in line with the view that to a certain extent delinquency is an expression of young people's need to exert control over their environment.

It has also been found that, compared with non-delinquents, offenders are less able to appreciate the perspectives of other people. Hence they have little appreciation of the victim's perspective, and in so far as victim–offender mediation schemes attempt to address offending behaviour, they do so through getting the perpetrator to see the consequences of their actions upon others. Sex offender treatment also involves increasing empathy with others. This is the reason why many of the attempts to determine what works in dealing with offenders have focused on programmes designed to improve offenders' cognitive skills. Ross and Fabiano (1985) have attempted to spell out the limitations in cognition experienced by offenders, as a result of which they developed a programme for the treatment and rehabilitation of offenders, under the heading, 'reasoning and rehabilitation'.

However, although the cognitive behavioural model is increasingly being adopted in North America and elsewhere, it is not a single unified method. As Vennard et al. (1997: 5) make clear, programmes with cognitive behavioural components can incorporate different elements. They draw on behaviour modification, in which socially acceptable behaviour and attitudes are rewarded, getting the offender to work on using internal thought processes to control their behaviour, role playing, training in problem solving and social skills training.

The STOP Programme

In the UK the 'what works' movement has had a number of adherents, and conferences have been held to consider results and pool experience. Understandably, the message that things do sometimes work has been especially welcome to a hard pressed Probation Service, and the Inner London Probation Service held its own conference for senior staff in 1995. A programme based on the 'reasoning and rehabilitation' approach, Straight Thinking On Probation (STOP), was initiated by the Mid-Glamorgan Probation Service in 1991. Like the approach of Ross and colleagues, this has involved sessions designed to teach cognitive skills and a range of social and self-control skills, negotiation, creative thinking and critical reasoning (Knott, 1995). The programme is being evaluated (Raynor and Vanstone, 1994), and reconviction data based on 12 months' follow-up showed that, *for those who completed the programme* (always an important qualification), actual reconviction rates of 35 per cent were better than the 42 per cent predicted for the participants concerned, and better than other forms of disposal (Knott, 1995: Table 5.5). In addition none of those who were reconvicted received a custodial sentence.

Reconviction Rates for Sentencing Revisited

Despite the claims of the 'what works' proponents and the possibility that some things do work, many remain sceptical about basing the justification for a rehabilitation approach to dealing with offenders on the likelihood that it will bring about a significant reduction in crime and offending (e.g. Institute for the Study and Treatment of Delinquency, 1996). While the adherents of the 'what works' school seek to provide grounds for optimism that some things do work, there is also research which suggests that, if the goal is a reduction in re-offending, then we have progressed little towards finding a solution to the problem of how best to deal with offenders. In 1994 the Home Office published the first major study comparing reconviction rates for different sentences for 15 years. This compared two-year reconviction rates for community service orders, probation orders (with and without 4A or 4B requirements)[2] and imprisonment. It concluded:

> The key finding of this report – in common with previous studies – is that there was little difference between actual and predicted reconviction rates, suggesting that sentence on its own did not have a major impact upon whether someone was likely to be reconvicted or not. There was no clear evidence to suggest that custody outperformed community penalties or vice versa in preventing reoffending. (Lloyd et al., 1994: 5)

This is, of course, reminiscent of the 'nothing works' verdicts of the past, suggesting that little has changed since the time of the review by Brody (1976). But it should be borne in mind that the analysis in this study is concerned with sentences in general, not with specific programmes. As indicated in Chapter 2, a distinction needs to be made between sentences, which cover many types of offender and are given for a number of reasons other than their rehabilitative potential, and the kind of programmes analysed by people like Ross, or Raynor and Vanstone. Indeed, the Home Office researchers acknowledge that 'there has always been variation in the quality of work with offenders, whether by the prison or probation service' (Lloyd et al., 1994: 5) and that it is quite possible that some probation and prison practice is more effective than others. Andrews et al. (1990) make a similar point when they note that 'The main effects of criminal sanctions on recidivism have been slight and inconsistent' (1990: 373), and 'the sanction and treatment services should be differentiated' (1990: 384). The same recognition was noted by a Home Office review of research on dealing with crime (Moxon, 1998).

Studies such as that by Lloyd, Mair and Hough also have to be seen in the context of the claim by the former Home Secretary, Michael Howard, at the Conservative Party Conference in October 1993 that 'prison works'. In the spring of 1997, at the start of a General Election campaign, two Home Office Statistical Bulletins were published. One reported that 57 per cent of offenders given community penalties in 1993 were reconvicted for a standard list offence[3] within two years of commencement of the sentence (Kershaw, 1997). The other reported that 53 per cent of all prisoners discharged in 1993 were reconvicted within two years (Kershaw and Renshaw, 1997). These were reported in the press as follows: 'Offenders spared jail "more likely to return to crime"' (*The Times*, 24 March 1997). In fact both the bulletins carefully explained that a range of factors can have an influence on recidivism. In addition it was noted that offenders discharged from prison were less likely than those starting community sentences to have 'pseudo-reconvictions'[4] and it is also necessary to take account of differences in the characteristics of offenders receiving community penalties and those sent to prison. Once these matters were taken into consideration the overall reconviction rates for custody and community penalties differed by only one percentage point after rounding – less than the statistical margin of error: 'This suggests that there is currently no significant difference between reconviction rates for custody and all community penalties' (Kershaw and Renshaw, 1997: para. 24 and Kershaw, 1997: para. 28).

This conclusion has been sustained by subsequent Home Office statistics for reconvictions of offenders sentenced or released from prison in 1995: 58 per cent of all sentenced prisoners discharged in 1995 were reconvicted of a standard list offence within two years, compared with 56 per cent of offenders who commenced community penalties in 1995 (Kershaw et al., 1999a, 1999b).

Does Anything Seem to Work?

So is anything effective in dealing with offenders? Before attempting to pull together some of the indications from research about what specific forms of intervention, if any, may be effective in reducing offending, it is useful briefly to take a broader perspective and consider possible explanations for why offenders carry on offending and why they stop, or desist from, offending.

Persistence and Desistance

In considering what may be most effective in reducing re-offending a sensible starting point might be to ask what factors are associated with re-offending and address those. While research has shown that a number of factors are associated with reconviction (which, of course, is not quite the same as re-offending), some factors seem to have been consistently more important than others, such as the influence of family and peers (Buickhuisen and Hoekstra, 1974; Phillpotts and Lancucki, 1979; Farrington and Morris, 1983). Just as there are many explanations for offending, so there are many reasons why people may stop offending, apart from undergoing a programme directed at treatment and rehabilitation. The study of *desistance* – why offenders stop committing crimes – has not attracted as much attention as the causes of offending and re-offending, although interest has grown in recent years. This helps to put the effectiveness of treatment programmes in perspective and draw attention to the fact that such programmes, while making a contribution to the reduction of re-offending may not be the only, or even the most important reason for crime reduction.

In the past there has been a notion that as young people mature, get jobs, and settle down with families they 'grow out' of crime (Rutherford, 1992), although there is relatively little evidence to support this hypothesis. The Cambridge Study in Delinquent Development, a longitudinal study of over 400 males, which looked at patterns of offending when the sample was aged 21, found that getting married was not related to a reduction in delinquency, although it was related to a reduction in some of the habits associated with offending, such as heavy drinking, sexual promiscuity and illegal drug use (Knight et al., 1977). Amongst the young male offenders who reformed, 'the breaking of ties with the male groups who had been their companions during adolescence seemed to have been a significant step in the process of change' (West and Farrington, 1977: 139). In a study of self-reported offending and desistance from offending, Graham and Bowling found that 'many young people had not completed the transition to adulthood by their mid-twenties' (Graham and Bowling, 1995: xii). Males lagged behind females in the maturing process associated with ceasing to offend and Graham and Bowling conclude that,

> If it is true that young people grow out of crime, then many will not do so by their mid-twenties simply by virtue of the fact that they (especially males) have not been able to grow up. (Graham and Bowling, 1995: xii)

The discrepancy between earlier suggestions that young people grow out of crime before their mid-twenties and Graham and Bowling's findings could be attributable to the change in employment and family patterns that has taken place in recent years. In the post-Second World War generation, because of successive governments' commitment to full employment, it was possible for most young people to have the prospect of getting a job and settling into a traditional family pattern. Since the 1980s there have been many areas where young people have stood little or no chance of achieving a settled employment pattern, and the patterns of stable family life that previously went with it. Whether this is the explanation or not, Graham and Bowling's research serves to remind us that ceasing to re-offend can be due to a variety of factors. They suggest that,

> Other factors which promote desistance are finding a sense of direction and meaning in life, realising the consequences of one's actions on others and learning that crime doesn't pay. (Graham and Bowling, 1995: xiii)

Of course, some of the programmes directed at the treatment and rehabilitation of offenders already seek to realise these objectives. But trying to help people attain a 'sense of direction and meaning in life' is a formidable undertaking, and there may be many different ways and means by which it is achieved. Graham and Bowling suggest that for females the best way to foster desistance from offending is by 'encouraging the natural processes of personal and social maturation', but that continuing to live at home protects young male offenders from persisting with crime. For those young men who leave home during their teenage years they suggest measures to prepare them better for life in the outside world, including bridging schemes such as 'foyers', which provide temporary accommodation coupled with training and employment opportunities, and better preparation for fatherhood and parenting (Graham and Bowling, 1995: xiv).

Guiding Principles for Effective Intervention

Is it possible to draw together the evidence from the research and say what kind of things work best in reducing offending? In answering this question we must bear in mind that past experience has shown that there is probably no universal solution, and that the best one can hope for is that some things may be effective in some instances. It is not possible to point to a single programme of intervention as the one that works. What does appear to be emerging is a degree of consensus about the kinds of intervention that are likely to be most effective, which can be used as a basis for putting forward some guiding principles. These are briefly summarised below, together with the references that support them.

Assessment, Matching and Risk Classification (Andrews et al., 1990; McIvor, 1990; McGuire, 1995; Vennard et al., 1997) Studies have consistently shown that the type and level of intervention must be matched to the individual offender. In particular there needs to be a degree of correspondence between the level of risk that an offender poses and the extent of any intervention, so that more intensive programmes are directed at higher risk individuals. This means that any form of treatment should be preceded by an assessment of the level of risk likely to be posed by an offender. The arrangements for doing this have been the subject of a Home Office research study (Burnett, 1996). In this instance the researcher did not examine whether the arrangements for matching various forms of intervention to individual offenders led to an improvement in effectiveness, although she did show that there were inconsistencies in assessment and allocation.

Responsivity   (Andrews et al., 1990; McGuire, 1995)   Responsivity means that programme workers should find what offenders respond to best and work on that. This generally means using methods which engage an offender in participating in the programme, rather than didactic teaching methods, or methods which lack any real structure or means of engaging a person.

Addressing Criminogenic Needs and Offending Behaviour   (Andrews et al., 1990; Vennard et al., 1997)   This principle involves targeting behaviours known to be associated with offending, such as drug or alcohol dependency, and poor social skills.

Programme Structure and Integrity   (Hollin, 1991; Lipsey, 1992; McGuire, 1991, 1995; Bottoms, 1995; Vennard et al., 1997)   The last chapter referred to the need to consider 'programme integrity' when evaluating the impact of treatment and rehabilitation programmes for offenders. Several studies in recent years have noted that the organisation, management, staffing and delivery of programmes are also related to their effectiveness in preventing reconviction. The guiding principle is that programmes need to have clear aims, be well structured and delivered in a consistent and reliable manner. For example, in an evaluation of Intermediate Treatment (IT) programmes for young offenders, the relatively ordered and authoritative staff approach, coupled with a high degree of care adopted by centre-based IT projects for those most at risk of custody ('heavy end' IT) was significantly more effective than the more fragmented individual packages developed elsewhere (Bottoms, 1995: 19–20). It was suggested that this finding reinforced the emerging trend towards a strong pro-social modelling approach in successful treatment projects. Thus the more effective programmes tend to be those in which there are clearly articulated links between the stated aims and the methods used, there is a structured programme and clear, directive treatment approaches, and the ingredients of the programme are carefully delivered as planned.

Cognitive Behavioural Components   (Gendreau and Ross, 1979; Garrett, 1985; Izzo and Ross, 1990; Hollin, 1991; Ross, 1991; Knott, 1995; McGuire, 1995; Vennard et al., 1997)   There is a body of evidence and opinion suggesting that, while no one form of treatment is uniquely able to reduce reconviction, those programmes which include a cognitive behavioural element appear to be the most promising. However, this is by no means a unanimous view, and it may be recalled that, in contrast to the references cited above, the work of Whitehead and Lab (1989) and Andrews et al. (1990) did not support such a conclusion. Furthermore, much of the evidence for the effectiveness of the cognitive behavioural approach has been adduced from meta-analyses – an approach which has its critics.

Multiple Techniques   (Gendreau and Ross, 1979; McIvor, 1990; McGuire, 1995)   Another common finding from the research is that more effective programmes are more often multi-modal. That is, they employ more than one approach or technique, and as a result address a variety of offenders' problems. As a guiding principle this is of dubious benefit, since it may be difficult to determine which element, or elements, in a multiple approach is most effective. This makes such programmes more difficult to evaluate and to replicate, and could result merely in throwing a mixed bag of approaches together in the hope that at least one of them will 'work'.

Community Based and Integrative   (McIvor, 1990; Hollin, 1991; McGuire, 1995; Vennard et al., 1997)   Several studies indicate that community-based programmes on balance yield more effective outcomes than those undertaken in institutions, the suggestion being that such programmes address offenders' behaviour and needs in the context of their day to day environment, and thus better equip them to deal with that environment and the problems that led them to commit offences. However, positive research results are by no means confined to community-based programmes and several studies (e.g. Garrett, 1985, referred to earlier) have indicated that programmes of treatment and rehabilitation undertaken in institutional settings do have value. This is important when we come to consider treatment and rehabilitation in a prison context in a later chapter.

Addressing Social Needs   (McIvor, 1990; Lipsey, 1992; Graham and Bowling, 1995)   Finally, it is apparent from a number of studies that a key element in successful rehabilitation is the addressing of social factors, such as education, training and employment, about which more will be said in the final chapter of this book.

Before moving on from what works in reducing offending, it is worth noting that, in addition to the principles mentioned above, several researchers have also given their judgement on what does not work. This includes traditional psychotherapy and counselling and one to one casework techniques (Lipsey, 1992; McGuire, 1995; Vennard et al., 1997) and several authors comment that measures which are purely punitive have been found to achieve little by way of reducing reconviction (Andrews et al., 1990; Lipsey, 1992; McGuire, 1995).

How Crucial is Effectiveness? A rights based approach to treatment and rehabilitation

So far this chapter has considered programmes for the treatment and rehabilitation of offenders purely in terms of their effectiveness in reducing re-offending, usually as measured by reconviction data. This is undoubtedly a valuable criterion, but is it, or should it be, the only one? Certainly there are those who believe so. In a consideration of the future for research on the Probation Service's work one reviewer says, 'However important other measures of success may be, reoffending is the key test for any probation programme' (Hedderman, 1998: 5). Are there dangers in becoming preoccupied with this as the sole basis by which to judge interventions? While one might consider that a programme in which offenders become more likely to offend should cease operations, should an initiative be closed down because, despite having other positive attributes, its participants have no worse a reconviction record than offenders dealt with using other measures?

These are essentially consequentialist considerations, justifying intervention on the basis of its outcomes. We saw earlier that other criteria might also be relevant. Programmes of treatment and rehabilitation need to be seen in a wider context of social and economic opportunity that may not be readily assessed by looking at the narrow criterion of impact on certain individuals. An alternative approach justifies treatment and rehabilitation on moral and ethical grounds. For example, Garland, addressing a conference organised by the Institute for the Study and Treatment of Delinquency (ISTD), suggested that 'The case for minimal punishment and constructive regimes was to be made on moral and political grounds, rather than utilitarian ones' (ISTD, 1995, 22: 14). Bullock, speaking at another ISTD conference,

> discussed how the answer to the question of 'what works?' depends on where we start with regard to justice or welfare models and how the aims of particular areas of the system will vary. (ISTD, 1996, 23: 16)

Such suggestions support those who would argue that treatment needs to be understood, not as a clinical term, but as how we treat people. On this basis right and proper treatment is an ethical rather than a utilitarian principle. Reviewing the legislation in the United States in the mid-1970s, Palmer (1977: Ch. 10) found relatively little judicial support for prisoners' rights to take part in rehabilitation programmes. Rotman (1986), nonetheless, has advanced a rights-based model of rehabilitation, arguing that the opportunity for rehabilitation is a right for the individual, whereas the need to demonstrate effectiveness is something that suits the needs of the state rather than the offender it deals with. Hence there is a contrast between the treatment paradigm and the justice paradigm. This should come as no surprise, since it will be recalled from Chapter 2 that the dominance of the treatment model originally came under attack, not just on empirical grounds, but also on ethical and theoretical grounds. Then the argument was the need to protect individuals from coercive treatment, ungoverned by due process. The other side of this argument is whether those who are duly coerced by the law have a right to the treatment that they could use as a basis for avoiding further offending. Such arguments have so far tended to revolve around prisoners' rights. McConville, for example, has argued that imprisonment as a means of incapacitation is the product of a political and moral vacuum:

> Containment means that we can't be bothered to engage the offender: 'It is too much trouble, too unreliable, and might make civic demands which I have neither the time nor the inclination to meet.'(McConville, 1998: 5)

But increasingly community sentences have been publicised as 'punishment in the community', with the Criminal Justice Act 1991 defining punishment as a restriction of liberty along a spectrum which starts in the community, of which imprisonment is only one part. Given such developments, the question of a right to take advantage of the opportunity to rehabilitate oneself could reasonably be extended to those given community sentences. Just as the medical model of treatment and rehabilitation was criticised on ethical, theoretical and empirical grounds, so any new approach to intervention needs to have firm theoretical, empirical and ethical foundations.

Conclusions

One thing is now fairly clear: it is not true to say that 'nothing works'. It probably never was, as the initiator of the doctrine, Martinson, himself acknowledged. In the mid-1970s work by Home Office researchers (Folkard et al., 1976; Brody, 1976) helped to establish the claim that 'nothing works'. Twenty-two years later a major review of criminal justice research gave official recognition to the end of this doctrine (Nuttall et al., 1998: 1). However, we are still a long way from being able to say what, if anything, does work. Indeed, it seems more likely that nothing works in a universal sense, but that some things can be effective in reducing the likelihood of reconviction for certain people in certain circumstances. The process of rehabilitation probably goes deeper and is more prolonged than we sometimes care to acknowledge. It has to be seen in a context where the factors associated with offending are embedded in a person's background, upbringing and social experience. When conviction occurs, the ensuing sentence is likely to expose the offender to a variety of interventions, some of which may even be conducive to further offending, such as spending time in a custodial institution in close contact with more experienced offenders. Taking part in even a good programme intended to deal with a person's offending may be all too short and limited an experience when set against the entirety of that person's existence to date. Other factors may be more important in altering the direction of a person's life, as the work on desistance indicates. In addition, unless there is a carefully planned follow-through, any benefits gained from a treatment programme may be superseded by a return to normal life. Although change may occur as a direct result of involvement in a treatment programme, immediate transformations may be too much to expect. It may be that work with an offender has to be looked at as a longer term process, in which specific programmes play their part.

Many of the programmes that seek to reduce re-offending are concerned with bringing about change in the individual. This tendency is apparent in the book edited by James McGuire (1995) which draws together much of the 'what works' material. In fact a reviewer of the book commented that,

> Its tight focus on cognitive psychology and the behavioural programmes which have stemmed from this approach to recidivism may irk some readers who would wish for socio-structural approaches to crime causation and crime prevention to be considered in any effectiveness debate. (Kemshall, 1996)

Not all the 'what works' literature consists of individualised solutions to offending. The point has been made earlier in this chapter that a number of the studies reviewed under the heading of treatment addressed social needs, but usually from the perspective of dealing with individual need. It is one thing to get an individual offender a job, but this is not the same as tackling unemployment. As argued elsewhere (Crow et al., 1989), programmes for the individual offender need to be seen as part of a broader attack on the conditions that give rise to crime. Programmes for offenders rightly take many forms and include economic and social provision, including education, training, jobs and housing. But unless they take place in circumstances which favour good educational, training and job prospects their impact may be no greater than that of Sisyphus rolling a rock uphill.

Further Reading

Important reading on what works can be found in the book edited by James McGuire, *What Works: Reducing Reoffending* (1995), and in the first part of the Home Office study, *Changing Offenders' Attitudes and Behaviour: What Works?* (1997), by Julie Vennard, Darren Sugg and Carol Hedderman. To understand the psychological background to some of the treatment approaches *Psychology and Crime* by Clive Hollin (1996b) is well worth reading, and a more detailed exposition of cognitive behavioural therapy can be found in the book of that name by Brian Sheldon. As I was writing this chapter the Home Office published a major review of what is known from research about the best ways of dealing with crime, *Reducing Offending: Research Evidence on Ways of Dealing with Offending Behaviour* (1998), directed by Chris Nuttall. Although much of the material can be found elsewhere, and is covered in this book, this review brings it together in a very useful manner, which will undoubtedly have implications for criminal justice policy. Chapter 8 on 'Effective Interventions with Offenders', by Julie Vennard and Carol Hedderman, is especially relevant and summarises the conclusions of their own earlier review of changing offenders' attitudes and behaviour, as well as other pieces of work.

Questions to Consider

- Can any conclusions be reached about the most effective ways of dealing with offenders?
- On what basis, if any, would you present the case for promoting the rehabilitation of offenders?

Notes

1 As with Martinson's earlier article, this can be found in the book of readings, *Offender Rehabilitation*, edited by Cullen and Applegate (1997) referred to in the Further Reading at the end of Chapter 2.
2 4A is a requirement to attend a probation day centre, and 4B a requirement to undertake certain specified activities; they tend to be used for more serious offenders than a straightforward probation order.

3   A standard list offence is one of a list of offences of which the details are recorded by the Home Office for the purpose of undertaking studies of criminal histories. The offences covered are all indictable offences, plus certain summary offences, such as criminal damage under £2,000 and assault on a constable.

4   These are convictions occurring after a sentence has started which relate to offences committed before the sentence in question commenced, which thus *appear* to be 'reconvictions'.

PART 2

THE INSTITUTIONS
OF TREATMENT

5

ON PROBATION

The Development of Probation

This chapter describes briefly the development and current concerns of the Probation Service in England and Wales, and then goes on to consider the service's role in the treatment and rehabilitation of offenders. The role of the non-statutory sector in working with offenders is referred to, and the chapter ends by looking at how the prospects for the Probation Service were developing at the end of the twentieth century.

The Probation Service has its roots in the activities of Church of England Temperance Society missionaries who started working in what were then police courts in the 1870s, although probation was already known in Massachusetts in the 1860s. The work of the missionaries was undertaken on a voluntary basis initially, first in London, then elsewhere. To start with, probation was associated with releasing offenders under recognisance of good behaviour. Early work included investigations, recommendations to the courts, home visiting and matrimonial conciliation, but soon involved prison after-care as well. Alcohol played a large part in the lives of those with whom the early police court missionaries worked, and this was the focus of much of their work.

In 1887 the work of the police court missionaries received its first official recognition in the Probation of First Offenders Act, which enabled courts to release offenders 'on probation' to the missionaries. This was followed in 1907 by the Probation of Offenders Act, which provided a statutory basis for probation work to replace the use of recognisance. But the Acts' essentially permissive nature meant that the appointment of officers and use of probation developed very unevenly. The service was still only partly funded by public money, and at this stage much of the work done by officers was concerned with social factors, such as finding homes and jobs for offenders.

The after-care of prisoners by probation officers developed as a result of the Prevention of Crime Act 1908, which also established borstal institutions, with a period of licence to follow training. In 1912 a significant step towards probation becoming an established profession was taken with the founding of the National Association of Probation Officers (NAPO). Another important development was the setting up of a Departmental Committee of the Home Office in 1922 to consider the 'Training, Appointment and Payment of Probation Officers'. This led to the Criminal Justice Act 1925, subsequently amended by the

Criminal Justice (Amendment) Act 1926. Following this, probation committees were set up on a local basis. At least one probation officer had to be available to every petty sessional division, and rules were introduced which governed the appointment and conditions of probation officers.

It was around this time that probation moved from being something whose use had been permitted and encouraged, towards something that was increasingly regulated, with officers' duties being progressively more defined, and the Home Office beginning to play a greater role. Nonetheless, the development of the service still depended on local initiative, which varied considerably. The Home Office sought to give a strong central lead, but had to tread carefully because the judiciary was wary of any initiatives that might prejudice their independence. However, in 1928 the Home Office issued a circular emphasising that probation was not just for first time offenders and could be equally valuable for adults as well as the young, and in 1930 it started an experimental training scheme for probation officers.

The use of probation increased during the 1920s and 1930s and the role of officers was extended to more matrimonial work, to acting as guardians *ad litem* in adoption cases, and to the supervision of people who failed to pay their fines. During this time also there was an important shift in the approach of probation work, away from the moral and material well-being of offenders and towards the treatment of individuals. This period, between the 1930s and 1960s, is described by McWilliams as one in which the Probation Service moved from the missionary phase of special pleading to the 'diagnostic phase' of probation work. In this time of change the basis for probation work shifted from metaphysics to science, the status of the offender changed from 'sinner' to 'patient', and the social inquiry report was 'transformed from a special plea for mercy to an instrument of objective professional appraisal' (McWilliams, 1986: 241). King (1964) describes the change as follows:

> The growth of other social services and the improvement of social conditions towards the end of this period (the 1930s) gradually made the old emphasis on work to deal with drunkenness and sheer poverty less necessary. . . . Interest in the medical and psychological aspects of crime and social inadequacy was growing fast.... This brought an increased emphasis on the importance of the personal and mental factors in delinquency and its treatment as opposed to the purely environmental. . . . The importance of diagnosis was increasingly recognised, and the gradual change in the attitude to treatment, once started, was to play a growing part in determining the nature of probation work in future. (King, 1964: 22–23)

Probation services subsequently came to adopt the casework approach to supervision. A Departmental Committee of the Home Office was established during 1934–36 to undertake a wide-ranging review of social services in courts of summary jurisdiction. This committee reviewed the whole position of probation at the time, proposing an official system of inspection of the work of probation officers and considering the organisation of the service and the appointment and training of officers. It also proposed that the increasing demands being made of the service were such that it should now become a full time public service and the remaining missionaries, selected and paid for by voluntary societies, were to disappear. The use of recognisance as a basis for probation, without proceeding to conviction, was also felt to be unsatisfactory and this was to be replaced by a legal order, 'which nevertheless should preserve the valuable element of "consent" which distinguished probation from all other forms of treatment of offenders' (King, 1964: 25).

Although the modern Probation Service could be said to have been largely established by the time of the Second World War, changes have continued up to the present. For example, until the Criminal Justice Act 1991 offenders were given a probation *order*, which was imposed in place of a sentence. The 1991 Act made probation into a sentence in its own right, and paved the way for the setting of nationally required standards of work. Section 38 of the Crime (Sentences) Act 1997 removed the necessity to obtain an offender's consent to probation and other community sentences. Although these changes have tended to increase the extent to which probation has become a centrally regulated service, it is worth noting that this is not new, but something that has been an element in the development of the Probation Service throughout its history.

The Probation Service at the End of the Twentieth Century

Organisation and Aims

At the end of the twentieth century there were 54 probation areas in England and Wales (although plans to make changes to the structure of the service will be referred to towards the end of this chapter). Each probation area was responsible to a Probation Committee composed of magistrates drawn from each of the petty sessional divisions covered by the area, and usually a circuit judge. Every service was headed by a Chief Probation Officer (CPO). In the past these had been drawn from the ranks of the Probation Service, but from 1994 it was possible to appoint a CPO who did not have such a background.

Without doubt the modern Probation Service has a difficult job, which is not made any easier by the fact that it is expected to carry out a wide variety of tasks, and to satisfy the needs of different groups of people. At one time it was common to describe the role of the probation officer as being to 'advise, assist and befriend' the offender, a phrase contained in the Probation of Offenders Act 1907, and because of this officers tended to be seen as primarily concerned with the offender. But they are also described as 'officers of the court', so are seen to have a duty to the public, and increasingly to be concerned with the victims of crime. The Home Office's Statement of Purpose for the Probation Service (Home Office, 1996c: 32) says that the responsibilities of the Probation Service are,

- to provide the courts with advice and information on offenders to assist in sentencing decisions;
- to implement community sentences passed by the courts;
- to design, provide and promote effective programmes for supervising offenders safely in the community;
- to assist prisoners, before and after release, to lead law-abiding lives;
- to help communities prevent crime and reduce its effects on victims;
- to provide information to the courts on the best interests of children in family disputes;
- to work in partnership with other bodies and services in using constructive methods of dealing with offenders.

Offenders on Probation

Although the service gradually acquired an increasing number of duties, its main work is criminal supervision of one kind or another (Table 5.1).

Studies have been done in the past on probationers and probation practice (e.g. Davies, 1969), but these have either become very out of date or were partial accounts based on research carried out in a few areas. The most recent attempt to obtain a more comprehensive picture was undertaken in 1994, involving a sample of 1,213 probationers in 22 probation areas (Mair and May, 1997).

Around seven out of ten (73 per cent) people on probation were male, 46 per cent of males and 39 per cent of females being under the age of 25 years old (Mair and May, 1997: 9–10). In the 1994 survey 93 per cent of respondents on probation were white. This is approximately the same as the proportion in the population as a whole, but other analyses have indicated that the proportions of black people dealt with by the criminal justice system and in prison are higher than in the population as a whole. The 1994 survey had a response rate of 61 per cent, and it may be that black probationers were less likely to respond to interview attempts, but the possibility remains that black

Table 5.1   *The work of the Probation Service*

	Orders and supervisions that commenced in 1997
Probation	50,700
Supervision under C&YP Act 1969	2,900
Suspended sentence supervision	550
Money payment supervision	4,800
Community service order	47,400
Community service (breach)	2,800
Combination orders	18,700
All court orders	**118,200**
Statutory pre- and post-release supervision	41,700
Voluntary supervision	8,200
All pre- and post-release supervision	**49,600**
All criminal supervision	**161,700**
Family court supervision	900
All supervisions	**162,600**
Pre-sentence reports	227,300
Criminal inquiries (e.g. bail inquiries)	61,000
Family court inquiries	36,300
Mediation work	8,300

Source: Home Office Statistical Bulletin, 12/98, Tables 1, 6 and 7, provisional data. Each person is counted only once in the totals even if they started more than one type of supervision.

offenders may be less likely to be on probation than receiving some other sentence, for whatever reason. Eighty-two per cent of probationers had a previous conviction. A high proportion of the family (40 per cent) and friends (about 75 per cent) of probationers had been convicted of a criminal offence. Probationers were particularly likely to be unemployed (only one in five of the 1994 sample had a job), to have been in a children's home, to be less well educated than the general population, to be in rented accommodation, and to be living on state benefit. About 40 per cent had problems paying bills. Almost half the 1994 sample said they currently had health problems or disabilities, and drug use was higher than in the general population. While nearly half the sample said they drank alcohol never or rarely, there was a minority for whom drink was a problem. The authors of the study commented that,

Irrespective of how these characteristics are related to offending, the poverty and deprivation exhibited by those on probation is an important factor which is likely to have implications for supervision and should not be forgotten or dismissed. (Mair and May, 1997: 30)

The National Standards for Probation Orders (Home Office, 1995c) suggest that as far as possible an offender should be seen on 12 occasions in the first three months of an order, and this appeared to have been followed in 83 per cent of cases involved in the 1994 survey. Later, probationers are more likely to be seen once a fortnight (40 per cent) or once a month (26 per cent) for sessions lasting half an hour (42 per cent) or an hour (38 per cent). Discussions during supervision are most likely to cover offending behaviour (63 per cent of respondents in the 1994 survey mentioning it) and the particular needs of the offender, for example relating to employment, money and accommodation problems, family and personal problems, and, where relevant, the consumption of drugs and alcohol (Mair and May, 1997: 37, Table 4.3). Over the last 20 years probation work has shifted from one to one counselling towards more group work, activities and special programmes.

One of the striking findings of the 1994 survey was that when asked why they thought they had been given a probation or combination order no one mentioned that it was to stop them re-offending. The most common response (27 per cent) was that the court wanted the offender to benefit from the services available while on probation. Nonetheless, two-thirds (67 per cent) agreed that 'Being on probation helps to keep me out of trouble with the law', and just over half (57 per cent) that 'Being on probation will help me to stop offending altogether' (Mair and May, 1997: 44, Table 4.7). One third had committed further offences since being on probation.

To Treat or Not to Treat?

Here we can only set the scene; for other and more extensive descriptions of the development and work of the service, see suggested reading at the end of the chapter. The treatment approach came to pervade the Probation Service for some 30 to 40 years around the middle of the twentieth century. The demise of the treatment model forced a major rethink in the service about the basis for its work. Several attempts were made to develop new models for probation practice. One was proposed by a group of probation officers working in south-east England who advanced the idea of what they referred to as 'Sentenced to Social Work' (Bryant et al., 1978). The 'medical model where the officer is expected to cure the offender's criminality' would be replaced by a clear distinction between the requirements placed on the offender by the court and the offering of services to help the offender (or 'client', as they were known in those days). Thus, in a redefined probation order the court would not only define the length of the order but *'the frequency of reporting to the Probation and After-Care Service'* (emphasis in original). There would be 'standard conditions', including the avoidance of further offences and notification of changes in address or employment, and 'special conditions' relating to residence in a hostel or medical treatment. The offender's consent to such a probation order would provide the basis for the *primary contract* between the offender and the Probation Service. In addition there could be a *secondary contract*, which would be negotiated on the basis of a joint assessment of the probationer's needs, regarding the provision of opportunities by the service. It was argued that under such an arrangement the court would have more confidence in the level of supervision and 'The offender would be treated as a more responsible individual, and by allowing him to choose social work help, the dignity inherent in self-determination would be recognised' (Bryant et al., 1978: 112).

The 'Sentenced to Social Work' approach was tried briefly over about two years in three different petty sessional divisions in Hampshire with, it was claimed, some success (Coker, 1984). Although it never became the norm for probation service practice, it is interesting to note that some of the proposals regarding the setting out of the requirements of a probation order can be found some 15 years later in the establishment of national standards for probation (about which more later). But despite Bryant et al. arguing that this would give courts greater confidence in the probation order, doubts about the order have continued to be expressed by policy makers.

Probably the best-known alternative to the treatment model was that put forward in the late 1970s by a criminologist and a probation research officer who was also a former senior probation officer. Following a conference in Sheffield, Tony Bottoms and Bill McWilliams published a paper, 'A Non-Treatment Paradigm for Probation Practice' (1979). Coming after the empirical studies undermining the traditional treatment model, their paper started by offering a theoretical critique of the model. They then went on to put forward a new paradigm, based on four key principles:

The Provision of Appropriate Help for Offenders   This involved the substitution of practical help, such as finding accommodation or employment, for treatment. In particular, Bottoms and McWilliams suggested that the treatment model involved 'objectification', the client being an object to be treated as the social worker or therapist saw fit. A non-treatment approach meant abandoning 'objectification' of the client and substituting a definition of 'help' based on what the client rather than the caseworker wanted.

Statutory Supervision of Offenders   It was the Probation Service's duty to supervise offenders, but whereas both the treatment model and the non-treatment paradigm involved 'an element of pressure', 'the help model obliges the client to make a series of moral and behavioural choices, but the worker does not reject the client whatever choices are made' (Bottoms and McWilliams, 1979: 178). The client was not a passive recipient of treatment, but an active agent.

Diverting Appropriate Offenders from Custodial Sentences   Bottoms and McWilliams claimed that 'The idea of saving appropriate offenders from going to prison where this seemed socially unnecessary has been a central part of the philosophy and practice of the Probation Service since its inception' (1979: 179). But they stressed that they did not see 'alternatives to prison' in purely rehabilitative terms. Whether or not someone received a custodial sentence was influenced by both the seriousness of the offence and the social needs of the offender. Within a given range of offence seriousness an offender with fewer social needs could end up in prison. It was therefore a matter of being prepared to '"hold" many offenders as successfully in the community as in prison, and more cheaply' (Bottoms and McWilliams, 1979: 182). Amongst other things, this involved rethinking the nature of the social inquiry report.

The Reduction of Crime   Bottoms and McWilliams pointed out that there had been a traditional expectation by the public that probation helped reduce crime, and that

> In a situation where poor people are often the victims of crime, and where there is some evidence of their increasing anxiety about such victimisation, we do not think that such expectations can be abandoned lightly. (Bottoms and McWilliams, 1979: 187)

However, if such reduction cannot be achieved by individual treatment then the only realistic answer is crime prevention. Because crime is predominantly social, crime reduction strategies must be social rather than individual, and the Probation Service must work with communities rather than individuals.

While Bottoms and McWilliams' principles did offer some guidance and were used as a basis for probation work in several settings, no overall paradigm or model replaced the treatment paradigm. Nevertheless, for much of the 1980s the Probation Service escaped the most severe stringencies imposed elsewhere in the public sector because of its law and order brief. However, the 1990s saw the arrival of cash limits, and more searching questions were asked of the service by Government. The Criminal Justice Act 1991 brought in a new sentencing framework based on a 'just deserts' model rather than on reforming the offender. In the era of treatment the word 'punishment' was little used. This changed in the latter part of the 1980s and during the 1990s. As mentioned in Chapter 1, the sentencing framework introduced by the Criminal Justice Act 1991 was based on degrees of punishment, where punishment was interpreted as meaning the restriction of liberty. Hence there was to be progressive restriction of liberty, ranging from discharges and financial penalties through community penalties to imprisonment, based first and foremost on the seriousness of the offence, with custody being reserved for the most serious cases. Consequently the sentences that involved the Probation Service – probation, community service orders and the new order enabling a combination of community service and probation – became 'punishment in the community'. Because sentencing was now based on offence seriousness, the nature of the reports prepared for the courts by the Probation Service altered, changing from social inquiry reports to pre-sentence reports. The Act marked a significant shift for the Probation Service, with less emphasis being placed on the offender's background and individual circumstances than on the offence and offending behaviour.

Because developments in recent years have shifted the focus of the Probation Service so much, it might be concluded that treatment and rehabilitation no longer play much part in the service's work. But individual probation areas have continued to develop and run a range of programmes that address offenders' needs and behaviour, as well as supervising them for the offences they have committed. These have included motor projects and sports counselling schemes, as well as the more traditional attempts to find housing and employment opportunities for offenders. However, such initiatives have become increasingly constrained by financial stringency. As far as treatment and rehabilitation are concerned the 'what works' movement described in the previous chapter has been an important and growing influence. The STOP programme in Mid-Glamorgan, based on the 'reasoning and rehabilitation' model of Robert Ross, has already been referred to (p. 69). The implications of this approach have been considered by Peter Raynor and Maurice Vanstone (1994), who referred back to the Bottoms and McWilliams' non-treatment paradigm, and put forward a revised and more modern version of it.

Raynor and Vanstone recognised that there had been criticisms of the 'reasoning and rehabilitation' approach. For example, its programme is a highly structured and prescriptive one, and Pitts (1992) has argued that effective programmes need to be adaptive and take account of individual needs. Nonetheless, Raynor and Vanstone claimed that the

introduction of the 'reasoning and rehabilitation' based STOP programme in the Mid-Glamorgan Probation Service was accompanied by
'early indicators of effectiveness' (Raynor and Vanstone, 1994: 395).
Given that probation services have adopted a non-treatment frame of
reference since the 1970s, Raynor and Vanstone ask what the implications are if it is found that certain forms of treatment *do* work. For
example, in the light of more recent knowledge the concept of appropriate help needs to be redefined into effectiveness which incorporates
a focus on helping individuals to stop offending.

Raynor and Vanstone suggested that a revised version of the
Bottoms and McWilliams' non-treatment paradigm needed to take seriously the status of offenders 'as moral agents responsible for their
actions' (Raynor and Vanstone, 1994: 399). This is more complex than
regarding intervention simply as treatment or non-treatment: there may
be various components to 'help'. So help needs to take account of other
people, not just the offender. 'Programmes like STOP also suggest the
need for some further clarification of the principle of informed consent,
which is central to any paradigm based on respect for persons' (Raynor
and Vanstone, 1994: 401), since it is not practicable to negotiate every
aspect of a treatment programme in advance.

Raynor and Vanstone put forward modifications to the Bottoms and
McWilliams' paradigm which 'respect moral agency and individual
choice, but recognise that the interests of communities and the needs of
victims properly limit the extent to which we can support the freedom
of offenders to choose continued offending' (Raynor and Vanstone,
1994: 402). A revised paradigm would therefore look like the final
column of Table 5.2.

The approach adopted by Raynor and Vanstone is important because
it is not just based on the consequentialist grounds of effectiveness, but
also seeks to incorporate a rights-based approach, which recognises the
rights and requirements of various parties: offenders, victims and communities alike. It is also reminiscent of the principles advanced by
Bryant et al. in their 'Sentenced to Social Work' model, which stressed
the dignity of choice.

The Mid-Glamorgan Probation Service's STOP programme is just
one programme, and if nothing similar had been developed elsewhere
in the Probation Service throughout England and Wales, Raynor and
Vanstone's ponderings about its implications would be of little relevance. The question therefore arises: to what extent has cognitive
behavioural training of the kind involved in the 'reasoning and rehabilitation' approach been developed elsewhere? Alongside the changes
moving the Probation Service towards punishment in the community
and all that it entails, the 'what works' movement had a growing influence during the 1990s. A study of the supervision of offenders by
probation officers found that two-thirds of senior officers were of the

Table 5.2 *Paradigms for probation*

Treatment paradigm	Bottoms/McWilliams' non-treatment paradigm (1979)	Raynor/Vanstone's revised non-treatment paradigm (1994)
Treatment	Help	Help consistent with a commitment to the reduction of harm
Diagnosis	Shared assessment	Explicit dialogue and negotiation offering opportunities for informed consent to involvement in a process of change
Client's dependent need as the basis for social work action	Collaboratively defined task as the basis for social work action	Collaboratively defined task relevant to criminogenic needs, and potentially effective in meeting them

Source: derived from Raynor and Vanstone, 1994: 402

opinion that officers were 'eclectic' in the methods of supervision they used (Burnett, 1996). On the other hand the study also reported almost one third of senior and supervising probation officers as saying that officers were increasingly adopting a cognitive behavioural approach. A similar conclusion was reached by the Chief Inspector of Probation when he said in his Annual Report for 1995 (HM Inspectorate of Probation, 1995) that the implementation of lessons from 'what works' research had been,

> piecemeal, fragmented and too dependent on local individual leadership. The Audit Commission, when looking at the Probation Service, found that the most successful programming too often failed to be replicated, exploited or transferred.

A survey of probation services' use of cognitive skills approaches found that most probation areas had developed or brought in programmes with a cognitive skills, or cognitive behavioural component (Hedderman and Sugg, 1997). Thirty-nine out of 43 services responding to the survey provided information on 191 such programmes, which most commonly targeted sex offending and motoring offences. However, it was also found that the terms 'cognitive skills' and 'cognitive behavioural' were used rather loosely, and many of the programmes did not meet the exacting standards required by such methods if they are to be effective in reducing offending. The results also indicated that offenders were not allocated to the programmes according to risk and need, and only 20 per cent of the programmes were based solely or mainly upon cognitive behavioural methods, suggesting that supervisors favoured using a range of approaches with such mixed groups of offenders. Only half the programmes had the necessary specialist expertise required to run this approach, and the monitoring of completion and compliance rates was inadequate. Only six areas had attempted an evaluation, but lacked sufficient numbers and comparison groups.

In the 1994 survey of probationers referred to earlier, the most commonly used programmes amongst respondents were alcohol management and counselling groups (30 per cent), probation day centres (25 per cent) and an employment or training unit (22 per cent) (Mair and May, 1997: Table 4.4). From the evidence available, it seemed that although parts of the Probation Service had taken up the 'what works' approach to treatment and rehabilitation, this lacked any consistent or co-ordinated framework of implementation and evaluation. In 1998 a Home Office plan set the Probation Service the goal of ensuring that every offender would be supervised in accordance with 'what works' principles by 2001.[1] This national initiative included 30 'Pathfinder' programmes developed as a variety of projects, as well as offending behaviour programmes and other services intended to reduce re-offending. The initiative had a budget of £21 million between 1999 and 2002, and a Joint Prison and Probation Accreditation Panel was set up to decide which programmes were effective and deserved accreditation for future use. Such a development may well increase the effectiveness of the service, but it is worth bearing in mind that many promising approaches to dealing with offenders have been pioneered by individuals and groups within the Probation Service, and the requirement that probation officers should follow approved programmes may limit their discretion, and the possibility for enterprising new initiatives. Introducing the Pathfinder programme, the Home Office Minister Lord Williams acknowledged that 'We must be realistic and robust. Not everything will have an instant effect. The causes of offending are often deeply rooted and difficult to tackle. The results of evaluation may be initially disappointing – but the information gathered will show the way forward.'[2]

The Non-Statutory Sector

Although this chapter is primarily about the contribution of the Probation Service to the treatment and rehabilitation of offenders, mention also needs to be made of the role of non-statutory agencies. Some of these are also referred to as voluntary agencies (although they commonly have paid, full-time staff as well as voluntary workers) and they are often registered charities. In recent years the phrase 'independent sector' has also come into use to indicate the actual or potential involvement of private companies as well as the more traditional 'voluntary organisations'. Non-statutory agencies have been working with offenders at national and local level alongside the Probation Service for many years, and indeed the Probation Service itself started life as a voluntary organisation. Some organisations have concentrated on a particular area: for example the Apex Trust has been primarily concerned with the employment of offenders, and training for employment. Some have concentrated most on acting as a pressure group for penal reform, such as the Howard League, and the Prison Reform Trust. Others, such as the Rainer Foundation[3] and NACRO, have delivered services to offenders. It is also possible to find a mixture of functions being undertaken within a single organisation: the Howard League has run projects for offenders, and NACRO has also done much to try to persuade the Government and public of the necessity of a positive rather than a purely punitive approach towards offenders, by issuing briefing papers and other material. Where such organisations have delivered services to offenders, these have usually been directed at assisting the offender's reform and rehabilitation, although this has not always meant an espousal of the treatment model as such.

The kind of contribution the non-statutory sector makes can be illustrated by reference to NACRO, which is the main national non-statutory body concerned with offenders and criminal justice issues. NACRO was founded in March 1966 at the time when the Probation Service took over the prison welfare and after-care work until then carried out by the National Association of Discharged Prisoners' Aid Societies (NADPAS). This addition to the work of the Probation Service had come about as a result of the recommendations of a report on *The Organisation of After-Care* by the Advisory Council on the Treatment of Offenders (1963). This report emphasised that it would be 'impossible for the probation and after-care service to undertake this formidable task unaided'. The Advisory Council recognised the potential of voluntary effort and expressed the view that if such potential was to be tapped effectively then NADPAS might well have a part to play as 'a new national voluntary organisation to co-ordinate such effort and stimulate public interest'. Consequently NADPAS became NACRO. NACRO also had a brief to explore new ways of working with offenders and in the 1970s it began to develop pilot schemes in housing, training workshops and education as models for others to follow. During the 1980s it began not only setting up pilot projects but, through development initiatives, to work with other statutory and non-statutory agencies in such areas as juvenile offending and initiatives for black offenders, and also diversified into working with prisons and in the area of mental health. It also encouraged the initial development of victim support schemes, and played an early role in the growing field of crime prevention. Indeed, the text under its title bears the inscription: 'for the care of offenders and prevention of crime'. NACRO has also addressed policy issues by developing research, setting up working parties and producing a wide range of briefing papers and publications.

Traditionally the work of the voluntary sector has been seen as supplementing that of the statutory sector: it operates in areas not covered by statutory provision, and tries out new things that, if successful, could then be integrated into mainstream statutory provision. But over the years the emphasis has changed somewhat, with the non-statutory sector more likely to be providing services that can be purchased in their own right. In 1990 the Government issued a paper, *Partnership in Dealing with Offenders in the Community* (Home Office, 1990b), which reviewed the relationship between the Probation Service and what was referred to as the 'independent sector', and since 1991 probation services have been expected to allocate up to 5 per cent (subsequently increased to 7 per cent) of their revenue budget to services provided by the independent sector.

Recent Developments and Future Prospects

> Probation work has changed a lot in recent years. The probation officer's role, which not so long ago was seen as 'to advise, assist and befriend' offenders – has now been re-defined considerably with the focus on protection of the public. 'Tackling offending behaviour' is now the over-riding purpose of statutory supervision, be it as part of a probation order or on post-release licence from a custodial sentence. (Broadhead, 1998: 993)

In recent years the service has faced a series of challenges. These have taken various forms, but at their core are the two key issues of control and funding. As the early part of this chapter indicated, there has been a tendency throughout its history for the Probation Service to become more regulated and for the Home Office to play an increasingly greater role. This has continued in recent years, with the Government, through the Home Office, seeking to exert more central control, first by requiring a Statement of National Objectives and Priorities (SNOP) during the 1980s and, since 1994, by setting National Standards for a range of activities undertaken by the Probation Service (Home Office, 1995a).[4] This has been accompanied by increasingly tight restrictions on probation expenditure since 1991, with limits being set on the amount of cash each service receives. Thus, in 1997 the number of court orders dealt with by the Probation Service rose by 2 per cent, while the number of probation officers in post fell by 2 per cent. This has meant that the service has been obliged to focus on statutory requirements and obligations, and some non-essential activities have been reduced. Thus, the extent of voluntary after-care has declined in recent years (Maguire et al., 1998), and imaginative special projects (e.g. the Hampshire Sports Counselling scheme) have had to give way to other, higher priority, activities. The service has also had to be aware of the potential for competition from the 'independent sector'.

The role of probation and the nature of probation work have also changed significantly, with much consideration being given to the work and organisation of the service in conjunction with the Criminal Justice Act 1991 and related discussion documents (Home Office, 1990a and undated, probably 1991). There has been a growing tendency for probation work to be less welfare oriented and more a matter of supervision of punishment in the community. This was highlighted during the mid-1990s, with discussion taking place about the possibility of replacing probation, and other sentences administered by the Probation Service, by a single 'community sentence' (Home Office, 1995b). Alongside this, the probation officer has become less of a caseworker and more of a case manager, and there have also been changes in the nature of probation training, which many in the service and elsewhere have seen as turning it from a professional social work qualification to a less demanding vocational course (Home Office, 1995b). Until 1995 those entering the service trained for a Diploma in Social Work, which has been replaced by a Diploma in Probation Studies following in-service training. The service has also become more involved in recent years in work with the victims of crime. This includes statements in pre-sentence reports about the impact of a crime on the victim, and victim contact work, the purpose of which is to provide information to the victim about custodial arrangements for the offender, and to ensure that the victim's concerns are taken into account when the conditions of an offender's release from prison are being considered.

There was discussion during the 1990s about reorganising the Probation Service, including reducing the number of probation areas and merging probation with the Prison Service. In August 1998 a consultation document, *Prisons – Probation Review* (Home Office, 1998c) was published, which considered the possibilities of greater integration of the Prison and Probation Services. At the same time the Government published another consultation document, *Joining Forces to Protect the Public* (Home Office, 1998e), which put forward proposals to change the structure of the Probation Service itself. Consideration was also given to renaming the service in a way that emphasised public protection as its central role. However, qualitative research carried out by MORI for the Association of Chief Officers of Probation suggested that amongst members of the general public, 'There is little sympathy with the move to change the name of the Probation Service' (MORI, 1998: 12). One member of the public said,

I think that they should be proud of what they do – there's nothing wrong with the name. (MORI, 1998: 12)

What was needed was to increase the public's knowledge about the work of the Probation Service and what it actually does. Despite this the Government announced that the name would be changed to the Community Punishment and Rehabilitation Service.

In April 1999 the Home Secretary announced that 42 local operational areas would replace the existing structure of 54 autonomous probation services, matching police force boundaries, and led by a Director who would be directly accountable to the Home Secretary.[5] Chief probation officers would continue to manage each area, but would become civil servants employed by the Home Office. Local probation boards would replace probation committees, with a more strategic role than the probation committees that they replaced. The Home Secretary would also appoint the Chairman of the Boards, and membership would reflect the local community and include representatives of the service's key partners. The Home Secretary would also have greater powers to direct and require necessary outcomes and standards of service delivery, and in future the service would be entirely funded by central Government, ending the arrangement whereby 80 per cent had been paid centrally and 20 per cent locally. Thus at the end of the twentieth century the Probation Service had experienced a transition from a voluntaristic, locally based service to a much more centralised service under the control of the Home Secretary.

The Probation Service in England and Wales has experienced constant change throughout its short history, but its development can be seen as having passed through three main phases. In the early days its work had underlying religious and moral principles, but it was work that addressed the material as well as spiritual poverty of offenders. In its second phase the service moved into a period where it became a professional social work agency guided by the rehabilitative ideal. In recent years it has moved into a third phase where it has become the agent of supervision in the community, with the requirements of the courts and the public coming before the needs of the offender.

A constant refrain in recent years has been that probation should not be seen as a 'soft option' and needs to become more 'credible' in the eyes of sentencers and the public. It will be recalled, for example, that Bryant and his colleagues (1978) in the south-east of England felt that if the probation order were to have more specific conditions this would increase courts' confidence in it. There has long been a tendency for non-custodial sentences to be compared with custodial sentences in terms of the degree to which they achieve certain goals, such as retribution or reducing reconviction. The framework of sentencing introduced by the Criminal Justice Act 1991 exacerbated this tendency by establishing punishment as the main criterion for sentencing. Consequently probation came to be judged by the extent to which it punished, rather than by claims to improve people or deal with the problems that underlie their offending.

There have been repeated demands, mainly from Government, that the courts and the public need to have 'confidence' in community penalties. This has been translated into an expectation that the Probation Service should supervise, contain and restrict the offender first and foremost. As a result of discussions related to the Criminal Justice Act 1991 the Probation Service put considerable effort into trying to satisfy this demand. Despite this, the Home Office Consultation Document, *Strengthening Punishment in the Community* said in 1995 that, 'Probation supervision is still widely regarded as a soft option' (Home Office, 1995b: para. 4.4). But this assertion was contradicted by the findings of the MORI survey referred to earlier which concluded that, 'Though some [members of the general public] see non-custodial sentences as an essentially "soft" option this view is not accepted by everyone. For the majority, non-custodial sentences have a part to play, mainly because of their rehabilitation potential' (MORI, 1998: 3).

One of the options considered by the Government in the consultation document was replacing probation, community service orders and combination orders by a single community sentence that would focus on the three objectives of restricting liberty, achieving reparation and preventing offending. Magistrates, judges and the Probation Service were happy to see both the substance and the presentation of community penalties improved, but were not enthusiastic about legislative change. One consequence of this was the development of initiatives in Shropshire and Teesside to strengthen the appeal of community sentences to sentencers, within existing legislation. These development projects provided sentencers with more information about the content of community penalties, gave sentencers an opportunity to specify what they would like pre-sentence reports to cover, invited them to comment on the range and content of community service provision, and provided them with feedback on completion rates. Sentencers responded favourably to the initiatives, and became more inclined to see community sentences as a way for offenders to make some amends for their offences, and as a way of reducing reoffending. On their side probation staff felt that the quality of their contact with sentencers had improved, but that more needed to be done regarding communication between probation officers and sentencers.

Despite these positive responses, the initiatives had a limited impact on sentencing. In Shropshire there was an increase in the proportion of offenders being fined and given community sentences at the Crown Court and a decrease in the proportion being imprisoned. Apart from this, however, there was no other evidence that the demonstration projects encouraged greater use of community sentences as an alternative to custody, and in Teesside the overall use of community penalties actually declined during the project. The only sentencing change common to both areas and both court levels was that the proportion of cases receiving a probation order with additional requirements rose, but this was largely at the expense of other community sentences and mainly associated with summary offences. The researchers concluded that while better communication and improved relationships between the Probation Service and sentencers could be achieved, 'the results of this study suggest that such improvements alone will not lead to a significant increase in the use of community penalties' (Hedderman et al., 1999: xiv).

The results of this research echo earlier findings that attempts to increase the use of non-custodial options tend to some extent to succeed at the expense of other non-custodial penalties, rather than as a replacement for the use of custody (see, for example, Pease et al., 1977; Crow, 1982). Such initiatives raise the question of whether community penalties can ever satisfy the same kind of expectations as a custodial sentence. It could be argued that prison and probation have some functions in common, but others which are different, and that criminal justice is best served by such a diversity of service functions, rather than all being judged by the same criterion.

However that may be, the inevitable consequence of the developments outlined above is that treatment and rehabilitation no longer seem to be at the centre of probation work. But attempts to address and change offending behaviour continue, both by seeking to improve offenders' material prospects, and by taking up some of the principles that have emerged from the 'what works' movement. More attention is likely to be devoted to probation research in future, whilst, as far as the Home Office is concerned, 'However important other measures of success may be, reoffending is the key test for any probation programme' (Hedderman, 1998: 5). At the heart of rehabilitation is the prospect of helping a person to change. The old rehabilitative ideal sought to impose change on the individual, with probation officers acting as change agents. As Raynor and Vanstone have indicated, this was a perspective on the offender as a passive recipient of the attentions of probation officers. They suggest that rehabilitation must now be seen to come from the offender him- or herself. The Probation Service can play a valuable role in enabling the offender to make this change, but it needs the opportunities and the resources to do so.

Further Reading

A history of the early development of the Probation Service can be found in Joan King's book, which although published in 1964, is still useful, as long as one bears in mind that it comes from the social case-work school of probation. Between 1983 and 1987 *The Howard Journal* published a series of four articles by Bill McWilliams, which cover the development of the Probation Service. The third of these covers 'The English Probation System and the Diagnostic Ideal' (1986). For a description of what the Probation Service does and how it works, see Dick Whitfield's *Introduction to the Probation Service* (1998). There is a good chapter on the constant tension between care and control in the Probation Service in Tim Newburn's *Crime and Criminal Justice Policy* (1995), and there is also a chapter on the Probation Service by Tim May (1994) in the first edition of *The Oxford Handbook of Criminology*. In the second edition of the handbook this has been replaced by a chapter by George Mair, which also contains a brief history of the service. Both are worth reading. Ian Brownlee's book, *Community Punishment: a Critical Introduction* (1998) is also worth reading in its entirety, and Chapters 3 and 4, on the changing role of the probation service, are particularly relevant here. Another book on the role of the Probation Service in the context of the emergence of community punishment is Anne Worral's *Punishment in the Community: The Future of Criminal Justice* (1997). For treatment and rehabilitation in particular, the key readings are the papers by Bottoms and McWilliams and by Raynor and Vanstone.

Questions to Consider

- What has replaced the treatment paradigm in probation?
- Do treatment and rehabilitation have a future in the Probation Service?

Notes

1   Home Office Press Release 360/98, 'Probation Service Can Help Design the Future for Crime Reduction', and *What Works: Reducing Re-offending: Evidence-based Practice*, available through the Home Office website at www.homeoffice.gov.uk.
2   Lord Williams, speaking at the 'What Works in Criminal Justice' conference, Manchester, 28 September 1998.
3   In fact the Foundation is the successor to the Church of England Temperance Society Mission. When the Home Office assumed full responsibility for the Probation Service in 1939 the Mission became known as the Rainer Foundation, after the Hertfordshire printer, Frederick Rainer, whose intervention prompted the Church of England Temperance Society into work in the police courts. It developed into an organisation providing residential care for young offenders.

4   Although it has been found that in general the setting of national standards has been beneficial. HM Inspectorate of Probation's report on the service's implementation of the Criminal Justice Act 1991 found that, 'National Standards had contributed to the provision of a more consistent, focused and developed approach to the supervision of offenders' (HM Inspectorate of Probation, 1993a: para 2.3 iii).

5   Legislation to enact these proposals was announced in the Queen's Speech of 17 November 1999.

6

IN PRISON

In order to afford anything in the nature of permanent protection, either the prison must keep the offender within its walls for the term of his natural life, or it must bring such influence to bear upon him while in custody that he will, on the day of his discharge, be an honest, hard-working and self-controlled man [sic], fit for freedom, and no longer an enemy of society. (Sir Alexander Paterson, 1951 edn.: 24)

This chapter does not attempt to present an extensive consideration of imprisonment. That has been done elsewhere (Cavadino and Dignan, 1997, for example). Instead we will briefly consider how treatment in prison has been seen since the arrival of the 'nothing works' doctrine. The chapter then goes on to consider a specific institution, Grendon Underwood, which both provides a very special example of treatment in prison, and raises questions about where treatment stands in relation to the prison system as a whole.

Prison as a Place of Treatment

Prison tends to be thought of primarily as a punishment, but custodial sentences are supposed to fulfil several functions. Traditionally these have been regarded as retribution, deterrence, containment and rehabilitation. Which of these is accorded the highest priority will vary depending on the prevailing penal philosophy of the time. The system of imprisonment with which we are familiar has not always been in existence. It only developed as one of the main ways of dealing with criminals just over two hundred years ago. Prior to that physical punishment was the norm, with execution being common. Foucault describes the shift that took place around the end of the eighteenth century from 'corporal' to 'carceral' forms of punishment, referring to prison as 'The gentle way in punishment' (Foucault, 1977). John Howard is widely regarded as a benevolent progressive reformer of prisons in the nineteenth century. But he and his supporters favoured a single cell in which the convict would be held in circumstances close to what we would now call solitary confinement, usually with the means for some form of labour in the cell. Today we would regard such conditions as less than progressive, being more concerned about the fact that there may be several people sharing a single cell. But what Howard and others were trying to achieve had a moral and religious impulse: convicts should be treated humanely, but should contemplate the error of their ways under appropriate moral guidance, and in isolation from other felons.[1]

Morgan (1997: 1144) suggests that prisons have three uses:

- the custodial – mainly remand prisoners, being held in custody 'to ensure that the course of justice proceeds to its conclusion';
- the coercive – mainly fine defaulters, because of their 'failure to comply with a court order';
- the punitive – in the famous dictum of Alexander Paterson, a reforming prison commissioner, 'Men come to prison *as* a punishment, not *for* punishment' (Paterson, 1951: 23).

Morgan goes on to distinguish between the reasons for sending people to prison and the objectives of prison. For many years prisons were regarded as a form of treatment and, as noted in Chapter 1, structurally and theoretically there are strong parallels between prisons and lunatic asylums. The treatment and training potential of prisons was enshrined in Rule 1 of the Prison Service, which advocated prisons as a place where inmates should be encouraged to lead 'good and useful lives'. The system of parole was very much part of this conception of prison, with its notion that release should in part depend on the extent to which an offender had responded positively to efforts to reform him or her.

The danger of such thinking is that it leads to the sending to, or keeping of people in, prison under the delusion that it is good for them and that it 'works'. As elsewhere, the loss of confidence in the rehabilitative ideal during the 1970s led to a reappraisal of the role of prisons, and this culminated in the work of the May Committee (1979) towards the end of the decade. In their evidence to the May Committee, King and Morgan (1980) suggested as an alternative to Rule 1 the term 'humane containment'. But the May Committee and others were not happy with this because of its negative implications, suggesting a policy of 'warehousing' criminals in circumstances that lacked a moral justification. May therefore adopted the phrase 'positive custody', but the concept never really achieved any meaningful development in practice. As Morgan has put it, '"humane containment" has been judged too stark a prospect, and "positive custody" too woolly' (Morgan, 1994: 901).

In this rather uncertain climate imprisonment made its way through the 1980s, on the one hand extolled (especially for more serious offenders) by a Government which laid claim to 'law and order' credentials, but on the other hand recognised as expensive and ineffective. An important shift occurred, however, during a meeting of Home Office ministers and officials at Leeds Castle, Kent in September 1987. The meeting has been reported by Lord Windlesham, a former Home Office minister and Chairman of the Parole Board, who described how, as the meeting progressed, ministers and officials contemplated figures produced by the Home Office Statistical Department forecasting an increase in the prison population to 60,000 in the foreseeable future and the prospect of it reaching 70,000 by the year 2000. It was resolved that 'such a situation would be intolerable, and must not be allowed to happen' (Windlesham, 1993: 239). Consequently the Home Office began to develop a policy which, by focusing more on the punitive aspects of community-based sentences, would reduce reliance on imprisonment. This resulted in the Criminal Justice Act 1991, with its sentencing framework of incremental loss of liberty based on a 'just deserts' approach. As far as prisons were concerned, however, the period of ambiguity about their role was brought to an abrupt end in April 1990 with the Strangeways riot and disturbances at other prisons, and the report by Lord Justice Woolf and Judge Stephen Tumim. This report (Woolf and Tumim, 1991) was a largely pragmatic and managerialist response to the circumstances which gave rise to the 1991 riots, and it sought ways to avoid a recurrence, rather than to look for a new creed for the prison system. Woolf and Tumim identified 'one principal thread' which linked the causes and complaints underlying the riots:

> It is that the Prison Service must set security, control and justice in prisons at the right level and it must provide the right balance between them. The stability of the prison system depends on the Prison Service doing so. (Woolf and Tumim, 1991: para. 1.148)

The recommendations of Woolf and Tumim covered such matters as closer co-operation between the different parts of the criminal justice system, an enhanced role for prison officers, levels of certified normal accommodation, access to sanitation, and improved standards of justice. However, they did stress that the Prison Service is part of the criminal justice system as a whole, and that 'The objectives of the Criminal Justice System include discouraging crime' (para. 10.24). Regarding rehabilitation, Woolf and Tumim favoured the formulation 'that the prisoner is properly prepared for his return to society' (para. 10.29), and Recommendation 72 stated that, 'The Prison Service and the Probation Service must work together to achieve the common objective of helping offenders to lead law-abiding lives' (Woolf and Tumim, 1991: 440). But it was emphasised that this 'does not mean a return to what came to be known as the treatment model' (para. 10.34). Under the old model of treatment 'it was thought appropriate to sentence an offender to a custodial sentence for reformative treatment, as if being a criminal was a curative condition'. Whilst an offender should not be sentenced to imprisonment for reformative treatment, Woolf and Tumim did regard it as part of the Prison Service's role to ensure, wherever practicable, that while serving a sentence a prisoner should have the opportunity of training. Woolf and Tumim also referred to the need to give special attention to certain groups of prisoners, including mentally disordered offenders, sex offenders and drug abusers. Although widely regarded as the way forward for the Prison Service at the time, the recommendations of Woolf and Tumin were not fully implemented.

Meanwhile, Michael Howard claimed at the Conservative Party Conference in October 1993 that 'prison works'. But this in no way signalled a return to the rehabilitative ideal. Rather prison was now seen, as in the United States, in terms of incapacitation, deterrence and punitive loss of freedom. Despite the fact that prison is commonly seen as punitive, treatment and rehabilitation have continued to have a place in the prison system, if a less prominent role than many might wish. Programmes of treatment within prison tend to be directed at specific groups, as will be seen in later chapters. Furthermore, in regard to imprisonment, as elsewhere in criminal justice, a more rights-based approach to treatment has tended to be adopted and, as in Raynor and Vanstone's paradigm of probation practice, this is a perspective which takes society's needs into account as well as those of the individual offender.

Morgan has placed such an approach in the context of what he describes as the 'new realism' in sentencing theory. This 'new realism' derives from the Criminal Justice Act 1991 and has three ingredients:

1   Custody is not justified on the grounds that it will make offenders better.
2   Deterrence as individual calculation has lost credibility.
3   The primary objective for sentencing is denunciation of, and retribution for, crime.

In relation to the first of these Morgan goes on to say that 'If treatment, training or rehabilitation is the object, it is accepted that these outcomes are *more likely* to be accomplished by the offender remaining in the community' (1994: 900, emphasis added). There is, however, a danger that in propounding such a view community sentences will be expected to justify themselves on the basis of their effectiveness, whereas prison will not. This raises again the issue mentioned in the last chapter about the criteria by which different sentences are to be judged. It is not uncommon for sentencers to take the view that because an offender has been given a community sentence and re-offended then community penalties have 'failed', and therefore prison must now be used, whereas it is unlikely that the reverse will apply.

Nonetheless, Morgan suggested that on this basis there was 'a real prospect of forging an alliance between "new realism" in sentencing theory and a "neo-rehabilitative" approach to prisons administration, with justice as the underlying leitmotif' (Morgan, 1997: 1150). The idea now is therefore to *facilitate* rather than coerce treatment or training, so that prisoners have the opportunity of addressing whatever personal shortcomings and social disadvantages are associated with their offending. This is what Rotman describes as a rights-based model of rehabilitation, 'humanistic and liberty centred' as opposed to authoritarian and paternalistic (Rotman, 1986). Garland expresses it in similar terms: 'The inmate is now said to be responsible for making use of any reformative opportunities that the prison might offer' (Garland, 1996: 458).

Such an approach is supported by practitioners as well as academics. Coyle, a former prison governor, has argued that the chance of re-offending is unlikely to be affected by the experience of imprisonment. What will affect it are the factors facing the offender on release, such as decent accommodation, the support of family and friends, and the likelihood of reasonable employment. 'The concept of rehabilitation as some sort of "coerced cure" was developed for the benefit of those who ran and worked within the prison system' (Coyle, 1992: 5). He goes on to suggest that a new framework has emerged, based on the recognition that the *act* of imprisonment is always negative, but every attempt should be made to make the *experience* of imprisonment as positive as possible. This recognises, among other things, the obligation to offer prisoners the *opportunity* to spend time in prison constructively and to prepare themselves for release.

> The concept of 'opportunity' is a recognition that in respect of rehabilitation, that is, of change from within, the prisoner is master of his own destiny. He is a human being with a free will, with rights and with responsibilities. The need is to give the prisoner, and for him to take, as much responsibility as possible for his own life and actions. (Coyle, 1992: 6)

This is why Prison Service policy documents have introduced new words into the prison vocabulary that are facilitating rather than prescriptive: 'provide', 'promote', 'encourage', 'enable'. The closing years of the twentieth century saw an emphasis on constructive regimes and purposeful activities,

> to reduce crime by providing constructive regimes which address offending behaviour, improve educational and work skills and promote law abiding behaviour in custody and after release. (HM Prison Service, 1999: 8)

This all sounds very hopeful, but in practice how far is it possible to implement such an outlook and approach? What resources are available, and how adequate are the opportunities for treatment, training and rehabilitation?

Treatment Opportunities in Practice

Prison is still seen by the Prison Service as a place where addressing offending behaviour occurs and where attempts are made to reduce re-offending. The Service's Statement of Purpose[2] says that,

> Her Majesty's Prison Service serves the public by keeping in custody those committed by the courts. Our duty is to look after them with humanity and to help them lead law-abiding and useful lives in custody and after release.

The Prison Psychology Service fulfils a variety of functions, including the assessment and treatment of offending behaviour. The service has pioneered several innovative treatment programmes, covering areas such as anger management, sexual deviancy, poor social skills, and drug and alcohol addiction.

However, since the decline of the rehabilitative ideal, therapeutic provision in prisons has been uneven. Treatment initiatives have often been dependent on the inspiration and enthusiasm of particular individuals or institutions to carry them forward, and for a long time programmes have tended to be *ad hoc*, and lacking a co-ordinated strategy, although there have been certain exceptions to this (see Chapters 7 and 9). In addition to the disappearance of an underpinning ideological framework, other developments have inhibited treatment and rehabilitation within prison. For one thing there was a substantial rise in the prison population during most of the 1990s, from 40,606 at the end of 1992 to 66,516 in the middle of 1998. This was counteracted to some extent in 1999 by the introduction of the early release of selected prisoners on home detention curfew monitored by electronic tagging, but by mid-1999 this covered only 1,854 prisoners. Another inhibiting factor came about following an escape by armed prisoners from Whitemoor prison in September 1994, followed by the discovery of Semtex explosives at the prison, and the escape of three life sentence prisoners from Parkhurst prison on the Isle of Wight a few months later, in January 1995. Inquiries were set up to investigate these incidents (Woodcock, 1994; Learmont, 1995) and the resulting preoccupation with security made it difficult to pursue more positive endeavours. Indeed Cavadino and Dignan have suggested that 'following the Woodcock and Learmont reports, the emphasis within prisons seems to be firmly on security at the expense of justice and humanity' (Cavadino and Dignan, 1997: 119), and in his annual report for 1996–97 HM Chief Inspector of Prisons, Sir David Ramsbotham said,

> While money has been made available to implement recommendations made in the Woodcock and Learmont reports, it has been cut, and continues to be

cut, despite the provision of some extra financial resources, from activities designed to help prisoners lead law abiding and useful lives in custody and after release. . . . In sum, while money and attention have been directed at the security part of the mission, the reverse has been true of the rehabilitation. (HM Chief Inspector of Prisons, 1998)

The rising prison population, restrictions on expenditure and a pre-eminent concern with security all meant that during much of the 1990s there were, with some important exceptions in the areas of drug misuse and sex offending, fewer resources available for activities directed at treatment and rehabilitation. Consequently schemes directed towards education, training and rehabilitation have received a lower priority. An *Audit of Prison Service Resources* published in 1997 found that the level of purposeful activity for prisoners had dropped over the previous two years, limiting the scope for reducing the risk of prisoners re-offending on release (HM Prison Service, 1997). There was a reduction in staffing in 1996–97, which led to the number of prison officers in post falling from 24,398 in 1996 to 23,058 in 1997, and a rise in the number of prisoners per staff member from 1.17 in 1993 to 1.41 in 1999 (Penal Affairs Consortium, 1999). It was only at the end of the decade that more funding was announced to help deal with the pressure on the prisons, with some of this being specifically directed towards treatment programmes. For example, in July 1998 the Home Secretary, Jack Straw, announced an increase of £660 million in expenditure on the Prison Service over the three years from 1999–2000 to 2001-02. Although most of this was for repair and maintenance work and additional prison capacity, £200 million was for an increase in purposeful activities, principally programmes to reduce substance misuse, accredited offending behaviour programmes, and improving basic skills. Despite such developments the Lord Chief Justice, Lord Bingham, speaking at a conference at the beginning of the year 2000, nonetheless felt compelled to call for more remedial treatment for persistent offenders at a time when only about 3,000 prisoners out of a total population of 66,000 (less than 5 per cent) were involved in treatment and rehabilitation programmes.[3]

Despite the limitations in terms of both overall aims and resources that existed in the prison system during the latter part of the twentieth century, there have been efforts to treat and rehabilitate offenders in a number of ways. Although there is a danger of too rigidly classifying practices, it is possible to identify three main areas of activity. The first is **treatment programmes** designed to address specific issues and offenders, such as anger management, drug misuse and sex offences. These have often involved various kinds of group work and cognitive skills training. Boddis and Mann (1995) refer to the use of two main cognitive skills programmes. The first was the Ross and Fabiano 'reasoning and rehabilitation' programme mentioned in Chapter 4. The second was an in-house 'thinking skills' programme, a highly structured course addressing impulse control, rigid thinking and problem solving, amongst other things. Anger management was the first programme to be developed nationally, with training courses for the staff involved, and careful piloting and evaluation. But in the mid-1990s Boddis and Mann described it as having declined as a national programme to the point where it 'appears to be in tatters' (Boddis and Mann, 1995: 65), with no standardisation of training and no programme identity. However, other programmes that started as *ad hoc* initiatives were developed nationally, becoming major investments in terms of both resources and policy expectations. These are the programmes addressing drug misuse and sexual offending, which will be considered further in later chapters.

The second main area of activities is concerned with what may be termed **social rehabilitation**, including education, training, and social skills programmes, designed to prepare offenders for when they are released. In recent years these have focused in particular on trying to increase ex-prisoners' chances of finding employment, and more will be said about initiatives involving social interventions in Chapter 10. An important feature of attempts to provide for the rehabilitation of ex-prisoners is the notion of throughcare. This is a process that begins at the point of sentence and continues until an offender completes a period on licence following their release. The term

> embraces all the assistance given to offenders and their families by the Prison and Probation Services and outside agencies and ties in with all the training, education and work experience they are given. (HM Prison Service, 1993: 5–6)

It is directed at equipping the ex-prisoner to return to society, get a job and a home and cope with life without re-offending, and includes all the support and help which is given to unconvicted prisoners and their families by the Prison and Probation Services and other agencies who work with offenders. Throughcare became especially important following the introduction of early release provisions in the Criminal Justice Act 1991, which led to the drawing up of a national framework for throughcare. This framework set out key throughcare tasks required for a successful resettlement, which included addressing addictions, budgeting, accommodation, employment problems, problems with reading and writing, relationship and family problems, low self-esteem, lack of relevant training, work experience or qualifications, lack of parenting skills, and discrimination experienced by the offender (HM Prison Service, 1993: 11). The framework went on to specify the role that each agency should play in addressing these matters.

The third main form of treatment activity may be identified as that involving **special provision and places**, such as special hospitals for the mentally disordered, and specialised therapeutic wings and institutions at Wormwood Scrubs, and Grendon Underwood. The remainder of this chapter looks in more detail at one of these institutions – the work and effectiveness of the therapeutic prison, Grendon Underwood.

Grendon Underwood

Therapeutic Communities

During and after the Second World War it was discovered that military personnel suffering from the trauma of battle stress could be helped to recover by working together in small groups in a community setting. This discovery gave rise to the 'therapeutic community'. In contrast to the individually centred psychoanalytic school of treatment, therapeutic communities are based on a social learning model of behaviour. They have several distinctive features, including an emphasis on self-help, usually with intensive group sessions, taking place over an extended period of time, and in circumstances where participants are isolated from outside influences. Therapeutic communities have arisen in a variety of settings. They were adopted as part of a new way of working with psychiatric patients in the 1960s, and they will be encountered again in the chapter on the treatment of drug misuse. The aim is to transform the whole person, rather than deal with just a particular problem that the person has (such as drug or alcohol abuse).

Background

While Grendon has been unique within the prison system as a thera-peutic prison, there are therapeutic wings at Wormwood Scrubs, and at Channings Wood and Lindholme for treating drug dependence. Grendon Underwood was opened in Buckinghamshire in 1962, and is classified as a category B training prison with certified normal accom-modation for 245 adult males. The prison has an Assessment Unit taking up to 26 referrals, and five therapeutic wings of between 35 and 42 prisoners, including a wing designed specifically for sex offenders (Wing G). Each of these wings operates as a separate therapeutic community. There is also a Healthcare Unit for up to 12 patients. Since the closure of workshops and the laundry there has been little employment at Grendon, the only work apart from therapy being cleaning and orderly duties. An HM Inspectorate of Prisons report noted that this was a source of boredom, and commented that the provision of a workshop would add the essential element of purposeful activity (HM Chief Inspector of Prisons for England and Wales, 1997: para. 23).

Aims

The booklet, *Grendon: a Therapeutic Prison* (HM Chief Inspector of Prisons for England and Wales, 1997, Appendix 1: 3) by HM Prison Service says there are three objectives to therapy at Grendon:

- to help each man improve his self-confidence and sense of worth;
- to help each man create positive relationships with others, helping him to move towards greater consideration and concern for the feelings and property of others;
- to help each man stop committing crimes.

The booklet also claims that 'the evidence is that they are all achieved', but detailed justification for this claim is not given and one needs to look elsewhere for support for this statement.

Regime

Therapy at Grendon consists of core procedures that regularly take place in all the wings, and additional procedures that take place from time to time, or only in some wings. The core procedures consist of small group sessions of up to eight men meeting three times a week, feedback from each small group to the rest of the wing to ensure groups do not become isolated, community meetings to discuss community matters and explore therapeutic issues arising from groups, staff meetings, and informal dialogues. Additional procedures include psychodrama, life and social skills classes, cognitive skills training to work on poor impulse control and repetitive interpersonal offending patterns, and art therapy. There are also socials and open days, drama and debating groups (see HM Chief Inspector of Prisons for England and Wales, 1997, Appendix 1: 5–7).

Population

Grendon receives about 200 referrals a year from other prisons, but by no means all are accepted as suitable. Indeed, one of the criticisms that has been levelled at Grendon is its ability to select its inmates. Of the last 300 receptions prior to September 1997, 29 per cent of those received had committed robbery as their main offence, 23 per cent homicide, 15 per cent sex offences and 14 per cent other violent offences (HM Chief Inspector of Prisons, 1998: Appendix 3, Figure 2). In a study measuring psychopathy a checklist was administered to 104 inmates admitted to Grendon for long term psychotherapy. Twenty-six per cent of the sample were classified as psychopaths, higher than previously found in UK prison samples, but 'consistent with the selection criteria for Grendon which emphasize the presence of 'personality disorder' or 'psychopathy' as a prerequisite' (Hobson and Shine, 1998). Cullen (1998: 6) points out that the offence profile of Grendon inmates has changed considerably over the years as a result of Grendon being expected by the Prison Service to undertake more work with life sentence prisoners. Twenty years ago only 17 per cent of inmates' main offences were for violence, with just 3 per cent for homicide and 7 per cent for sexual offences. The shift towards 'heavy end' offenders was also noted in a study undertaken by Gunn and Robertson (1987).

Research

In its relatively short history Grendon Underwood has probably been subjected to more research than any other prison. Several studies have demonstrated the positive effects that Grendon has had on prisoners' attitudes and behaviour, but initial findings on reconviction rates were not encouraging. However, the picture has changed in the last few years, with positive findings on reconviction emerging from more recent studies. Newton (1971) compared reconviction rates of prisoners who had spent time at Grendon with a matched sample from Oxford prison and, as Genders and Player delicately put it, 'Her results were not encouraging for those who seek to promote and justify the purpose of the therapeutic regime as the reduction of recidivism' (Genders and Player, 1995: 14). Gunn and Robertson (1987) carried out a controlled reconviction study on a sample of Grendon men who had been at liberty for at least a year, and again ten years later. It was concluded that, while there were changes in the psychological test scores of men while they were in Grendon, therapy appeared to have no significant impact on subsequent patterns of offending when compared with prisoners from other prisons with similar probabilities of reconviction.

A study by Genders and Player looked at the Grendon population and its flow through the prison system. Genders and Player say that, although Grendon is described as a therapeutic community, 'Therapy at Grendon is not *primarily* directed to the prevention of crime . . . the principal undertaking of therapy is to facilitate and promote the welfare of each individual inmate' (Genders and Player, 1995: 12). Nor is it a strictly 'medical model' in the traditional sense. There is considerable emphasis on self-governance and democracy. A distinguishing feature of Grendon as a therapeutic community is its holistic approach to the individual. Genders and Player do not attempt to evaluate Grendon in terms of reconviction. They argue that the impact of a specific period of therapy such as Grendon has to be seen in the wider context of the men's careers. But Genders and Player conclude that it is not only possible to run a therapeutic prison within the modern prison system, but it is also desirable:

> but the conditions for a *therapeutic prison* can only be met if a balance is struck between individual and community interests in ways which foster communitarian principles of social organisation. (Genders and Player, 1995: 228; emphasis in original)

Despite the negative findings of earlier studies, and Genders and Player's avoidance of reconviction as a major focus of their study, two studies have produced positive findings in recent years. Dr Eric Cullen (1994), a consultant forensic psychologist found that therapy at Grendon was significantly related to lower reconviction rates, that there was a relationship between time in therapy and rates of reconviction, with 18 months appearing to be the threshold for greatest improvement, and that the most positive effect was for those prisoners who left Grendon under parole supervision. Marshall (1997b) examined 700 prisoners who had been admitted to Grendon between 1984 and 1989. These prisoners were compared with 142 men who had applied for Grendon but not been admitted, and with a group of over 1,400 men from the general prison population who were similar to the admitted group in terms of age, offence type and sentence length. Comparison of the general prison group with the non-admitted applicants indicated that, although the general prison group had similar characteristics to those admitted to Grendon, Grendon had been selecting prisoners at higher risk of reconviction. This 'means that previous reconviction studies which have compared Grendon prisoners with the general prison population have not been comparing like with like'. Comparing the 'not admitted' and 'admitted' groups, it was found that the admitted group had a significantly lower reconviction rate. Therefore, 'As no selection takes place between going onto the Waiting List and being admitted to Grendon, the different reconviction rates suggest the existence of a "treatment effect"'. This research also found that reconviction rates were lower for prisoners who stayed for longer periods and there also appeared to be some reduction in reconviction rates for sexual and violent offences, but these were less clear.

As Cullen (1998) found, an important consideration is where men go to on leaving Grendon. Of the 189 men discharged from Grendon in the year ending April 1995, only 14 (8 per cent) were released directly into the community. The majority of men left Grendon because they fell foul of one of the rules forbidding drink, drugs, sex or violence (and could therefore be regarded as not being a fair test of treatment effectiveness), or because they had been transferred, either by choice, or as part of their sentence plan. Cullen explains that it is Home Office policy to transfer almost all Grendon 'graduates' to other prisons before release in order to test them in conditions of lower security, but in the course of this period their risk of re-offending rises. Newton and Thornton (1993)[4] found that being released directly into the community from Grendon was related to the avoidance of further conviction. Of a sample of 150 men, those released direct from Grendon on parole were significantly less likely to be reconvicted within two years of release than those transferred to other prisons before release. Those who were released direct from Grendon but not on parole were also less likely to reoffend. The implication is that the benefits of Grendon are lost when men are transferred to other prisons, but it may also be that those men least likely to succeed are also those who are more likely to fall foul of the rules or opt for transfer, quite apart from Home Office policy. Sir David Ramsbotham, HM Chief Inspector of Prisons, commented on this matter in his report on Grendon Underwood. Noting that 'figures show that those who go back into the prison system, after a Grendon course are twice as likely to re-offend as those who are released into the community directly', he commented that former Grendon prisoners whom he had met elsewhere told him that after they were transferred from Grendon nothing was done to follow up the work there, 'because other prisons do not appear to understand what the treatment had entailed' (HM Chief Inspector of Prisons, 1997, Part A: 8–9). The report went on to recommend an expansion of direct release, allowing for 'a gradual weaning from therapy and a gradual resettlement into the community' (Part A: para. 15).

Management: an Uneasy Balance

It has been recognised for many years that Grendon sits rather uneasily within the prison system as a whole, and there is tension between its therapeutic needs and the demands of a system that is geared towards other objectives as well and is constrained by limited resources. The prison has undergone a number of reviews and reappraisals of its role. It was initially run by a Medical Director, but since the recommendations of the Advisory Committee to Review the Therapeutic Regime at Grendon (ACTRAG) in 1985, it has been run by a Governor like other prisons, with a Director of Medical Services.

A report by HM Chief Inspector of Prisons for England and Wales (1998) voiced concerns about some aspects of the institution, saying he did not think that the work was 'being adequately directed or supported by senior management' (HM Chief Inspector of Prisons for England and Wales, 1998: 7). In contrast to Genders and Player, the report of the inspection expressed concern at 'the fact that too much wing management was left to therapists rather than experienced prison staff . . . the apparent domination of a medical approach to the task . . . and that too much responsibility was vested in the medical authorities'. The inspectors recommended that there should be a single body responsible for ensuring the effectiveness of all therapeutic units within the Prison Service.

Grendon Underwood is no stranger to the struggles between differing perspectives. As noted above, Grendon has a dual structure, with the medical authorities on the one hand and the mainstream elements within the Prison Service on the other. Cullen referred to 'the conflict between proponents of the traditionalist psychiatric/medical power model and supporters of more integrated, cognitive behavioural, multi-modal treatment approaches' (Cullen, 1998: 10), saying that the medical hierarchy 'continues to fight a rearguard action against any changes which could be perceived as eroding the primacy of the medical model and management' (Cullen, 1998: 4). He also explained that when it comes to judging Grendon's success the traditionalists have taken the view that 'personal insight and the re-integration of personality' are a sufficient target for Grendon, while the alternative view holds that reconviction is an entirely appropriate and relevant outcome measure (Cullen, 1998: 9). Despite these difficulties the Home Office has approved the commissioning of a second therapeutic community prison, something recommended by Woolf and Tumim (1991: para. 12.211 and recommendation 123). This may be because, as Cullen points out, 'the sole prison which can offer hard empirical proof of its efficacy is Grendon' (Cullen, 1998: 3).

Conclusion

The prison system has clearly reached a point where the treatment of offenders is not its main *raison d'être*. Nonetheless, much therapeutic activity can and does take place in custodial establishments, and more indications of this will become apparent in the chapters on sex offenders and drug misusers. Rather than being a treatment, prison has become a place where treatment may occur. It has also been stated by

Woolf and Tumim and others that the Prison Service should be preparing inmates for a law-abiding life on their return to the community. This places emphasis on the importance of rehabilitation as well as treatment *per se*. It means that there is a need for imprisonment to prepare the way for the eventual re-integration into the community of the prisoner who has served his or her time. This involves addressing the ex-prisoners' material needs on release, such as housing, training and employment. But it also involves a mutual acceptance, first on the part of the ex-prisoner of the rights of other members of society to live free from crime and the fear of crime, and second by members of society that ex-prisoners having completed their punishment have the right to an opportunity to lead law-abiding lives. This may be hard for both parties.

Further Reading

Rod Morgan's chapters (1994, 1997) in both the first and second editions of *The Oxford Handbook of Criminology* are a good basis for general reading on this aspect of treatment and rehabilitation. On various aspects of the use of psychology within prison, the collection of papers by McGurk, Thornton and Williams *Applying Psychology to Imprisonment* (1987) is useful, especially Chapters 10, 11 and 13. On Grendon the book by Genders and Player (1995) is a must, and the paper by Eric Cullen (1998) for the Prison Reform Trust is also worth reading.

Question to Consider

- Should treatment and rehabilitation be part of the purpose of imprisonment, or should we just concentrate on making prison conditions as humane and positive as possible?

Notes

1 If the opportunity arises, a visit to Lincoln Gaol enables one to see something of the cells, and the prison chapel in which convicts were literally compartmentalised so as to avoid contact with other inmates.

2 The Prison Service's Statement of Purpose can be found on the Home Page of the Prison Service website: http://www.hmprisonservice.gov.uk/

3 'Jails should offer remedial treatment, says Bingham', *Daily Telegraph*, 28 January 2000. The research is also cited in 'Grendon: a therapeutic prison', a guide published by HM Prison Service, and contained as an appendix in a Prisons Inspectorate report on the prison (HM Inspectorate of Prisons, 1997).

4 This study by Newton and Thornton is unpublished. It is cited by Cullen (1998: 9), and the information has been confirmed by personal communication. The research is also cited in *Grendon: a Therapeutic Prison*, a guide published by HM Prison Service.

PART 3

TREATMENT IN PRACTICE

7

THE TREATMENT OF SEX OFFENDERS

> The panic about sexual crime has followed the classic pattern for such panics: the denial of the existence and extent of the problem; a growing fear as the facts become clearer; the knee-jerk response of tougher policing and harsher sentencing; and finally some small signs of a more considered and planned criminal justice response. However, it is difficult to argue that there now exists a coherent and effective policy towards sex offenders. (Sampson, 1994b: 119)

This chapter looks at the nature of sexual offending and of sex offenders before reflecting on the work done with sex offenders in prison and in the community. What is known about the effectiveness of this treatment is also considered. It is impossible to consider the prospect of successful treatment and rehabilitation without also taking into account the considerable public disquiet about the presence of sex offenders in the community and attempts to obtain and control information regarding their whereabouts. This is discussed in the concluding section of the chapter.

Offences and Prevalence

Sexual offending takes a variety of forms, including rape, buggery, indecent assault, incest, unlawful sexual intercourse and procuration. Other sexual activities, including indecent exposure and prostitution, are also controlled by law. As with other offence categories, it is important not just to see sexual offending as a category of offence, but to recognise its relationship to other offending and offensive behaviour. Although classified as a separate offence category, violence is an element in some sexual offences. Other sexual offences, such as voyeurism and obscene telephone calls, represent attempts to obtain gratification by controlling and demeaning, rather than involving direct physical violence. West (1996) points out that a number of violent offences may have a sexual element but not be classed as sexual offences. Sexual offences also need to be seen in relation to domestic violence, since many sexual offences involve people who know each other, and two thirds of recorded rapes and about half of offences of indecent assault have taken place at the home of the victim or suspect (Watson, 1996).

As with all offences, the true extent of sexual offending is unknown. But in the case of sexual offending there are particular problems because of the reluctance of victims to report an offence, and also because of the difficulty of proof in many cases. In 1997 there were 33,200 recorded sexual offences, accounting for under 1 per cent of all notifiable offences. About three-quarters of recorded sexual offences are cleared up. The number of recorded sexual offences has risen at a slightly faster rate than recorded crime in general since 1987, at around 3 per cent a year, but the number of offences of rape rose at about 10 per cent a year over the same period. This higher increase in the number of recorded rapes is thought to be partly due to an increase in victims being prepared to report such offences and partly to changes in police recording practices which make the recording of rape more likely (Home Office, 1998a: para. 2.32). The Crime and Public Order Act 1994 introduced the offence of rape of a male, and 347 such offences were recorded in 1997.

A total of 6,400 offenders were found guilty or cautioned for sexual offences in 1997, over half (53 per cent) for indecent assault on a female. The number of offenders convicted for rape in 1997 was 650, including 45 for male rape. In 1997, 55 per cent of those found guilty of sexual offences received a sentence of immediate custody, compared with 37 per cent in 1987. The use of custody increased by 7 per cent for all indictable offence groups between 1992 and 1997, but the increase has been most marked for those convicted of sexual offences, at 16 per cent. The average length of sentences of imprisonment for sexual offences has also increased: whereas the average length of a prison sentence for a sexual offence for a male aged 21 and over was 34.5 months in 1987, it was 39.7 months in 1997 (Home Office, 1998a: Table 7.16). Sixteen per cent of offenders sentenced for sexual offences received a probation order in 1996.

What Are Sex Offenders Like?

It is virtually impossible to produce a picture of sex offenders, partly because a wide range of offending behaviour is involved, and also because any profile of the characteristics of sex offenders will inevitably be based on those who are caught and convicted, who may not be typical of sex offenders in general. Stereotypes such as the dirty old man and the predatory stranger can be dangerous, because they can lead potential victims to believe that they are safe with people who are not like this. A high proportion of victims of sex crimes know their attacker, with so-called 'date rape' becoming a particular cause of concern in recent years. Grubin (1998) reports that in the case of child sex abuse, the majority of child molesters sexually assault children they know, with about 80 per cent of offences taking place in the home of either the offender or the victim. Undoubtedly some sex offenders are disturbed or inadequate individuals who cannot form satisfactory relationships (West, 1996), but there are also indications that sex crime is more widespread than had at one time been realised, and that those who commit such crimes are often not noticeably different from the population in general. It has been estimated that about one man in 60 born in 1953 had a conviction for a sexual offence (including those of a less serious nature) by the age of 40. For more serious sexual offences the ratio is one in 90. Using five cohort samples of men born from 1953 to 1973 it has been estimated that in the population in 1993 at least 260,000 men aged 20 or over had been convicted of a sexual offence, including those of a less serious nature (Marshall, 1997a).

In recent years it has been recognised that sex offending occurs amongst quite young people. It has been estimated that adolescent sex offenders account for up to a third of all sex crime (Grubin, 1998: v), and that about a fifth of sex offences are committed by juveniles (Rutter et al., 1998: 113). In November 1997 a boy aged 13 became the youngest person to be put on the newly instigated sex offenders register (see p. 134), and in July 1998 a boy who raped a five-year-old girl when he was 12 years old was sentenced to three years' detention under the Children and Young Persons Act. There are indications that people who commit sexual offences may themselves have been the victims of sexual abuse when young, and that this may be a factor predisposing to sex offending (Watkins and Bentovim, 1992), but Grubin suggests that the relationship is a complex one and that 'the simple answer to the question of how childhood sexual abuse contributes to adult sexual offending, is that we do not know' (Grubin, 1998: 31). Camden and Islington Health Services run a Young Abusers Project, and its Clinical Director reported that the average age of those interviewed had dropped from 17 years old in 1992 to 12 in 1996, with serious sexual abuse sometimes being committed by boys as young as six.[1] Boys seen by the project had frequently suffered some form of abuse themselves: 40 per cent had suffered serious physical abuse, 81 per cent had been seriously emotionally abused, 71 per cent neglected, and 37 per cent had harmed themselves in some way.[2] In 1998 a thematic inspection of Probation Service work with sex offenders expressed concern that, 'The largest and most worrying gap in provision was for adolescent sexual offenders, responsibility for whom did not lie solely or principally with the probation service' (HM Inspectorate of Probation, 1998: para. 1.10).

Sex Offender Treatment

The response to offending reflects, implicitly or explicitly, the theory which is held regarding the nature of either a specific crime or of crime in general. Therefore, how one thinks sex offenders should be treated is likely to depend on what is thought to be the reason for their offending. One view is that sexual offending is a personality disorder, that those who commit such offences are in some way deranged or 'sick' and that they need treatment of a psychiatric or psychological kind. Another view is that sex offenders know perfectly well what they are doing, and that what they are doing is evil, and they deserve severe punishment. Whereas the first view may have had some currency in the past, in recent years the emphasis has shifted towards the second perspective. The 1980s and 1990s saw a growing tendency towards 'bifurcation' in criminal justice policy (see Chapter 2), with sexual and violent offenders being singled out for the most severe penalties.[3] A third view may be that sexual offending is not that abnormal and that, since most sexual offences are perpetrated by men, they are an extension of the way that men exercise power over women (and also on occasions over children), and that more fundamental changes are needed than can be effected by either individual treatment or severe punishment. Prentky (1995) has put forward a model of sex offending which brings together several predisposing psychological factors, including lack of empathy, cognitive distortions and antisocial personality. This leads to the adoption of several modes of treatment depending on what are assessed to be the most important predisposing factors. Marshall and Barbaree (1990; see also Sampson, 1994b: Ch. 1) have advanced an integrated theory of sexual offending which brings together the biological propensity for male aggressive sexual behaviour, psychological theory concerning poor socialisation, and the context produced by sociological variables, such as society's attitudes towards sex and women. This integrated approach, involving both background factors and the more immediate considerations that give rise to sexual offending, has formed the basis for the treatment of sex offenders in recent years.

Criminal justice has responded with an ambivalence about sex offenders which has been summed up by Donald West: 'The notion of treatment for sex offenders, unless it is by castration, is unacceptable to many people, since it suggests evasion of just deserts' (West, 1996: 63). He went on to note that 'Treatments are also limited by the uncertain state of scientific knowledge of the causes of deviant sexuality and the complex linkages that can occur between violent and sexual impulses' (West, 1996: 66). Nonetheless, alongside the increasing use and length of imprisonment, there has been a recognition that something more than punishment is needed to tackle the behaviour of sex offenders on a long term basis, and the past decade has also seen the development of more and better-planned programmes for the treatment of sex offenders.

West (1996) divides the treatment of sex offenders into three broad types:

1   suppression of the male libido, usually by the use of substances to reduce the function of testosterone in maintaining sexual drive, but this can only be done for a limited time;

2   correction of inappropriate sexual arousal using orgasmic recondi-
    tioning, by discouraging sexual arousal by inappropriate stimuli;
3   cognitive programmes, akin to those described in Chapter 4,
    using group sessions, role play, and similar social learning tech-
    niques in order to get the offender to confront and deal with his
    offending behaviour. This third technique is currently the one most
    commonly used.

In an article reviewing treatments for sex offenders in prison, Ditchfield
and Marshall (1990) also offered a typology of sex offender treatment at
that time, identifying three main types: psychotherapy, behavioural
regimes and social skills training. Epps (1996) has described treatment
programmes as having three parts: assessment, intervention and relapse
prevention. But he emphasised that these are not completely distinct
and separate activities, since assessment is inevitably part of the intervention process, and to some extent the whole of a treatment
programme is directed towards relapse prevention. Treatment for sex
offenders is undertaken both in prison, and by the probation service in
the community. The treatment itself may be carried out by specially
trained professionals, but a variety of criminal justice professionals who
do not have specialist training have to deal with sex offenders and make
important decisions about what needs to be done.
    Consequently, because sex offenders vary considerably and present
a range of concerns, some form of sex offender classification is essential.
A number of schemes have been developed; these have been reviewed
by Fisher and Mair (1998), who concluded that none of them entirely
fulfilled the essential requirements of being reliable, efficient, pertinent
to a large number of offenders and simple to administer: 'none of the
schemes could be used in practical criminal justice situations'. However,
Fisher and Mair did suggest that some could be the basis for further
development, and that work might be carried out to investigate the best
forms of classification for use on a day to day basis by criminal justice
professionals.

Sex Offenders in Prison

There are two main areas for consideration regarding sex offenders in
prison. One is management and the other is programmes to deal with
their offending. Sex offenders are usually segregated from other inmates
for their own protection under Rule 43. This of itself can be problematic,
since it often means that such offenders have restricted access to normal
prison facilities (Sampson, 1994a). Prior to 1990 attempts to treat sex
offenders within prison tended to be *ad hoc*, unco-ordinated, and largely
the result of initiatives by staff at some establishments. In 1989 the

Prison Department commissioned a survey which showed that 63 prisons in England and Wales were operating some kind of specialist provision for sex offenders, although Sampson (ibid.) suggests that this should not be taken to indicate that there were 63 fully functioning treatment programmes operating. It is likely that the nature and quality of initiatives at this time was very variable.

The Prison Service Strategy

Following this survey, in 1991 the Prison Service announced a strategy for treatment programmes for sex offenders in custody, the Sex Offender Treatment Programme. Reviewing the research background in the strategy document, David Thornton, Head of Programme Development Section, Directorate of Inmate Programmes, identified three characteristics of initiatives for sex offenders to date that deserved to be taken into account:

–   Comprehensive programmes using cognitive behavioural methods appear to be the most promising.
–   Short programmes are particularly prone to poor results.
–   More generally, correctional research contains many examples of programmes which sound good on paper but where offenders' actual experience of treatment was quite different from that which had been intended. (HM Prison Service, 1991: paras 4.3–4.5)

The core programme was originally introduced in 20 prisons, with extended programmes at a small number of establishments for those who present the greatest risk. Six prisons have been designated for assessment and allocation. The goals of the programme[4] are to get offenders to accept responsibility, to develop motivation, and to increase empathy. The programmes are cognitive behavioural in approach, designed to challenge offenders' denial of their behaviour. The cognitive element involves recognising the patterns of distorted thinking which allow the contemplation of illegal sexual acts and understanding the impact of sexually abusive behaviour on its victims, while the behavioural component of treatment involves reducing sexual arousal by inappropriate fantasies of forced sexual activities with children and adults (Beech et al., 1998a: 5). There are 200 hours of structured treatment in 20 blocks, as follows:

Blocks 1–4:   establish group rapport
Block 5:   offenders recall accounts of their offences
Blocks 6–9:   develop victim empathy
Blocks 10–20: direct towards relapse prevention.

The extended programme runs after the core programme, focusing on the management of negative emotion, and relationship and intimacy skills. Success is measured by changes in offenders' attitudes. Sex offenders tend to be cognitively very distorted, to engage in denial of the offence, claim memory loss, claim the offence was consensual, and deny a sexual motivation for what they did. Some group members try to undermine group sessions. The treatment uses peer group pressure and some people seek to deflect this by making a joke of it, or intimidating other group members. Because it is not possible to offer treatment to all convicted sex offenders thought to be in need of it, cases are selected using a risk classification algorithm (Grubin and Thornton, 1994). The treatment is delivered by a broad range of staff, including prison officers, probation officers and teachers who have been given training. Specialists, usually psychologists, are involved, mainly to ensure treatment integrity. Because non-specialist staff are not able to make clinical decisions in the same way as a professional specialist the prison programme relies on detailed treatment manuals and set decision-making procedures, which some see as limiting its flexibility, but others claim enhances its consistency (Grubin and Thornton, 1994: 65). Although early results indicate that the programme has had positive effects on the attitudes and cognition of those who have taken part, at the time of writing it is too early to say whether it is successful in reducing reconviction (Vennard and Hedderman, 1998: 107).

A total of 2,247 prisoners had completed the sex offender treatment programme by 31 March 1997,[5] and a further 671 convicted sex offenders completed treatment during 1997–98.[6] In May 1998 the Prison Service published its business plan for the coming year, which set out the 'key performance indicators' (KPIs) for 1998–99. This included KPI 7, to ensure that there are 680 completions of the sex offender treatment programme in 1998–99 (HM Prison Service, 1998c).

Sex Offenders and the Probation Service[7]

The Probation Service has been undertaking work with sex offenders for a number of years, but for some time it tended to be undertaken by concerned and dedicated individuals, rather than being part of an integrated policy. The work increased after the Criminal Justice Act 1991 extended post-release supervision for sexual and other violent prisoners, and it has achieved greater significance as a result of more emphasis being placed on the service's role in protecting the public. Probation officers work with sex offenders subject to community sentences and with sex offenders receiving custodial sentences during and after their release from prison. At the end of 1996 there were 9,091 sexual offenders on the caseloads of probation services, with 4,753 of these in the community and 4,338 in prison (HM Inspectorate of Probation, 1998: 31).

There have been two thematic reports by HM Inspectorate of Probation, one in 1991 and the second in 1998. The report in 1998 commended the work the Probation Service had done with sex offenders, although the growth of work in this area had outstripped the development of sex offender policies and strategies in recent years. At the time of the report probation hostels were holding 430 charged or convicted sex offenders. In a sample of 337 sex offenders studied during the inspection, 93 per cent had not been reconvicted of a sexual or violent offence while under supervision or in an approved hostel. However, increasing public agitation about a small number of predatory sex offenders was making it more difficult for hostels to continue work with sex offenders, and ten hostels said they were no longer able to continue taking such offenders because of actual or threatened attacks, with more of the 100 or so approved hostels likely to follow. As noted earlier, the Probation Inspectorate report highlighted work with teenage sex offenders as something that required more attention in the future. However, the report also noted that 'The combination of rising caseloads and reductions in resources had led areas to find efficiency savings and to review the way in which services were delivered. At the time of the inspection, some were reviewing the continued existence of specialist teams working with sex offenders' (HM Inspectorate of Probation, 1998: 29). Such reviews of resourcing, together with public antagonism, give rise to the worry that there may be a reversion to the more *ad hoc* arrangements that existed formerly, and this would hardly be a reassuring development, especially since the report noted that only a minority of services had sought opportunities to explain and promote their sex offender work to the public (HM Inspectorate of Probation, 1998: 15)

Sex offender treatment within the probation service is commonly based on a model put forward by Finkelhor (1984), which challenges sex offending behaviour. Sexual offending is seen as a result of the perpetrator moving through several stages:

- First, there is the motivation to abuse, arising from sexual arousal to inappropriate stimuli.
- Next, there is the overcoming of internal inhibitions, which often involves rationalisation of the behaviour, such as, 'she wants it really'.
- The third stage is the removal of external inhibitions to offending by seeking opportunities which make abuse possible.
- Finally, there is the overcoming of victim resistance by the use of physical force, manipulation or control.

Treatment is undertaken using a series of working assumptions about the nature of sexual offending and sex offence perpetrators, which are based on clinical experience and research undertaken over a number of years. In particular it is assumed that the perpetrator's offending is repetitive and forms an addictive cycle of behaviour which develops over time, and that the offender will habitually engage in denial of the behaviour. The aim of treatment is not so much to 'cure' the behaviour as to give perpetrators the means of controlling their behaviour in future, to accept responsibility for their behaviour, to identify risk situations and to give them the skills required to manage risk. This perspective is important since the approach to treatment is now very different from what it used to be. It is no longer based on an active therapist and a passive 'patient' or subject. The onus is now on the offender to do something about their offending behaviour. In other words we have moved from a positivist frame of reference, where perpetrators can't help what they do because they are the victims of forces outside their control, to one where the perpetrator is seen as a rational agent with the free will to make choices. It also follows that to stand any chance of success, offenders have to be motivated to confront and do something about their behaviour.

Research on the Treatment of Sex Offenders

An earlier chapter drew attention to the problems of measuring the success of intervention attempts by reference to reconviction rates. Studies of the effectiveness of work with sex offenders have these problems to contend with, but also have other problems that are more specific to sex offending:

- Because much sexual offending goes unreported and offending can go on for some time without coming to official attention, sex offending has especially low and changeable detection rates.
- Where sex offenders are concerned, much longer follow-up periods than usual are necessary because the risk of reconviction persists for a much longer time (Ditchfield and Marshall, 1990; Marshall, 1994; Hedderman and Sugg, 1996). For most offence groups the greatest chances of reconviction occur within two or three years of sentencing and the reconviction rate then tails off noticeably. Where sex offences are concerned, failure can occur for many years, perhaps as long as 16 years after release, so the traditional two-year follow-up period is of very limited value.
- The main offence recorded may be a non-sexual offence; it may be an offence of violence with a sexual background (Marshall, 1994).
- Because it is a relatively rare occurrence, sex offender treatments

often involve quite small numbers, so there can be problems ensuring that any differences in reconviction rates between different groups are statistically significant.

- Treatment programmes depend on offenders being motivated. They are therefore likely to attract those who want to do something about their offending behaviour. This means that the results may not be generalisable to all sex offenders (Ditchfield and Marshall, 1990).
- The effects of treatment may vary for different types of sex offender (rapists may respond differently to child molesters, for example). But treatment programmes often include different types of sex offender, so again there is the problem of knowing whether what works with one type of sex offender can be transferred to another type of sex offender (Ditchfield and Marshall, 1990; Marshall, 1994).
- In any one treatment programme a mixture of methods is often used. Consequently, if treatment is effective, there is the problem of determining *which* component of treatment is working (Ditchfield and Marshall, 1990).

In a study of 13,000 offenders discharged from prison in 1987, 402 (3 per cent) were recorded as sexual offenders. The study supports the idea that a person should be considered a potential sexual recidivist if he/she has *ever* been convicted of a sexual offence, regardless of whether the current offence is a sexual one: 'A person serving a sentence for a non-sexual offence who has a history of previous sexual offending is as likely to be reconvicted of a sexual offence as someone serving a sentence for a sexual offence but with no previous convictions for such offences' (Marshall, 1994: 27).

Forty-two studies of sex offender recidivism were examined by Furby, Weinrott and Blackshaw (1989) in what was claimed to be an exhaustive review at that time. After a discussion of methodological issues, the results of the studies were considered in relation to three main questions:

- How many sex offenders continue to commit crimes?
- Is clinical treatment for sex offenders effective in reducing recidivism rates?
- Are recidivism rates different for different types of sex offender?

Because of the methodological problems involved the authors had difficulty in coming to unequivocal conclusions about any of these matters. However, the authors do say that they were able to identify several suggestive trends:

- The longer a follow-up period is, the greater is the percentage of men who will have committed another crime (though not necessarily a sex offence).

- There is no evidence that clinical treatment reduces rates of sex re-offending in general, and no appropriate data for assessing whether it may be differentially effective for different types of sex offender.
- There is some evidence that recidivism rates may be different for different types of sex offender. For example, the recidivism rate for paedophiles tends to be lower than that for exhibitionists and assaultive offenders (rapists).

Marshall and Pithers (1994) suggested that the review by Furby et al. was unnecessarily gloomy. They argued that many of the programmes which Furby et al. reviewed were outdated and had been superseded by more modern methods of treatment based on the more efficacious cognitive behavioural model. Furthermore, the review disproportionately involved treated sex offenders from programmes in the United States, which 'is thought to have the highest rate of interpersonal violence and criminal activity in the world' (Marshall and Pithers, 1994: 14), and *untreated* sex offenders in Europe. Finally, some of the studies covered the same groups of (unsuccessfully) treated offenders, thereby double counting failure. Marshall and Pithers suggested that more recent, relatively well-controlled evaluations have shown that treatment can be effective, but it must be comprehensive, cognitive-behaviourally based, and include a relapse prevention component.

In a review of the literature on sex offending against children Grubin (1998) said that although the general perception is that sex offenders carry a high risk of sexual re-offending, in reality recidivism rates for sexual crime are relatively low. About 20 per cent of those who are convicted of sexual offences against children are reconvicted for similar offences over a 20-year period, in contrast to non-sexual offenders, who are reconvicted at a rate of about 50 per cent over two years and 60 per cent over four years. But there are certain groups of offenders amongst whom re-offending rates are substantially higher, and therefore risk assessment needs to be a high priority. Although Grubin concurred with Marshal and Pithers that the pessimism expressed by Furby et al. was overstated, he said that it was not yet clear just how effective modern treatment will be, and that the kind of problems referred to earlier mean that the interpretation of the results of treatment will always be problematic. Consequently he concluded that 'treatment of sex offenders on its own will not solve the problem of sexual re-offending' (Grubin, 1998: 41). Ackerley, Soothill and Francis (1998) studied reconviction rates amongst a sample of 7,401 males convicted of an indictable sex offence, and distinguished the most serious sex offences (such as rape and unlawful sexual intercourse with a girl aged under 13) from the, relatively speaking, less serious sex offences (such as indecency between males, unlawful sexual intercourse with a girl aged between 13 and 16, procuration and bigamy). For the 'serious' group just over 20 per cent (23 per cent) were reconvicted for any sexual offence within 20 years, of which the great majority (86 per cent) were reconvicted within ten years. For the 'less serious' sexual offences just under 20 per cent (18 per cent) were reconvicted of any sexual offence within 20 years, again with over 80 per cent of these occurring within ten years of the original conviction. On the basis of these findings the authors conclude that a ten-year period of extended supervision for sex offenders after they have served their sentence would not be unreasonable.

Alongside the Sex Offender Treatment Programme mentioned earlier, in 1991 the Home Office established a sex offender treatment evaluation project, STEP, covering treatment in prisons and in the community. The community-based evaluation covered seven programmes, four of which involved short term intensive treatment of between 50 and 60 hours, two were longer term 'rolling' programmes adding up to an average of 59 hours of therapy, and the seventh was a privately run long-term residential programme involving an average of 462 hours of therapy. This last programme targeted highly deviant offenders (Beech et al., 1996; Hedderman and Sugg, 1996). The offenders who took part were assessed before and after treatment using psychometric tests designed to measure their attitudes and behaviour related to sex offending, locus of control, self-esteem and assertiveness, ability to empathise with victims, sexual obsessiveness and willingness to admit to sexual deviance.

The initial measure of effectiveness involved comparing changes on these measures before and after treatment for the 59 offenders who completed pre- and post-testing with a control group of 81 non-sex-offending adult males. Reports on the results of this phase of the study (Beckett et al., 1994; Beech et al., 1996; Hedderman and Sugg, 1996) said that, on the basis of the measures used, over half the sample appeared to have benefited from treatment. However, while short term programmes had a beneficial effect on men with low levels of deviancy, long term therapy was needed in order to be successful in producing change in highly deviant men. It was also found that it would be unwise to use instruments that measure reduction in denial as the only measure of effective treatment. The regimes that were most likely to have a therapeutic impact on offenders had 'high levels of cohesiveness and task orientation; a clear structure and explicit rules; and an atmosphere where members felt encouraged and where they did not feel they were being treated solely as sex offenders' (Beech et al., 1996: 25). Results of the two-year follow-up found that of 133 offenders who had been referred to one of the seven community-based treatment programmes, only 11 (8 per cent) had been reconvicted, five of whom were convicted of an offence of a non-sexual and non-violent nature (Hedderman and

Sugg, 1996). This rate of reconviction was much lower than would have been expected using a reconviction prediction score. The results of the reconviction study indicated a relationship between the likelihood of reconviction and the measures of deviancy and attitude change used earlier. A further evaluation of the Sex Offender Treatment Programme within six prisons (Beech et al., 1998b; Beech et al., 1998a) found that 53 out of 77 men tested (67 per cent) showed a treatment effect in relation to admittance of deviant sexual interests and offending, pro-offending attitudes, predisposing personality variables and relapse prevention skills. The researchers concluded that,

> Using these rigorous criteria to judge treatment effectiveness, the study found that over two-thirds of the sample were successfully treated with regard to a reduction in pro-offending attitudes, with one third of men showing an overall treatment effect. (Beech et al., 1998a: 7)

Not too surprisingly, treatment was most successful for low deviancy/low denial offenders than for high deviancy/high denial men, and longer term treatment of around 160 hours produced results which held up better after release than short term therapy of about 80 hours, particularly for highly deviant sex offenders. The next phase of the research involves two-, five- and ten-year follow-up of reconviction rates.

Monitoring Sex Offenders in the Community

The monitoring of sex offenders in the community can take different forms and involve various groups of people (Hebenton and Thomas, 1996: 107). Traditionally it has involved some form of supervision by police and the Probation Service. Like all offenders imprisoned for serious offences, sex offenders have been subject to supervision arrangements on release, which were extended to cover the whole of the sentence by Section 44 of the Criminal Justice Act 1991. Arrangements have also been in place in England and Wales to enable local authorities to have notice of the discharge from prison of a person convicted of offences against children (Hebenton and Thomas, 1996). In 1964 a Home Office circular mentioned that 'it has been the practice of the Home Office for many years' to inform a local authority when a prisoner convicted of incest is due for release, and outlined arrangements to include those convicted of any sexual offence against a child listed in Schedule 1 of the Children and Young Persons Act 1933, or any offence against a child involving cruelty or ill-treatment (Home Office, 1964: paras 6 and 7).

There have been growing attempts in recent years in the United

States and the United Kingdom to let victims and witnesses know about when and where an offender may be released. *The National Standards for the Supervision of Offenders in the Community* allow victims to express any concerns they would wish to have taken into account when the conditions attaching to an offender's release are being considered (Home Office, 1995a: para. 7.13). In the United States, as of September 1995, 46 states had provision for the registration of sex offenders with law enforcement agencies in the community in which the offender plans to reside (National Victim Center, 1996) but, as Hebenton and Thomas (1997) have noted, most of these were enacted between 1990 and 1996, and practice varies widely. In the United Kingdom, the Sex Offenders Act 1997 established a registration scheme. Section 2 of the Act provides for the notification of the names and addresses of sex offenders to the police. The periods for which registration is required are a minimum of five years for those offenders cautioned or convicted and sentenced to a non-custodial sentence, seven years for a custodial sentence of less than six months, ten years for a custodial sentence of six to 30 months, and an indefinite period for those given custodial sentences of over 30 months. It was estimated that if the Act had been in force in 1993, 125,000 men in the population would have required registration. For 25,000 this would have been for life (Marshall, 1997a).

The register came into operation in September 1997, and one of the most important issues regarding registration is the verification and updating of information (Hebenton and Thomas, 1997: 33). The provisions of the Sex Offenders Act were confined to those cautioned or convicted on or after the Act came into force at the beginning of September 1997 and those serving a custodial sentence at the time of implementation, and did not apply to some 100,000 sex offenders with criminal records pre-dating implementation (Power, 1999). This gave rise to further legislation in Section 2 of the Crime and Disorder Act 1998 enabling the police to apply for a 'sex offender order' if it is deemed necessary to protect the public from serious harm by the offender. Further provision to extend the supervision of sexual offenders is also contained in the Crime and Disorder Act 1998, ss. 58–60 of which enable courts to order extended periods of post-release supervision of up to ten years. Power, in an article reviewing the legislation enacted during the 1990s regarding sex offenders and its implications, states that, 'In the short and medium terms, however, the fact remains that numerous offenders have been released, and others will be, who, depending on the dates of conviction and release, are subject to no control, or to registration under the 1997 Act and relatively short periods of post-release supervision' (Power, 1999: 10).

The topic that has attracted most attention in recent years has been whether to notify the public in general regarding the whereabouts of a convicted sex offender: (community notification). This practice developed in the United States, and was related to a notorious case in which a young girl was murdered by a convicted sex offender, as a consequence of which legal arrangements for the notification of the presence of a sex offender in a community have often been referred to by the media as 'Megan's Law'. At the end of December 1996 there were, to the knowledge of the US National Victim Center, 14 states with community notification statutes, although the exact form that such arrangements took varied. For example, California and New York had a special telephone line that members of the public could call to obtain information regarding a specific offender, and details of the Californian information system are available on an Internet web site. A directory listing registered offenders is distributed to local law enforcement agencies and is open to public inspection.

The media has carried a growing number of reports about the notification of the whereabouts of sex offenders to schools, play groups and the local community in general, of which the following are a selection:

Schools sent list of local paedophiles

Ten schools in Southampton and four in nearby Portsmouth have been sent files, including photographs, on two men living near them in what is thought to be the first police led initiative of its kind in Britain. The offenders had not been told about the files.

Daily Telegraph, 18 October 1996

Schools may be told when a paedophile moves near

David McLean, Home Office Minister, was consulting on the possibility of making police information on the whereabouts of paedophiles more widely available. Pressure on the Government to consider American-style community notification orders for sex offenders has been growing since the conviction of paedophile Howard Hughes for the murder of seven-year-old Sophie Hook.

Daily Telegraph, 19 December 1996

Mob hounds out paedophile

Police intervened on behalf of a convicted paedophile and drove him to a secret location yesterday after the hostel in Stirling where he has lived since Christmas was besieged by a mob of 70 chanting mothers and grandmothers.

Guardian, 11 January 1997

Council warns of paedophile

More than 8,000 parents in south-east London have been warned that
a 'very dangerous' convicted paedophile has moved into their area

Guardian, 27 March 1997

'Give paedophiles town of their own'

A town built for paedophiles who have served their sentences but are
likely to pose a risk to children was proposed yesterday by a former
senior prison official

Daily Telegraph, 11 April 1997

Freed childkiller flees from angry neighbours

A convicted paedophile appeared last night to have been driven from
his home by an angry mob after police said that he posed a
considerable threat to young men and boys.

The Times, 29 September 1997

Worried parents jam website as state outs sex offenders

Across America, states are posting the names, faces and addresses of
released violent sex offenders on the Internet. Yesterday Virginia joined
a rapidly expanding trend that gives parents the power to find
potential neighbourhood predators at the click of a mouse. Within
hours the website had been jammed by callers.

Civil liberties lawyers expressed fears about a loss of privacy and a
potential for harassment by neighbours or vigilantes that could make
the rehabilitation of sex offenders so difficult they could be driven to
repeat their crimes.

The Times, 31 December 1998

Following the murder of an eight-year-old girl, Sarah Payne, in July
2000 the *News of the World* published details and photographs of known
paedophiles, which resulted in an innocent man, Ian Armstrong, being
attacked because he looked like one of those identified.

In 1997 Middlesbrough Council gave consideration to the possibility
of banning known sex offenders from local authority housing. In the
same year a campaign by villagers at Hawthorn, near Pontypridd, prevented a convicted paedophile from being rehoused on their estate, and
led Rhondda Cynon Taff Council to ban similar offenders from living in
its houses. Subsequently the Chartered Institute of Housing issued

guidance to councils urging them to consider very carefully before applying blanket bans on sex offenders. The guidance said,

> Many professionals will accept that successful resettlement and reintegration within society, for which settled housing is a key requirement, can make an important contribution to managing the risk that sex offenders may pose, either following release from a custodial sentence or as part of a community sentence. Exclusion policies may make this process more difficult to achieve. . . . Local housing authorities will need to consider whether additional specialist accommodation is needed in their area as part of their strategic role. The provision of such accommodation could make an important contribution to the rehabilitation of offenders and long term community safety. (Chartered Institute of Housing, 1998: paras 2.1 and 3)

Further research on practice in three areas in providing stable housing for sex offenders has emphasised the importance of housing provision being made available by multi-agency partnerships which are able to own the problems and the solutions jointly (Cowan et al., 1999).

Although the Criminal Justice Act 1991 provided for the extended supervision of sex offenders following release from prison, as noted earlier it did not cover offenders convicted prior to the Act's implementation. This led to considerable public hostility during 1998 when two sex offenders, Robert Oliver and Sidney Cooke, were released from prison and there were angry demonstrations outside police stations and probation hostels where it was thought such people might be. This prompted the Government to review arrangements for the post-release monitoring of high profile sex offenders, and in May 1998 the Home Secretary announced the setting up of a new national steering group on high profile sex offenders. This group would identify such offenders in advance of their release, oversee their handling following their release and consider any funding necessary to meet the likely additional accommodation costs (Home Office press release, 5 May 1998). There have also been court cases concerned with whether or not the police have the right to disclose the whereabouts of convicted sex offenders to third parties. In one case the police informed a caravan site owner of the presence on the site of a couple convicted for sex offences, and they were forced to leave.[8] In the course of an appeal it was made clear that such disclosures should be on the basis of exceptional grounds, and that there is no policy of general disclosure. In so ruling, Power points out,

> the court has clearly set its face against the adoption in the United Kingdom of an approach akin to the United States' so-called 'Megan's Law', a permissive federal law which most American states have adopted whereby the police can inform entire communities of the presence of sex offenders in their area, with all that implies for offenders' safety and rehabilitation. (Power, 1999: 13)

The degree of media attention and public anxiety that has centred on a few high profile cases has a significant bearing on treatment and rehabilitation. First, as the Chartered Institute of Housing and the Probation Service have noted, it makes successful rehabilitation and re-integration more difficult if convicted sex offenders cannot be found places in either hostels or local authority housing, where they can be adequately supervised. It raises the likelihood that serious sex offenders will avoid notification and end up where they are more of a danger to the public. The knowledge that sex offenders will never be accepted back into the community could affect treatment programmes themselves. Offenders may think that there is little point in undertaking programmes to control their behaviour if these will be of little benefit in helping them to live a normal life in the long term. Programmes for the treatment of sex offenders depend on the perpetrators themselves being motivated and willing to exercise control over their behaviour. West points out that 'Men who have been rejected by families and former employers and who endure an isolated lifestyle with no stake in the normal community have correspondingly little to lose by a failure to resist sexual temptations' (West, 1996: 57). It has also been suggested that panic about the dangers posed by paedophiles, fuelled by the media and politicians, could in itself have harmful effects on children's development. In a survey of 200 parents in four British cities, almost two-thirds of parents (63 per cent) responded that their fears about the risks posed by strangers led them to restrict the movements of their children 'way too much'.[9]

In conclusion, it may be said that, after a period in which the availability of treatment programmes for sex offenders was patchy, a more co-ordinated response has developed, involving structured programmes of treatment. These focus on challenging the offenders' behaviour in a way that aims to get them to accept responsibility for, and exert control over, their actions. So far it is difficult to tell how effective treatment programmes have been, for methodological reasons and because long follow-up periods are needed, but there have been indications that they can have a beneficial effect. Meanwhile growing public anxiety about the presence of certain sex offenders in the community has also made successful resettlement more difficult to achieve.

Further Reading

During the 1990s there were significant developments in the treatment of sexual offenders and in public policy and legislation concerning such offenders. The literature evolved rapidly, and anything written has been at risk of becoming out of date quickly. However, some of the more fundamental considerations about the nature of sexual offending are still relevant. Probably the best starting point for further reading is the book, *Sex Crime: Sex Offending and Society* (2000), by Terry Thomas. Thomas is one of the United Kingdom's leading writers on the topic, and the book looks both at the general problem of sexual offending and at specific aspects of the issue, including policing, the courts, and the operation of a sex offenders register. Less recent but another useful reference is Sampson's *Acts of Abuse: Sex Offenders and the Criminal Justice System* (1994b). There are also chapters in books that are useful, including Prentky's chapter in *What Works: Reducing Reoffending* (1995), edited by James McGuire, the chapter by Epps in Clive Hollin's edited collection of papers, *Working with Offenders* (1996), and Donald West's chapter in *Dangerous People* (1996), edited by Nigel Walker. Anne Worral's, *Punishment in the Community: The Future of Criminal Justice* (1997), also contains a chapter about sex offenders. *Assessing Men Who Sexually Abuse*, by David Briggs and others, is a handbook used by those working with sex offenders, and another handbook, by Alec Spencer, *Working with Sex Offenders in Prisons and through Release to the Community* (1999), looks at the work done with sex offenders both before and after their release from prison.

Questions to Consider

- How much importance should be attached to treatment when considering public policy options to reduce sexual offending?
- What are the implications for the treatment of sex offenders of telling members of the public that convicted sex offenders are living in their area?

Notes

1   *The Times*, 9 May 1997.
2   *Guardian*, 25 February 1998.
3   For example, Section 2(2)(b) of the Criminal Justice Act 1991 provides that where the offence is a violent or sexual one, a custodial sentence may be 'for such longer term (not exceeding the permitted maximum) as in the opinion of the court is necessary to protect the public from serious harm from the offender'. Section 44 of the Act also provides that following release on licence from prison, sex offenders should be supervised in the community for the full term of their sentence, rather than receiving unconditional release after three-quarters of the sentence, as is usual. Almost 250 sex offenders started such statutory supervision in 1996 (Home Office, 1997c).
4   The information which follows is based on a presentation by members of the Prison Service at the British Criminology Conference, Loughborough University in July 1995, and a report of a conference held in HMP Brixton in March 1997 (Richardson, 1997).
5   Joyce Quin in a written parliamentary answer to Alan Beith, MP on 23 July 1997.
6   Joyce Quin in a parliamentary answer on 19 June 1998.
7   I am grateful to probation officers in the South Yorkshire Probation Service who have

given presentations on their work with sex offenders, which have been very helpful to me in drafting this section.

8   R. v. *Chief Constable of North Wales*, ex p. AB and CD, (1998) 3 All ER 310, CA.
9   *Independent*, 21 July 1998.

MENTALLY DISORDERED OFFENDERS

In this chapter consideration is given to the definition of mental disorder, and the various points in the criminal justice process at which decisions are taken about how those thought to be suffering from such disorders should be dealt with. The adequacy of provision for treating the mentally disordered in prison and in the community, and the extent to which the mentally disordered are diverted from the mainstream criminal justice process into a more appropriate mental health setting are discussed. Recent developments in provision for mentally disordered offenders, especially those with a severe personality disorder, are also reviewed.

The treatment of mentally disordered offenders needs to be discussed in any consideration of the treatment and rehabilitation of offenders. Not only is it a topic of continuing public concern and interest, but in the past the way society has dealt with the mentally disordered has had close parallels with the way that offenders have been dealt with. There are parallels between the development of the prison system and the asylum, and consideration of mentally disordered offenders involves two major systems of policy: criminal justice and health.[1] One of the main problems regarding such offenders is establishing the part that should be played by each of these systems in dealing with the mentally disordered who break the law. This is due in large part to the fact that mentally disordered offenders present some difficult dilemmas, and society has often responded to such offenders in an ambiguous manner. So, for example, questions arise as to whether such offenders knew what they were doing and were responsible for their actions, whether they can be 'cured' or merely controlled, whether they should be in prison or in hospital. Dealing with mentally disordered offenders also involves two main professions, the legal profession and the medical profession, and raises questions about who is best placed to make a judgement about what needs to be done.

The perpetration of a horrific crime is often followed by speculation that the perpetrator must be mad. This happened, for example, in the wake of killings at a school in Dunblane, Scotland, in 1997. Initial speculation about the mental state of the perpetrator, Thomas Hamilton, was followed by the announcement that Hamilton had no history of mental illness, although this does not preclude the possibility of an undiagnosed personality disorder. In recent years public concern and media coverage have focused on a number of cases where people with a history of mental disorder are known to have been responsible for killing others. As a consequence much discussion has revolved around the concept of dangerousness and the need to contain and control certain mentally disordered people, versus the rights of the mentally disordered themselves. However, the majority of cases involving the mentally disordered are much less dramatic. How disordered offenders need to be dealt with legally and socially depends very much on how one conceives of the relationship between offending and mental disorder. Does mental disorder in some way predispose people to offend, or are the mentally disordered prone to commit offences much as other people are? If the latter, might they then be regarded as being, to some extent at least, responsible for their offences? This latter possibility prompted the advent of a 'hybrid order' to deal with both the offending and the mental disorder. It can happen that a psychiatric condition is not diagnosed until remand or after conviction (Staite et. al, 1994: 3). Peay (1997: 687) has suggested that offence categories among disordered offenders mirror those amongst the 'normal' offending population. It may nonetheless be that those with certain types of mental disorder are more likely to be apprehended because they occupy a marginal social position and their condition makes them more 'visible' to the authorities and the public in general.

Mental Disorder

Mental disorder has been classified in a number of ways, and has both medical and legal definitions. In medical practice psychiatric disorders have traditionally been divided into psychoses, neuroses and personality disorders, and more recently maladaptive behaviours (Goldberg et al., 1987: Ch. 4). The first two involve deterioration from a presumed healthy state, whereas the third relates to characteristics that remain constant. Psychoses have included those disorders traditionally regarded as 'madness', in which strange beliefs and perceptions, with delusions and hallucinations, may be attended by violent and destructive behaviour. Neurosis is not a particularly helpful term these days, since it referred originally to a supposed disease of the nervous tissue giving rise to 'weak nerves', which is known to be no longer the case. Neuroses are mainly defined now as *not* being accompanied by delusions of the kind that accompany psychoses, and it is thus a way of saying 'non-psychotic'. Neuroses include such things as depressive illness and anxiety.

The treatment of the mentally disordered will, of course, vary depending on the nature of the disorder, the circumstances of the person concerned, and to some extent at least on the resources available nationally and locally. In so far as the disorder calls for medical intervention, this most often takes the form of medication. Electroconvulsive therapy (ECT) is used occasionally for severe depressive states (about 1,300 treatments a week), and very rarely neurosurgery is used to cauterise areas of the frontal lobe (about 30 patients a year). But the main thrust of treatment in recent years has focused on the management of mental disorder, preferably in a community setting, by providing supportive services, and where necessary rehabilitation in the form of suitable accommodation. Ongoing medication may form part of this community-based provision. The treatment and rehabilitation of the mentally disordered offender is on the same basis as far as possible, but is more problematic where severe personality disorders and Prison Service establishments are involved.

Given the nature of this book, we are more concerned with legal than with medical definitions of mental disorder. The Mental Health Act 1983, s. 1(2) defines four main types of psychiatric disorder:

> *mental disorder* – meaning mental illness, arrested or incomplete development of mind, psychopathic disorder and any other disorder or disability of mind;
> *severe mental impairment* – meaning a state of arrested or incomplete development of mind, which includes severe impairment of intelligence and social functioning, and is associated with abnormally aggressive or seriously irresponsible conduct on the part of the person concerned;
> *mental impairment* – meaning a state of arrested or incomplete development of mind (not amounting to severe mental impairment) which includes severe impairment of intelligence and social functioning, and is associated with abnormally aggressive or seriously irresponsible conduct on the part of the person concerned;
> *psychopathic disorder* – meaning a persistent disorder or disability of mind (whether or not including significant impairment of intelligence) which results in abnormally aggressive or seriously irresponsible conduct on the part of the person concerned.

These definitions are not unproblematic, however, since there is some overlap and room for interpretation. The term 'mental illness', in particular, causes confusion. Although it accounts for the majority of people detained in hospital it is not defined by the Act. Jones (1988) suggests that 'the question of whether a person is to be placed in this category is therefore entirely a matter for clinical judgement'.

It has been estimated that at any one time around one in six adults in the UK has a mental health problem such as anxiety or depression (Department of Health, 1998b), and that six million people a year receive treatment for a medically defined mental illness (Mental Health Foundation, 1990). Expenditure by the NHS and social services on mental health is approximately £3 billion a year. However, less than 1 per cent of the population suffers from severe mental illness, such as schizophrenia or manic depression. A ten-year follow-up study of 1,056 mental patients with a diagnosis of schizophrenia, affective psychosis or paranoia who were discharged from mental hospitals in Stockholm in 1986 found that there was an over-representation of criminal convictions among the patients. Of those who were 40 years old or younger at the time of discharge, nearly 40 per cent had a criminal record compared with less than 10 per cent of the general public, with violent crimes occurring most frequently (Belfrage, 1998). However, as suggested earlier, it could be that arrest and conviction occur more often amongst such a group because they attract more attention and an official response. Also, the conclusions of the study have been challenged on the basis that, because the institutions sampled contained more patients admitted as a result of violent offending, there was the likelihood of exaggerated rates of violent behaviour (Lindqvist and Allebeck, 1999). Lindqvist and Allebeck were the authors of an earlier study of the same population (Lindqvist and Allebeck, 1990), and they contended that 'an epidemiological study like ours reveals the relatively low risk of homicidal behaviour by schizophrenics, while descriptive studies, such as Belfrage's, present absolute figures that appear appalling when based on high risk populations backtracked for many years' (Lindqvist and Allebeck, 1999: 451). As a result they concluded that, although mental disorder is associated with an increased rate of violent behaviour, as measured by criminal records, self-report or other information, 'it is also clear that the increased risk is modest and that most patients with mental disorders are not violent' (ibid.: 451). The extent to which certain mentally disordered people pose a danger to others is considered further later in this chapter.

While mental illness is not uncommon, and the more lurid cases involving the mentally disturbed attract a lot of attention, the proportion of people coming before the courts who are known to be mentally disordered is relatively small. In a study at a south London magistrates' court where 38,000 cases were dealt with during 1988, only 70 cases were identified as involving mentally disordered people (Browne et al., 1993: 107), and an assessment of almost 3,000 detainees at seven London police stations found that only some 3 per cent were suspected of suffering from some form of mental disorder (Robertson et al., 1993, cited in Burney and Pearson, 1995).

The Legislative Framework and the Criminal Justice Process

The Mental Health Act 1959 set out arrangements for joint working between health and social services and, to a lesser extent, the criminal justice system. It was amended by the Mental Health (Amendment) Act 1982, which was then consolidated by the Mental Health Act 1983, and reference now is usually to the Mental Health Act 1983. However, in September 1998 the Labour Government announced the setting up of a group of experts to undertake a 'root and branch review of the 1983 Mental Health Act' (Department of Health press release 98/391, 22 September 1998). A consultation paper was issued in November 1999, outlining the main features to be included in a new Mental Health Act (Department of Health, 1999a). These included the scope and structure of compulsory powers (paras 9–24), the forms of treatment that should attract specific safeguards (para. 25), the notion of incapacity (paras 27–28), and matters relating to offenders in general (paras 43–44) and prisoners in particular (paras 45–46). Concerning this last point, the consultation paper says, 'The priority must be to ensure that all those with mental disorder of a severity which would attract compulsion outside prison are transferred to a suitable hospital facility. The [expert] Committee therefore recommends the introduction of a right of prisoners to an assessment of their mental health needs.' The main points in the criminal justice process at which decisions are taken regarding mentally disordered defendants and offenders as they exist at present are set out in Figure 8.1.

A consideration of this process is important because it affects how, when and where a person is dealt with, and therefore has significant implications for their likely treatment and rehabilitation.

Diversion from Criminal Justice

Section 136 Mental Health Act 1983 empowers a constable to take a person who is in a public place, and who appears to be suffering from mental disorder and to be in immediate need of care and control, to a 'place of safety', in the interests of the person or for the protection of others. The person may be detained there for up to 72 hours for examination and for arrangements to be made for his/her treatment or care. Note that the person does not have to have committed an offence for this to happen (Jones, 1988: 195). A place of safety normally means a hospital, mental nursing home, residential home for the mentally disordered 'or any other suitable place'. Where a police station is used, it should be for as short a time as possible until other arrangements can be made (Jones, 1988: 194). Research by Rogers and Faulkner (1987) suggested that the use of s. 136 was very erratic, that clearer policies regarding its use needed to be implemented, and that its use needed to be more closely monitored. In particular they noted that the provision seemed to be disproportionately used for Afro-Caribbean people.

Other research has focused on the crucial role that the police play

Figure 8.1   *Mentally disordered offenders and the criminal justice process*

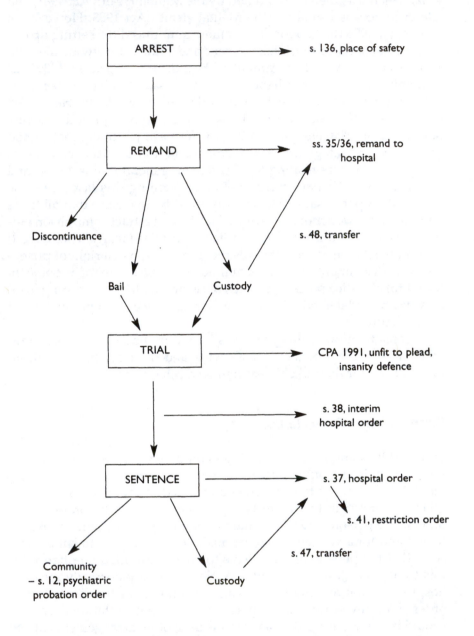

ARREST ⟶ s. 136, place of safety

REMAND ⟶ ss. 35/36, remand to hospital

Discontinuance

s. 48, transfer

Bail   Custody

TRIAL ⟶ CPA 1991, unfit to plead, insanity defence

s. 38, interim hospital order

SENTENCE ⟶ s. 37, hospital order

s. 41, restriction order

s. 47, transfer

Community
– s. 12, psychiatric
probation order   Custody

(unless otherwise stated, sections refer to the Mental Health Act 1983)

when mentally disordered people are taken into custody. The police are at the forefront in identifying whether or not someone is mentally ill, but seldom have the necessary training to enable them to make such an identification. Gudjonsson et al. (1993) in research for the Royal Commission on Criminal Justice drew attention to the need for better identification of the mentally disturbed and training for those likely to be involved in dealing with them, such as custody officers. Like juveniles, mentally disordered people when being interviewed by the police must be accompanied by an 'appropriate adult' (who may be a social worker, medical person or relative). However, supposing that a person is identified as requiring the presence of an appropriate adult, the research by Gudjonsson et al., and that by Palmer and Hart (1996) has called into question whether the role of the appropriate adult in such cases is sufficiently clearly defined and whether those who most often fulfil such a role know what to do and are adequately trained. Palmer and Hart noted that in their study the appropriate adult often did little more than observe what happened and seldom intervened in any meaningful manner: 'a lot of times they just sit in the interview and twiddle their thumbs and make a few notes' (Palmer and Hart, 1996: 64). A Home Office circular (66/90, supplemented by 12/95) urged statutory authorities to use their powers to divert mentally disturbed people from the criminal justice process, but Palmer and Hart reported that the circular had not been widely available to the police in South Yorkshire, where they carried out their study (Palmer and Hart, 1996: 73–75). However, a report of research carried out by the Home Office Research and Statistics Department in the custody suites of seven Metropolitan police stations offered more reassuring conclusions, and suggested that the police had 'actively and positively responded to the messages in Home Office Circular 66/90' (Robertson et al., 1995: 4). In some areas, such as Hull, Barnet and Birmingham, arrangements have been developed involving psychiatric and other agencies to identify and divert mentally disordered people at the police custody stage. A study of cases in Scotland (Duff, 1997) reported that while, in theory, the prosecution service decides which offenders should be diverted from prosecution, in practice selection is largely determined by the police. It is suggested that the key to expanding diversion from prosecution into psychiatric care is to require the police to provide more information.

Although the police may have a key role to play in diverting the mentally disordered from the criminal system and into the health system, many mentally disordered people are nonetheless likely to come to court. In recent years a number of court-based schemes have been developed to enable a person who appears to be mentally disturbed to be diverted to hospital. These take various forms (Penal Affairs Consortium, 1998), and include psychiatric assessment schemes at Clerkenwell (James and Hamilton, 1991) and Bow Street and

Marlborough Street magistrates' courts (Joseph and Potter, 1993), those where a psychiatric nurse is in attendance, as in Islington (Burney and Pearson, 1995) and Sheffield, and multi-agency assessment panels, first developed in Hertfordshire (Hedderman, 1993). Since April 1993 the Home Office has made funding available to meet the costs of psychiatrists or community psychiatric nurses attending magistrates' courts, and funding was provided for 53 such schemes in 1996 (Penal Affairs Consortium, 1998: 10). Palmer and Hart (1996), amongst others, have argued for the extension of such schemes, and have suggested that similar provision might also be located at police stations.

Remand for Psychiatric Reports

The emphasis has been for some time on avoiding remand in custody for a psychiatric report, but the main concern is that the provisions for doing this are not used as much as they might be.

> S. 35 Mental Health Act 1983 permits remand to hospital for reports. S. 36, remand in hospital for treatment, is only available to the Crown Court in cases of mental illness or severe mental impairment.

There were 322 remands under these sections in 1989. The Mental Health Act Commission has noted that remands to hospital could be used more in place of remands to custody (Mental Health Act Commission, 1991).

Section 48 allows *transfer* to hospital from remand in custody for prisoners suffering from mental illness or severe mental impairment, who are deemed to be in need of urgent psychiatric treatment. The use of such transfers has increased in recent years from 77 in 1987 to 494 in 1997. Research on 370 remand prisoners transferred to hospital under s. 48 in 1992 found that, on average, the transfer was initiated 35 days after being remanded in custody (Mackay and Machin, 1998). However, this average reflected the fact that in a small minority of cases (10 per cent) the period was considerably longer, at over 200 days. For over half the sample (56 per cent) the request for transfer was initiated within 25 days of their being remanded in custody. The most common diagnosis for those transferred was schizophrenia, in around half of the cases. In addition to mental illness, 15 per cent of the sample were also diagnosed as suffering from personality disorder. Following transfer, 12 per cent of the people involved were returned to prison because they were no longer considered to need hospital treatment and 5 per cent were released on bail following a period in hospital. Three-quarters of the people transferred were subsequently convicted, with most of the remainder having charges dropped or withdrawn. Of those convicted, over half (57 per cent) were given restricted or unrestricted hospital orders (see p. 150), and 15 per cent were imprisoned. The research also found that the increased number of transfers under s. 48 in recent years appeared to be incorporating more prisoners charged with less serious offences and was probably due to a greater awareness and better identification of the needs of mentally disordered offenders. There are also some specialised bail hostels that can take people who are on remand and suffering from mental disorder, but more are needed than are currently available.

Plea

An important consideration, and one about which there has been much discussion, is whether a mentally disordered person is fit to plead or can be determined to be guilty. The legal provisions are governed by the Criminal Procedure (Insanity) Act 1964, as amended by Criminal Procedure (Insanity and Unfitness to Plead) Act 1991 (see Peay, 1997: 682–685):

> Unfit to plead – The 1991 Act requires unfitness to be determined by a jury on the evidence of two or more doctors. If the person is found unfit then a new jury determines a 'trial of the facts'.
>
> Not guilty by reason of insanity – the person is labouring under such a defect of reasoning that s/he did not know what s/he was doing.[2]
>
> Not guilty by reason of diminished responsibility – The Homicide Act 1957 s. 2(1) enables a defendant to be found not guilty of murder but guilty of manslaughter by reason of diminished responsibility where the defendant was suffering from substantially impaired responsibility for his/her acts.

Disposal

Section 12 Mental Health Act 1983 provides for **probation orders** with a condition of psychiatric treatment. However, not all psychiatrists are happy about the constraints of a probation order being imposed on a patient's treatment.

Section 37 Mental Health Act 1983 provides for a **hospital (or guardianship) order**, without conviction, but

(a) the diagnosis must be agreed by two doctors, and
(b) one of the doctors must be willing to offer a hospital bed within 28

days, and in the meantime the patient must be kept in a place of safety, usually a prison.

If it is agreed that hospital admission is desirable but neither doctor is able to offer a bed, then under s. 39 of Mental Health Act 1983 the court can request a health authority to provide information about a hospital placement. Problems can arise when the offender is suffering from an untreatable disorder, such as certain kinds of personality disorder, because hospitals are essentially places for treatment, not containment. As Staite et al. (1994: 6) point out, 'a person with a psychopathic disorder may only receive treatment under the Mental Health Act 1983 if he or she is "treatable". Just as there is no objective test for mental illness, there is no objective test for "treatability".' Prins argues that the 'nothing works' doctrine has extended to work with mentally disordered offenders, and that there is a 'continuing climate of nihilism in the treatment of offenders and offender-patients. Psychiatrists and others seem to be reflecting this attitude in the view held by some of them that, for example, psychopaths should no longer be managed in the hospital system.' (Prins, 1993: 7). It is not, therefore, too surprising that 'Many, if not most, "disordered" offenders do not receive the therapeutic "hospital order" disposal' (Peay, 1997: 668). As a result, where the court deems that public protection demands it, the only option may be imprisonment.

Section 38 Mental Health Act 1983 permits an **interim hospital order**, so that proper assessment can be carried out before the responsible medical officer agrees to admit. The provision is little used.

Section 41 provides that where a hospital order is made by a Crown Court, a **restriction order** may be imposed, which means that the offender cannot be transferred or discharged without the authority of the Secretary of State, or in certain circumstances of a Mental Health Review Tribunal. About 120 restricted patients leave hospital on conditional discharges each year to be supervised in the community. Some 13 per cent of restricted patients conditionally discharged for the first time between 1972 and 1993 were convicted of a standard list offence within two years of release. This included 2 per cent convicted for a grave offence.[3] Twenty-seven per cent were convicted of a standard list offence within five years, 5 per cent of whom were convicted of a grave offence. The two- and five-year reconviction rates have been lower since 1987 and it is suggested that this may be due to a number of factors, including diversion of mentally disordered offenders from the criminal justice system and more effective supervision of conditionally discharged restricted patients (Kershaw et al., 1997). A study of the supervision of restricted patients in the community showed that it was seldom possible to identify cases where preventive action could have been taken, but the restriction order was regarded as effective in making possible continuing treatment with medication for people with mental illness (Home Office, 1995d).

Section 45A, inserted by the Crime (Sentences) Act 1997, s.46, pro-vides for **hospital and limitation directions**, commonly referred to as 'hybrid orders'. This was first proposed in the White Paper, *Protecting the Public* (Home Office, 1996a) for 'those who are considered to bear a significant degree of responsibility for their offences' (para. 8.12). It allows the Crown Court to pass a prison sentence on a convicted offender diagnosed as suffering from treatable psychopathic disorder, while at the same time ordering his or her immediate admission to hos-pital for treatment. The effect of this is for the person to be regarded as if he or she had been sent to prison, but he or she in fact goes to hospi-tal as if transferred under s. 47 of the Mental Health Act 1983. This means that if the person fails to co-operate with, or respond to treat-ment, they can then be sent to prison to serve out their sentence. Cavadino has argued that this puts the convicted psychopath in a triple no-win situation. The offender is sent to hospital even if he or she would prefer a straightforward determinate prison sentence then,

> Once in hospital, if you fail to co-operate with treatment you will go to prison to serve out your sentence. Supposing everything goes wonderfully well and you are cured? Your shining reward will be – a transfer to prison to complete your sentence. Best of all, perhaps, if you fully co-operate but no effective treatment is provided, you can *either* be transferred to prison *or* remain detained in hospital indefinitely. (Cavadino, 1998: 7)

Transfers from Prison to Hospital

Section 47 Mental Health Act 1983 allows transfer from prison to hospi-tal where the accused has been sentenced to imprisonment, and s. 48 allows for transfer from prison to hospital where the accused has been remanded in prison. The number of transfers under these sections rose from 180 in 1987 to 767 in 1993, since when it has remained at around 750 transfers annually. However, a high proportion of transfers (two-thirds in 1997) are of untried or unsentenced prisoners, some of whom return to prison on discharge from hospital (Kershaw and Renshaw, 1998). The use of these sections varies across the country, a shortage of hospital provision being an important factor. A report of the House of Commons Health Committee has referred to the 'extreme pressure on acute beds' and 'individuals in prisons who were ill enough to be trans-ferred to secure mental health units, but for whom no place was available' (House of Commons, 2000: 1). It is also recognised that 'The majority of mentally disordered prisoners do not come within the Mental Health Act criteria for transfer to hospital'. For such prisoners the Prison Service aims 'to provide them with access to the same range and quality of health care services as the general public receives from the NHS' (Criminal Justice Consultative Council, 1997: 3), but it is acknowledged that a number of things need to be done before this aim can be achieved.

The Treatment of Mentally Disordered Offenders

In Prison and Hospital

There are three high security hospitals (formerly known as *special hospitals*): Broadmoor, Rampton and Ashworth (formed in 1990 when Moss Side and Park Lane merged). These hold patients who require treatment under secure conditions because of their 'dangerous, violent or criminal propensities'. On 1 April 1996 three new Special Health Authorities were established to manage the three special hospitals – rather as other NHS hospitals are now managed by NHS Trusts. A High Security Psychiatric Services Commissioning Board has been formed to advise the NHS Executive on commissioning high security psychiatric services. At the time of writing the future of the special hospitals was under review. Although suggestions that they may be replaced by a network of smaller units appeared to have been ruled out by the Government in favour of reform of the existing system, a House of Commons Select Committee nonetheless recommended that the special hospitals be closed and replaced by 'eight smaller, regional based units, fully integrated with existing medium secure, low secure and general mental health service provision' (House of Commons, 2000).

Restricted patients cannot be discharged without the consent of the Secretary of State or a Mental Health Review Tribunal. The number of restricted patients in detention in all hospitals in 1997 was 2,694, of whom 1,203 were detained in high security, special hospitals and 1,491 in other hospitals. However, while the number of patients in high security hospitals has remained at around 1,000 over the past decade, the number of restricted patients in other hospitals has more than doubled from 656 in 1987. Consequently the *proportion* of restricted patients in high security hospitals fell from 62 per cent in 1989 to 42 per cent in 1999:

A major study was carried out in the late 1980s to determine the extent of mental disorder amongst the prison population. In a 5 per cent sample of the sentenced prison population (2,042 prisoners serving six months or more) Gunn, Maden and Swinton (1991) diagnosed 37 per cent of all males (40 per cent of adult males and 33 per cent of young males), and 56 per cent of all females in the sample, as having psychiatric disorders, but it should be noted that the diagnoses went wider than the Mental Health Act classifications.

Table 8.1 *Restricted patients detained in hospital at 31 December*

Type of hospital	1989	1999
High security hospital	1187	1193
Other hospitals	722	1664
All hospitals	1909	2857

Source: Johnson and Taylor, 2000a and b: Table 1

Of the 37 per cent of all males the following diagnoses were made:

23% substance misuse;
10% personality disorder;
6% neurosis;
2% psychosis;
0.8% organic disorders.

(The figures add up to more than 37 per cent because some individuals had more than one disorder.)

It was estimated that over 9,000 of the 46,500 prisoners at that time may have been suffering from a significant mental disturbance, and 3 per cent of the sample were diagnosed as being in need of urgent transfer to hospital (around 1,100 prisoners sentenced to six months or more nationally), but one of the most striking characteristics of the diagnoses is the high proportion attributed to substance misuse. In the years since the survey was conducted this has become a source of concern in its own right.

More recently studies have been carried out suggesting a high prevalence of mental disorder amongst the remand prison population. In a 1995 study it was found that 53 per cent of unsentenced young male offenders were suffering from some form of psychiatric disorder,[4] including substance misuse. In a study of three Young Offender Institutions and 13 adult men's prisons psychiatric disorder was diagnosed in 63 per cent of a sample of 750 prisoners. The main diagnoses were:

substance misuse	38%
neurotic illness	26%
personality disorder	11%
psychosis	5%

(Again, more than one diagnosis was possible.)

Four hundred and fourteen inmates were judged to have an immediate treatment need and it was concluded that mental disorder was common among unconvicted male prisoners. Extrapolation of the results suggested that the remand population as a whole contained about 680 men who needed transfer to hospital for psychiatric treatment, including about 380 prisoners with serious mental illness (Brooke et al., 1996).

In another study in HMP Durham reported at the same time, 26 per cent of 569 men aged 21 and over awaiting trial had one or more current mental disorders (excluding substance misuse). The prison reception screening process identified only 34 men with mental disorder, compared with the researchers' 148. The researchers identified 24 who were acutely psychotic, but prison screening identified only six of these. One hundred and sixty-eight men required psychiatric treatment, 50 of whom required urgent intervention. Of these 50, 17 were placed on the hospital wing. It was concluded that not only was the prevalence of mental disorder high in this population, but that the numbers identified at reception were low, and subsequent management poor (Birmingham et al., 1996).

It is generally recognised that prisons are not the best places to treat mentally disordered offenders, for several reasons:

- They constitute a management problem, which makes demands on the service's stretched resources.
- Insufficient staff are trained to treat such offenders.
- With the possible exception of places like Grendon Underwood, prison conditions hardly constitute a therapeutic milieu.

Gunn et al. said,

> Prisons are not equipped to provide anything more than 'first aid' care for individuals suffering from severe mental illness. At one end of the spectrum, they are prevented from prescribing to seriously disturbed patients who refuse medication. At the other, they do not have the resources to provide a full multi-disciplinary assessment and treatment package for patients with a chronic mental illness such as schizophrenia. As 'total institutions' prisons resemble the old asylums. (Gunn et al., 1991)

In evidence to the House of Commons Select Committee on Health Dr John Reed said, 'care for mentally disordered people in prison is frankly a disgrace. There is no other word to describe it. It is appalling' (House of Commons, 2000: para. 205).

However, there will continue to be some mentally disordered offenders within the prison system, for one reason or another, for whom provision has to be made. Some provision for the mentally disordered does exist within prison, including a wing at Grendon Underwood. The Prison Service also has plans to develop further therapeutic provision, including two new therapeutic community facilities for sentenced adult males with personality disorders, and a new unit for women (Criminal Justice Consultative Council, 1997: 3). Nonetheless, reporting the results of a programme of inspections two prison inspectors concluded that

> The quality of services for mentally ill prisoners fell far below the standards in the NHS. Patients' lives were unacceptably restricted and therapy limited. (Reed and Lyne, 2000: 1031)

Of 13 prisons with inpatient beds in England and Wales inspected during 1997–98 no doctor in charge of inpatients had completed specialist psychiatric training, only one prison had occupational therapy input, and two had input from a clinical psychologist. The inspectors recommended that, at a minimum, it was necessary that inpatient care in prisons be given by doctors and nurses with appropriate training, and that patients meeting the criteria for transfer to the NHS be transferred promptly. They also suggested that 'An alternative strategy would be to transfer all mentally ill prisoners who require specialist mental health care to the NHS, whether or not they meet the criteria for detention under the act' (ibid.: 1034).

In response to a proposal by Her Majesty's Chief Inspector of Prisons that responsibility for delivering health care should be shifted from the Prison Service to the NHS, a Working Group of the NHS Executive and the Prison Service recommended that departmental accountabilities should remain the same, but there should be a formal partnership between the NHS and Prison Service, with the aim of ensuring that standards in prison health care centres matched those in the NHS, and avoiding the isolation of clinical staff working in prisons (Department of Health, 1999b). To develop this partnership a prison health policy unit was set up within the NHS Executive, and a task force was appointed to help prisons and health authorities identify the health needs of prisoners in their area and to agree prison health improvement programmes.

In the Community

Regional Secure Units   The *Report of the Committee on Mentally Abnormal Offenders* (Butler Committee, 1975), recommended the setting up of Regional Secure Units (RSUs) in each region of the NHS. The report said that such units 'are required for those mentally disordered people, offenders and non-offenders alike, who do not require the degree of security offered by the special hospitals . . . but who, nonetheless, are not suitable for treatment under the open conditions obtaining in local psychiatric hospitals'. The units were seen as one solution to overcrowding in special hospitals and to mentally ill offenders ending up in prison.

However, their development was very slow to start with, and has always fallen short of the minimum of 2,000 beds recommended by the Butler Committee. In January 1991 there were only 635 permanent RSU beds. The Government announced an increase in the money available for building medium secure psychiatric units from £3 million to £18 million in 1992–93. But the Reed review of services for mentally disordered offenders suggested that at least 1,500 places were required for those too ill for prison, but for whom a special hospital place was not necessary (Department of Health/Home Office, 1992: recommendation 11.274). A more recent development has been that, following the Reed report, in order to compensate for the shortage of RSUs and the fact that they are often at a distance from the populations they serve, there has been a growth in the number of local secure units (LSUs; see Department of Health/Home Office, 1992: Annex 1).

The number of mentally disturbed prison inmates moved into secure hospitals has increased in recent years, from 326 in 1990–91 to 715 in 1994–95. Even so there have been continuing reports that people who could be in places of psychiatric treatment are in prison. In a letter to John Battle, MP on 20 February 1996 the Director General of the Prison Service said that on 20 January 1996, 163 prisoners were awaiting transfer to a psychiatric hospital; 853 mentally disordered prisoners were occupying beds in prison health care centres, and 1,380 were requiring some form of mental health care but not transfer to hospital or inpatient treatment in a prison health care centre (NACRO, 1996: 9). In October 1996 it was reported that sentencing on a convicted sex offender had been delayed due to a shortage of secure psychiatric beds because prisons were transferring more disturbed inmates to hospitals, and 'There is a widely recognised shortage of medium security beds in the system' (*Guardian*, 23 October 1996: 5).

It has been argued that the movement to close down mental hospitals in recent years has led to some people re-emerging in the criminal justice and prison system. This is sometimes referred to as the 'transcarceration hypothesis', and is based on the notion that one institution tends to get substituted for another. For example, in the United States it was reported that,

> At the end of 1968, there were 399,000 patients in state mental hospitals and 168,000 inmates in state prisons. Within a decade, the hospital population fell 64 per cent to 147,000 and the prison population rose 65 per cent to 277,000. (Steadman et al., 1984: 475)

However, various factors may account for the rise and fall of institutional populations, and co-variations do not necessarily mean that there is a direct causal relationship between a decrease in one population and an increase in another. Fowles (1993) suggests that it is difficult to sustain the transcarceration hypothesis on closer examination of the data, and finds little unequivocal evidence to support it on the basis of information for England and Wales.

Diverting Mentally Disordered Offenders: an Achievable Goal?

An important aim of legislation and policy in recent years has been as far as possible to divert the mentally disordered from (a) the criminal justice process, and (b) prison, or at least to facilitate their transfer from prison into community facilities and health service provision. Although this is an eminently sensible goal, there are many reasons why diversion is difficult to achieve in practice. These include the problem of identifying a mentally disordered offender at the appropriate time, the availability of resources, the problem of whether or not someone is regarded as 'treatable', and public anxiety about the mentally disordered in general. Reference was made earlier in this chapter to the fact that the mentally disordered are a relatively small proportion of the total number of people dealt with by the criminal justice system. Consequently any one court or police station will have to deal with the mentally disordered relatively infrequently, and this in itself means that it is difficult to ensure the effective operation of procedures to deal with an occasional event. As Burney and Pearson have put it:

> A relatively tiny number of people passing through a myriad of decision-making points in the criminal justice system cannot be dealt with by posting a gatekeeper, like a cat at a mousehole, at every opening. (Burney and Pearson, 1995: 308)

They go on to suggest that in such a situation what is needed is a combination of access to specialised advice and assessment services and a high level of general awareness of the problems of the mentally disordered throughout the criminal justice system.

In 1992 a national survey was carried out in England and Wales to assess the extent and nature of psychiatric assessment schemes based at magistrates' courts for the early diversion of mentally disordered offenders from custody (Blumenthal and Wessely, 1992). The survey found that there were 48 schemes in existence, with another 34 under development at that time. However, problems were identified: lack of adequate transport arrangements, difficulties with hospital admissions, an over-dependence on key people, and little liaison between health, social services and members of the criminal justice system. Another survey carried out by NACRO in 1996 (Penal Affairs Consortium, 1998: 11) identified 194 diversion schemes around the country. While this growth is encouraging, it has been pointed out that future funding for some of these schemes is uncertain (Penal Affairs Consortium, 1998: 11). Furthermore, the local nature of such developments means that a mentally disordered person may encounter very different circumstances in one area than they would in another area. Consequently, although diversion schemes have developed in recent years, Staite et al. (1994: 11) suggest that 'Development of diversion from custody projects has tended to be piecemeal. Practitioners should aim to develop not a diversion project but a diversion system.'

This point is echoed by Laing when she refers to the fact that 'a vast array of differing schemes have emerged across the country; however, they have been developed on a purely ad hoc and unco-ordinated basis' (Laing, 1999a: 817). Laing also raised the important issue of ensuring that, in diverting the offenders, adequate consideration be given to the needs and rights of the victims of their crimes, and argued for the introduction of a formal and mandatory system of victim impact statements, thereby perhaps improving the victim's satisfaction with the operation of the criminal justice system (ibid.: 814).

There is also the question of what mentally disordered people are being diverted to, and whether appropriate provision exists for their treatment elsewhere. Blumenthal and Wessely (1992: 1325) commenting on their national survey of provision say that 'Many of the schemes currently operating have adequate provision for psychiatric assessment, but inadequate arrangements for follow-up treatment and care of the offender once diverted from custody'. Grounds goes one step further and suggests that,

> The simple view that in principle all those who are mentally disordered ought to be diverted from the criminal justice system into psychiatric care in the health service is both impractical and fails to take into account the heterogeneity of psychiatric conditions and clinical needs. (Grounds, 1991: 38)

And Shapland has argued that,

> We shall always have mentally disordered offenders in . . . the penal system not because of lack of facilities, but because of intrinsic contradictions in our ideas about mental disorder and its relation to offending. (Shapland, 1991)

For the time being at least, the need seems to be to continue pursuing the goal of diverting the mentally disordered from criminal processes and custody wherever possible, but also to make appropriate provision for the fact that criminal justice agencies are likely to continue to encounter and have to deal with those who suffer from mental disorder. The Penal Affairs Consortium (a consortium of 35 groups involved in working with offenders) suggests that,

The task is now to extend and consolidate diversion initiatives, to develop the improved range of hospital and community based facilities which is needed to increase their effectiveness, and to ensure that the process of diversion is effectively integrated into mainstream services. (Penal Affairs Consortium, 1998: 12)

Mentally Disordered Offenders and Dangerousness

Although for some time there has been a policy of attempting to divert the mentally disordered from penal institutions, in recent years another policy – that of closing mental institutions and providing 'care in the community' – has attracted significant attention. This has come about because concern has been awakened by cases in which those who are mentally disordered have killed people. These include the cases of Christopher Clunis who stabbed Jonathan Zito to death in an unprovoked attack in 1993, John Rous who killed a social worker at the hostel where he was staying, Wayne Hutchinson who went on a rampage, killing two people and wounding three others, and Martin Mursell who attacked his mother and killed his stepfather. The Zito Trust, set up by Jayne Zito following her husband's death, has chronicled such cases, claiming that between 1992 and 1997 104 homicides were committed by people known to the mental health services before the homicide took place (Zito Trust, 1997).

Cases such as these have often been blamed on the policy of 'care in the community'. The parallels between the development of the prison and the development of the lunatic asylum meant that by the mid-twentieth century many mentally disordered people were kept in large Victorian institutions, often in poor physical conditions and with little prospect of an early cure and return to the outside world. This led reformers to call for an end to such conditions, and it was argued that many of those in the asylums could, given proper care and support and a tolerant community, be resettled into society. During the 1980s many of the large, old institutions were indeed closed, but it was thought by many that the main justification for this was the fact that they were very expensive to run, rather than a result of zeal to improve conditions for the mentally disordered. Consequently, it was suggested, insufficient planning and resources went into the policy of 'care in the community'. In particular, it was difficult to ensure that former mental patients always followed their regime of medication. The Zito Trust (1998) has estimated that 70 per cent of psychiatric patients discharged from hospital will stop taking their prescribed medication within two years, and concluded that non-compliance with medication was a major contributory factor in the breakdown of care leading to homicide. The argument is that this, together with the possibility that there were some mentally ill people who needed to be kept in modern, secure institutions for the protection of the public and themselves, created a situation in which killings became more likely.

There is, however, another perspective. It could also be pointed out that the people who are at most risk of harm are the mentally disordered themselves, either through neglect or self-harm and suicide attempts. For example, there were 240 suicides in England by mental patients between June 1993 and December 1994 (Royal College of Psychiatrists, 1996). Also, since people who are not mentally disordered commit homicides, the question is whether someone is more at risk from a person with a mental disorder than from anyone else. The studies by Belfrage (1998) and by Lindqvist and Allebeck (1990)were mentioned earlier in this chapter. Research by Taylor and Gunn has shown that in fact the number of homicide convictions of people considered to be mentally disordered has fallen to half that in 1979, prior to the closure of the old asylums (Taylor and Gunn, 1999). The number of killings committed by the mentally disordered fell proportionately from almost half in the early 1960s (48 per cent in 1963), to little more than one in ten (11.5 per cent) by the mid-1990s. In general the reconviction rate for restricted patients who committed sexual and violent offences is lower than that expected for comparable discharged prisoners and those sentenced to community sentences (Johnson and Taylor, 2000b: paras 18–21).

Whether or not the killings that have occurred in recent years can be attributed in whole or in part to 'care in the community', they have served to reinforce the public perception of the mentally disordered as dangerous people, and to increase calls for greater protection of the public and a more restrictive approach towards mental disorder. The concept of dangerousness has regularly accompanied discussions over the years about how to deal with the mentally disordered. It was one of the themes of the Butler Committee's deliberations. At the heart of this debate is the dilemma over 'false positives' – people who are held in institutions who if released would not constitute a danger to themselves or others, and 'false negatives' – those who are released who do constitute a danger. The dilemma is accentuated by the difficulty of being able to predict behaviour with sufficient accuracy to be sure that the right decision is being made.[5] It could be argued that the only safe course in such a situation is to err on the side of caution and accept that some people will be held securely who do not need to be. But if this were to happen, the rights of many non-dangerous people could be abrogated.

The dilemma was highlighted by the consequences of a famous case in the United States during the 1960s. Having served a prison sentence Johnnie Baxstrom was diagnosed as a dangerous epileptic who, it was felt, was unsafe to release into the community. He was compulsorily detained in a secure hospital rather than being released at the end of his prison term. But in 1966 the US Supreme Court ruled that his detention was unlawful and he was released. Because the ruling was relevant to others detained in the same way, 967 supposedly dangerous patients were also released into the community. The 'Baxstrom patients' as they became known were followed up and it was found that 80 per cent of the male patients and 75 per cent of the female patients subsequently committed no assault against anyone. In other words, there were at least three 'false positives' for every 'true positive'. The researchers also worked out that, but for the Supreme Court ruling, the Baxstrom patients would have been detained for a further seven years on average, and that non-assaultive patients would have been subjected to some 5,400 person-years of unnecessary secure detention (Steadman and Cocozza, 1974: 78).

The Baxstrom case has been discussed at some length, with differing views being taken about its implications. The Butler Committee, for example, took a cautious view, but recognised the dilemma:

> How many probably safe individuals should cautious policy continue to detain in hospital in the hope of preventing the release of one who is still potentially dangerous? (1975: para. 4.13)

Bottoms (1977), on the other hand, contested the Butler Committee's interpretation of the data regarding the Baxstrom patients and emphasised the high proportion of false positives that would be required to stand a reasonable chance of safeguarding against the danger that may be posed by a very small number of truly dangerous people. Bottoms mentions that, 'In the research sample of male Baxstrom patients, there were no cases of subsequent homicide, although in the full Baxstrom male population of 920 cases, *three were re-admitted after causing a death*' (Bottoms, 1977: 79; emphasis added). In the climate of the 1990s it is these three cases that would catch the headlines and receive much attention and publicity. It would be pointed out how awful those three deaths were, and how much suffering had been caused for family and friends. In other words society may have become more prepared to accept the false positives in order to avoid the fatal true positives. It could still be asked, however, whether it is ever going to be possible to achieve a state of complete certainty and security.

Finding a Way Forward?

The concern about cases involving attacks and killings by mental patients prompted consideration of the options for improving the way that the mentally ill are treated in the community. For example, a

compulsory treatment order to impose treatment in the community
without the consent of the person concerned has been suggested.
However, it has also become apparent that a more far-reaching review
of services for the mentally disordered is needed. Following its election in 1997 the Labour Government was reported as saying that 'care
in the community' was deemed to have failed[6] and a major strategy
review was in progress. In July 1998 the Health Secretary announced
that the Government was seeking to develop a 'third way' to treat the
mentally ill which was somewhere between 'care in the community'
and simply locking patients in asylums.

In 1998 the Government's strategy document, *Modernising Mental
Health Services* (Department of Health, 1998b), placed the emphasis on
modernising mental health services to ensure that they would provide
safe and effective care for the mentally ill in the most efficient and cost-
effective way. A series of measures to reform the existing arrangements
was announced, underpinned by an extra £700 million to be spent on
mental health services over the next three years on top of the £3 billion
spent annually. Specific measures included the provision of 24-hour
helplines, a network of assertive outreach teams staying in contact
with patients in the community, extra hospital beds, more staff and
more secure places. More controversially it was announced in
February 1999 that legislation would be brought in to give courts the
powers to order the indeterminate reviewable detention of 'dangerous
people' with severe personality disorders. Later that year the Home
Office and Department of Health issued a consultation paper,
*Managing Dangerous People with Severe Personality Disorder: Proposals for
Policy Development* (Department of Health/Home Office, 1999), setting out two broad options for dealing with people who could be
assessed as posing a risk to the public as a result of severe personality
disorder. The first option would build on existing arrangements within
the health and prison services, facilitating greater use of the discre-
tionary life sentence and extending its availability to a wider range of
offences. It would also remove the requirement that people with
severe personality disorder should be 'likely to benefit from hospital
treatment' in the case of individuals detained in civil proceedings. The
second option would introduce new powers in civil and criminal proceedings to provide for a new indeterminate detention of dangerous
severe personality disorder individuals, plus powers for supervision
and recall following release from detention. Under this option a new
specialist service would be established to manage people with severe
personality disorder. It was estimated that there were around
2,000–2,500 people who could be assessed as having a dangerous and
severe personality disorder, although most of these would be in prison
or hospital at any one time. However, a House of Commons Select
Committee expressed reservations at how this figure had been arrived

at (House of Commons, 2000: para. 156), believed that the link between severe personality disorder and dangerousness was 'extremely tenuous' (ibid.: para. 154), and felt itself unable to support either of the options put forward by the Government. It is therefore apparent that the treatment of mentally disordered offenders (in all senses of the term 'treatment') continues to be in a state of flux, with satisfactory outcomes for the mentally disordered and the general public still in question.

Further Reading

A good starting point for those interested in mentally disordered offenders is Jill Peay's (1997) chapter on this topic in *The Oxford Handbook of Criminology*. On the legal side, Genevra Richardson's book, *Law, Process and Custody: Prisoners and Patients* is a detailed consideration of the processes of decision making within custodial institutions. For anyone wanting to take the subject seriously an essential text is *Offenders, Deviants or Patients?* by Herschel Prins. Extensive consideration of the topic of diversion can be found in *Care or Custody? Mentally Disordered Offenders in the Criminal Justice System*, by Judith Laing (1999b). Also on the topic of diversion, *Diversion from Custody for Mentally Disordered Offenders: a Practical Guide* (1994), by Catherine Staite, Neill Martin, Michael Bingham and Rannoch Daly, is written by people with first hand knowledge and experience of the problem, and is therefore more practically than academically oriented.

Questions to Consider

- When mentally disordered offenders are treated – what is being treated, the mental disorder or the offending behaviour?
- Why are so many mentally disordered offenders in prison despite the fact that there seems to be widespread agreement that they should not be there?

Notes

1 The same is true of drug-misusing offenders, who are considered in the next chapter.
2 This is governed by what are referred to as the McNaghten Rules, first established in a famous case in 1843, which put the onus on the defence, and applied a strict interpretation of insanity, such that it had to be shown that the defendant did not know what s/he was doing, or did not know that it was wrong.
3 Grave offences are a subset of standard list offences covering all indictable-only

offences which have a maximum sentence of life imprisonment, including homicide, serious wounding, rape, robbery, aggravated burglary and arson endangering life.

4 Ann Widdecombe, parliamentary answer, 22 January 1996.

5 The Governor of one secure institution is reported as saying that probably 50 per cent of his patients could be released into the community without danger; the problem is knowing which 50 per cent.

6 J. Hibbs, and C. Hall, 'Search for "third way" to treat mentally ill', *Daily Telegraph*, 30 July 1998.

9

THE TREATMENT OF DRUG MISUSE

The first part of this chapter considers some of the terms used in relation to drug misuse, and describes the legislation relating to drug misuse. The next section describes the background against which the treatment of drug misuse takes place, including the development of the drug scene over the last 30 years, the prevalence of drug misuse, statistics relating to law enforcement and sentencing, and some of the organisations involved in dealing with drug misuse. The chapter then describes some of the policy initiatives that have taken place in recent years, and moves on to look at the treatment of drug misusing offenders and research relating to its efficacy.

Definitions and Legislative Context

Definitions

The use of drugs is widespread and takes many forms, including the smoking of tobacco and the drinking of alcohol, and a wide variety of drugs are prescribed by doctors and can be bought over the counter. The use of drugs, whether legally available to the public or not, can cause problems in many ways, and a number of terms are used in connection with problems arising from drug use, including misuse, abuse and problem drug use. The term used most commonly is 'drug misuse'. It is hard to define misuse in objective terms, other than in relation to legality and illegality. Nonetheless, this is the term that will be adopted here, despite its subjective nature.

A term widely used in connection with drug misuse is 'addiction'. This refers to specific features of drug use and its cessation:

- the onset of withdrawal symptoms when a drug of addiction suddenly ceases to be taken;
- the need to increase the dose of a drug in order to achieve the same effect;
- dependence – a psychological craving for the drug.

The principal focus of this chapter will be the main drugs of addiction, such as heroin, and those for whom drugs may be said to have become a significant problem, either by their own definition or that of society.

Drug use can be problematic for a variety of reasons apart from addiction, including the fact that many drugs are illegal, that a drug habit can be expensive and that drug use can lead to various physical and mental health problems This chapter is also concerned with a legal definition of drug misuse, which relates to those drugs controlled by the Misuse of Drugs Act 1971.

Legislation

The main legislation controlling the use of drugs at the present time is the Misuse of Drugs Act 1971. The Act divides controlled drugs into three **classes**:

> Class A – including what are sometimes regarded as the 'hard' drugs, such as heroin, morphine and cocaine, but also including hallucinogens, such as LSD, MDMA (Ecstasy) and the active ingredients of cannabis, the tetrahydrocannabinols;
> Class B – including cannabis and cannabis resin, amphetamines, barbiturates and weaker opiates, such as codeine;
> Class C – includes benzodiazepines – which are the most commonly prescribed minor tranquillisers (for daytime relief) and hypnotics (to promote sleep) – including Valium, temazepam and Mogadon.

Controlled drugs are also divided into five **schedules**, which determine the extent to which the Government will authorise their production, supply, import and export. Thus, drugs in Schedule 1 (such as cannabis and hallucinogens) are the most strictly controlled. These drugs can only be possessed or administered in accordance with a Home Office licence, which will be granted only in exceptional circumstances, such as for research. In Schedule 5 are those drugs that are considered to pose minimal risk of abuse and are available in a pharmacy without prescription. The schedules in between cover a range of drugs and controls that determine whether a substance is available on prescription, can be imported or exported with or without authority, and administered to another person with lawful authority.

The **offences** that can be committed with drugs controlled by the Misuse of Drugs Act 1971 are,

- possession;
- allowing premises to be used for the supply of drugs;
- cultivation or production;
- supply to another person;
- import and export.

The last three are referred to as 'trafficking' offences and, together with allowing premises to be used for supply, attract more severe penalties.

The **maximum penalties** for the misuse of a controlled drug are determined by:

- the class of drug involved;
- whether the offence is one of possession, 'trafficking' or 'allowing premises';
- whether it is dealt with summarily (before a magistrates' court) or on indictment (before a Crown Court).

This is summarised in Table 9.1.

Table 9.1

| Offence | Type of trial | Class of drug | | |
		A	B	C
Possession	Summary	6 mths &/or £5,000 fine	3 mths &/or £2,500 fine	3 mths &/or £1,000 fine
	Indictment	7 yrs &/or unlimited fine	5 yrs &/or unlimited fine	2 yrs &/or unlimited fine
'Trafficking'	Summary	6 mths &/or £5,000 fine	6 mths &/or £5,000 fine	3 mths &/or £2,500 fine
	Indictment	Life &/or unlimited fine	14 yrs &/or unlimited fine	5 yrs &/or unlimited fine

Although The Misuse of Drugs Act 1971 is the main legislation controlling drug misuse, various other laws are also relevant. These include:

Medicines Act 1968, which governs the manufacture and supply of medicines;

Road Traffic Act 1972, which makes it illegal to be in charge of a motor vehicle while unfit to drive through drink or drugs;

Customs and Excise Management Act 1979, which penalises unauthorised import or export of controlled drugs;

Controlled Drugs (Penalties) Act 1985: increased maximum sentence for trafficking in Class A drugs from 14 years to Life;

Intoxicating Substances (Supply) Act 1985, controlling the supply of solvents to those under 18 years of age;

Drug Trafficking Offences Act 1986 and Drug Trafficking Act 1994, which provide for the seizure of assets that cannot be shown *not* to come from the proceeds of drug related crime. The number of confiscation orders grew from 200 in 1987 to 1560 in 1996, yielding a total value in 1996 of £10.5 million (*Home Office Statistical Bulletin* 10/98, para. 70).

The Drug Scene in the United Kingdom

Historical Background

For much of the twentieth century drug addiction in the UK was limited to a fairly small number (around 500) of what were termed 'therapeutic' addicts – people who had become dependent on opiates during the course of medical treatment – or to members of the medical profession. The situation changed in the 1960s when much popular and professional attention was directed at drugs, partly because of the association with lifestyles at the time, and partly because there had been what then seemed to be a dramatic upsurge from a few hundred addicts to around 3,000 registered opiate addicts. This was thought to be in part the result of irresponsible prescribing by a small number of doctors and resulted in the introduction of stricter controls, and the Misuse of Drugs Act 1971.

Known and presumed use gradually increased during the 1970s, but it was the early 1980s that saw a significant increase, to around 12,000 registered addicts by the middle of the decade. Estimates of regular users far exceeded this figure, ranging up to some 50,000 (Pearson, 1987). But it was not just the size of the problem that attracted attention. The 1980s 'boom' was also identified as having a particular character. As in the 1960s it was the use of opiates that attracted special attention, but the new users primarily took the drug by smoking rather than by injection at first. The new users were also increasingly likely to be working-class young people in certain rundown areas of towns and inner cities, rather than the more middle-class 'hippies' associated with the 1960s, and in some areas specific housing estates were identified as being at the centre of the problem. These areas were often characterised by high levels of poverty and social stress, poor social provision and high levels of alienation amongst the young.

In the 1980s drug misuse also came to be associated with other issues. Partly because of the characteristics of the new heroin users, and partly because of the economic climate of the time, drug misuse was associated with high unemployment and the development of an informal economy (e.g. Fazey, 1988; Parker et al. 1988) and, later in the decade, with other social problems such as the growth in homelessness. Studies indicated a close link between heroin misuse and neighbourhood levels of social deprivation (Pearson, 1987; Dorn and South, 1987). Another association that developed during the decade was the link between drug misuse and crime, both organised crime related to drug supply, and crime by users to support a habit. This had not been so marked in the past (Mott, 1989). Thus, what appeared to develop during the 1980s was a triangular relationship between drug misuse, social deprivation and criminal activity in a way which meant that drug misuse was no longer an isolated issue; it had come into the mainstream of social and economic concerns. This is a simplified description of the development of the 'drug scene' in the UK, but the way in which problem drug use developed over the years was closely related to the development of youth culture. In a situation where many young people did not have formal links with the mainstream economy in the form of a regular job, they became less likely to define their drug use as problematic, and many drug users did not feel culturally at odds with their drug use (National Local Authority Forum on Drug Misuse, 1988: 10). However, the emergence of a stereotype of what has been termed the 'normal' drug user has been challenged (Pearson, 1990).

Developments in the size and nature of drug misuse in the 1980s also affected responses to it. For one thing, the social context of increasing drug misuse meant that the largely medical response, which had predominated in the past, was no longer sustainable. Instead the focus shifted towards a more community-oriented approach, which emphasised the role of education. Where the medical profession was involved, it was increasingly in the context of working with other professionals and agencies. As the decade progressed there was also a growing awareness on the part of drug agencies of the significant role played by the criminal justice process in their work, something that was highlighted at the end of the decade by the Government's Green Paper on *Punishment, Custody and the Community* (Home Office, 1988) and the imminent Criminal Justice Act 1991.

The drugs scene was also characterised by several important developments in thinking during the 1980s. One of these involved a debate over whether problem drug use was best tackled by trying to reduce demand for drugs, or by restricting their illegal supply. Of particular importance, however, was the move from thinking primarily in terms of treatment towards putting more emphasis on prevention, a process given impetus by a report of the Advisory Council on the Misuse of Drugs (1984), and followed by a report from the Association of Local Authorities. Drug misuse prevention had several aspects, including the mounting of public education campaigns, a stress on community involvement, and the development of activities to divert people from drug misuse. Another development in the drug scene during the 1980s that came to overshadow all the others was the advent of AIDS/HIV as a major source of concern, particularly as those who had started using heroin by smoking it turned to injecting. This gave rise to what became known as the harm reduction or harm minimisation approach to drug misuse. While primary misuse prevention could be argued to be essential to harm reduction, it was now suggested that the priority needed to be, once again, a public health concern, which concentrated on stemming the spread of AIDS, to which injecting drug misusers were now significant contributors (Stimson, 1989).

In summary, then, the two decades preceding the 1990s saw:

- a growth in the prevalence of drug misuse, and by a much wider range of social groups;
- a changing social and economic context;
- changes in drug fashions, especially the increase in polydrug use;
- a shift from traditional (medically dominated) treatment to prevention and control (supply side interventions);
- the advent of HIV and AIDS.

Prevalence of Drug Misuse

The evidence of research carried out during the 1990s was that drug use became increasingly widespread, particularly amongst young people, and was not restricted to socially marginal groups (Leitner et al., 1993; Parker, 1995). Successive British Crime Surveys have produced the results of self-reported use of prohibited drugs amongst the population. These showed that just under one third of all those aged between 16 and 59 said they had ever used an illicit drug. However, amongst young people, aged between 16 and 29, the proportion rose to almost half (Table 9.2).

Table 9.2   Drug misuse declared, 1994–98[1]

Year of BCS	Age group	Drug use ever %	Drug Use Last Month (%)
1994	16–59	28	6
	16–29	43	14
1996	16–59	29	6
	16–29	45	15
1998	16–59	32	6
	16–29	49	16

Table 9.2 also indicates that a distinction needs to be made between those who have *ever* used drugs illicitly, and those who have done so recently, with only a quarter of 16–29-year-olds saying that they had used drugs in the last year and 16 per cent that they had done so within the last month. Cannabis was the most commonly used prohibited drug,

having been tried by 42 per cent of 16–29-year-olds at some time, and by 14 per cent within the last month (Ramsay et al., 1999). There are also gender differences, with males being 1.4 times more likely to have ever taken drugs than females (Ramsay and Partridge, 1999). In a representative study of 7,722 schoolchildren aged between 15 and 16 covering the whole of the UK, 42 per cent (45 per cent of boys and 40 per cent of girls) said they had taken drugs. Amongst this sample Northern Ireland had the lowest (26 per cent) and Scotland the highest (55 per cent) rate of 15–16-year-olds who said they had used drugs; for Wales the rate was one in three (33 per cent) and for England 41 per cent (Miller and Plant, 1996).

Given such findings, it is hardly surprising that reference has been made to the 'normalisation' of illegal drug use as a recreational pastime amongst young people (Parker et al., 1998). On the other hand, there have also been indications that the rise in youthful drug use is not an inexorable one. Levels of drug misuse were found not to have changed very much between the 1994 British Crime Survey and the 1996 British Crime Survey, leading the Home Office Minister, George Howarth, to comment that this showed that at least drug misuse was not 'escalating out of all control' (Home Office, 1997a). Surveys of up to 40,000 school pupils carried out over several years by the Schools Health Education Unit have reported that illegal drug use peaked in 1995, fell from around a third in 1996 to about a quarter in 1997 (Balding, 1998), and decreased further to 21 per cent in 1999 (Balding, 2000). Another study, based on a survey of over 2,500 15- and 16-year-old boys and girls, also reported that most forms of drug misuse had declined between 1995 and 1999. Amongst the boys, those reporting any use of illegal drugs had decreased from 40 per cent to 33 per cent, and for girls the reduction was from 45 per cent to 40 per cent (Plant and Miller, 2000). It is also worth noting that although large numbers of people may have reported that they have tried drugs, the proportion who use drugs frequently and for whom they have the potential to become a problem may be much lower (Newburn and Shiner, 1997). Alcohol use, for example, is common, but alcoholism is less so.

Drug Addiction

Under the Misuse of Drugs (Notification of and Supply to Addicts) Regulations 1973 doctors were required to notify the Home Office of the particulars of people who were addicted to 14 controlled drugs, all of them opiates apart from cocaine. This Addicts Index was subject to various shortcomings, including the incompleteness of coverage and lack of practical use. It was therefore discontinued from April 1997 under the Misuse of Drugs (Supply to Addicts) Regulations 1997.

Instead notification of the treatment of people is recorded by the Department of Health's Regional Drug Misuse Databases (DMDs) in England and the Scottish and Welsh DMDs. In 1996, the last year in which the Addicts Index operated, the number of notified addicts was 43,400, of which 18,300 were new notifications, the numbers of both new and renotified addicts having increased steadily during the first part of the 1990s (Corkery, 1997). One group of researchers has estimated that, since the British Crime Survey suggests that around 4 million people use illicit drugs each year, this means that 'around 3 per cent of the drug using population could be defined as problematic users' (Edmunds et al., 1998: iii).

Drug Misuse and Crime

Some reference has already been made to the relationship between drug misuse and crime, which became more noticeable during the 1980s. This is not the place for an extensive discussion of that relationship, but some points are relevant to a consideration of the treatment of drug misuse. The first point is the complex nature of the relationship. Illegal possession of drugs is, by definition, an offence, and this means that people who may commit no other offence become criminalised by virtue of their drug use. But what is usually of more concern is the likelihood that once drug use moves from an occasional recreational activity to being a more serious problem, it can lead to other criminal involvement, such as the more serious offences of supplying drugs to others, and committing crimes in order to obtain the large sums of money needed to maintain a habit. Brain, Parker and Bottomley (1998) reported that in a study of crack cocaine users the annual drugs bill per person was £20,000, and that acquisitive crime such as theft, shoplifting, fraud and burglary was the single most important source of funding. Any treatment programme therefore is not just a matter of tackling a health issue, and detoxifying a user, but can involve trying to unravel a difficult set of social and criminal relationships. It is significant in this context that there has been a shift over the years from drugs being regarded as principally a health issue, with the Department of Health leading on policies for tackling drug misuse, towards the Home Office coming to the forefront in such matters.

In recent years research has tended to confirm that there is a relationship between drug misuse and crime. A study of people arrested for a variety of crimes (Bennett, 1998) found that, on the basis of several measures, drug use and crime were strongly correlated. It was found that almost two-thirds of arrestees who provided a urine specimen tested positive for a drug apart from alcohol. Excluding alcohol, arrestees held for property offences were more likely to test positive than arrestees held for other offences. Of those held for burglary in a dwelling, 11 per cent tested positive for opiates, but 26 per cent tested positive for alcohol. Almost half of arrestees who said they had used drugs in the last 12 months believed that there was a connection between their drug use and crime. In particular there was evidence for the idea that crime is committed to support drug use. Arrestees who said that their crime and drug use were connected reported illegal incomes that were two to three times higher than those who said that their crime and drug use were not connected. Further analysis indicated that the use of heroin and crack cocaine was particularly likely to result in increased illegal activity. Although many people with a serious drug problem probably commit offences (other than use of illegal substances) and there is undoubtedly a proportion of offenders who take illegal drugs, it is not possible to be entirely sure about the causal relationship between drug misuse and crime. In a review of the literature Hough summarises the position by concluding that,

> our current knowledge about the volume and cost of drug-related crime is so patchy that all we can say with any certainty is that problem drug misuse is responsible for a significant minority of crime in England and Wales. (Hough, 1996: 18)

Law Enforcement, Courts and Sentencing

There were approximately 150,000 drug seizures in the UK in 1998[2]. The drugs involved are shown in Table 9.3:

Table 9.3   *Drug seizures in 1998*

Drug	No. (in 000s)	Per cent
Cannabis	113.8	75
Amphetamines	18.3	13
Heroin	14.9	10
Ecstasy-type	4.7	3
Cocaine	5.0	3
LSD	.6	0
Total	149.9 *	100

*More than one drug may be involved in a seizure.

In the courts the number of offences dealt with in 1998 was as shown in Table 9.4.

Table 9.4   Drug offences in 1998

Offence	No.	Comment
Unlawful possession	115,232	Of which, 89,129 (77 per cent) for cannabis
Trafficking offences	18,269	Includes unlawful production of drugs other than cannabis, unlawful supply, possession with intent to supply and unlawful import or export
Permitting premises to be used for unlawful purposes	825	
Total number of persons dealt with for drug offences	127,840	As the same person may be dealt with for more than one offence this total is less than the sum of the above types of offence

Sentencing for drug offences in 1998 is summarised in Table 9.5.

Table 9.5   Sentencing for drug offences in 1998

Disposal	No. (in 000s)	Per cent of those found guilty
Total cautioned	59.7	
Total compounded*	0.6	
Total found guilty	67.0	
Absolute/conditional discharge	8.8	13
Fine	29.0	43
Probation/supervision	6.3	9
Community service order	3.7	6
Suspended sentence	0.5	< 1
Combined order	1.7	3
Immediate custody	10.8	16
Other	6.3	9

*Customs & Excise cases dealt with by payment of a penalty in lieu of prosecution.

On 30 June 1998 the population under sentence in Prison Service establishments for drugs offences in England and Wales was 7,900 (Corkery, 2000: para. 67).

Organisations

Finally in this section giving some background to the treatment of drug misuse, it is worth noting that in addition to the statutory agencies dealing with drug misuse, such as the police, Probation Service and hospitals, there are several specialist agencies:

- The Advisory Council on the Misuse of Drugs (ACMD) was established under the Misuse of Drugs Act 1971 to provide independent advice to the Government. The Council has 36 members, and is comprised of academic experts and practitioners. Working groups produce authoritative and widely quoted reports on various aspects of the drugs problem.
- The Institute for the Study of Drug Dependence (ISDD) is a widely respected information source on drugs and their misuse. It has an extensive library, carries out research into drug misuse, and publishes the drug scene's national 'trade magazine', *Druglink*.
- Release is an organisation which was founded in the heyday of 1960s alternative culture. It is now a national organisation with a special expertise in the practice of the law as it relates to drug misuse, and runs a 24-hour emergency helpline.
- The Standing Conference on Drug Abuse (SCODA) is an 'umbrella' body, which was originally set up to represent the interests of, and provide a forum for, non-statutory agencies and projects working in the drugs field, but it later broadened its remit to include statutory services as well.
- In 2000 the ISDD and SCODA joined together to form Drugscope.

Policy Initiatives towards Drug Misuse

Rising concern about drug misuse and its consequences during the later part of the twentieth century, particularly in relation to drug-related crime, resulted in several national and local policy initiatives. Some of the main developments are described in what follows.

The Drugs Prevention Initiative

In the late 1980s the Home Office funded two experimental drug misuse prevention projects in Birmingham and Bristol to investigate the possibilities of bringing agencies based in local communities together to prevent, rather than merely respond to drug misuse. The main means by which the projects sought to achieve this was the development of diversionary activities that could provide people with an alternative to drug taking. These projects demonstrated the feasibility of such an approach, but also produced some important lessons for future work (Crow, 1991). In 1990 the Home Office followed its funding of the projects in Bristol and Birmingham with its own Drugs Prevention Initiative to further a community-based approach to drugs prevention. In the first phase, between 1990 and 1995, 20 small teams were set up to inform, encourage and support local communities in resisting drug misuse. In all they supported more than 2,000 drugs prevention projects, drawing support from a range of statutory and non-statutory services, local volunteers and business people. A second phase of the initiative was started in 1995 to run until 1999 as part of a broader strategy, Tackling Drugs Together (see below). In this second phase 12 bigger teams, covering larger geographical areas in England, were to deliver local action within a national programme of work directed at reducing drug misuse. The teams were to find out whether and how different approaches could have an impact on knowledge, attitudes and behaviour in relation to drug misuse, and the initiative was supported by 17 independent research studies to help identify good practice about the most effective approach to drug misuse prevention in a community setting in order to influence future policy and practice. As a result of a new Government anti-drugs strategy Tackling Drugs to Build a Better Britain, launched in 1998 (see p. 177), the Drug Prevention Initiative was replaced by the Drug Prevention Advisory Service in April 1999. The Service works with Drug Action Teams to help young people resist drug misuse and protect communities from the adverse criminal and social consequences of drug misuse. It is supposed to facilitate links between drug misuse prevention and related activities, such as tackling social exclusion, crime and disorder partnerships, and health action zones, and provides funding and expertise to assist the development and evaluation of projects designed to find the best ways of preventing drug misuse.

Tackling Drugs Together

In 1995 the Government published a White Paper, *Tackling Drugs Together*, a strategy for the period 1995–98 (Central Drugs Coordination Unit, 1995). The focus of the strategy was on three areas:

- reducing drug related **crime**: this included the reduction of drug misuse in prisons, involving mandatory drug testing and the introduction of effective treatment services.
- reducing the availability and acceptability of drugs to **young people**: an additional £5.9 million was made available to schools in 1995–96 to train teachers and support innovative projects in drug

education and prevention, £1 million to be available to develop services for young people at risk of drug misuse, and the Home Office's Drugs Prevention Initiative was to be expanded.

- reducing the **health** risks and other damage related to drug misuse: this included ensuring that drug misusers had access to advice, counselling, treatment and rehabilitation. While abstinence was to be the ultimate aim, steps would continue to be taken to reduce the spread of HIV and other diseases communicable by drug misusers.

At a national level the strategy was to be co-ordinated between those Departments involved with drug misuse by a Ministerial Sub-Committee of the Cabinet on the Misuse of Drugs. Locally the strategy was to be carried forward by Drug Action Teams (DATs) composed of senior representatives from the police, prisons, local authorities, the Probation Service, and health authorities. Drug Reference Groups (DRGs) would provide local expertise to the DATs and harness local communities to tackle drug misuse. Some £8.8 million was to be available to the DATs for development work over the three years of the strategy. Rather than just being 'tough on drugs' it highlighted the importance of education, advice and improving treatment services, and it emphasised partnership in dealing with drug misuse. Although the approach was an improvement on previous policy, it came at a time when many areas already had local forums for co-ordinating drugs issues, and some clarification of working arrangements was necessary.

Tackling Drugs to Build a Better Britain

Following the General Election in May 1997, the new Government issued another White Paper, *Tackling Drugs to Build a Better Britain* in 1998 (HMSO, 1998). Described as a ten-year strategy for tackling drugs misuse, this had four main elements:

- *To help young people resist drug misuse.*
  Since almost half (48 per cent) of 16–24-year-olds questioned in 1996 had ever used illegal drugs, a principal objective of the first aim was a reduction in the proportion of people under 25 reporting use of illegal drugs in the last month and previous year.
- *To protect communities from the adverse consequences of drug related behaviour.*
  The key objective of this part of the strategy was to reduce levels of repeat offending amongst drug misusing offenders, and one of the main means of achieving this would be to increase the number of offenders entering treatment programmes as a result of arrests and the court process.

- *To enable people with drug problems to overcome them.*
  The key objective here was to increase the participation of drug misusers, including prisoners, in drug treatment programmes which have a positive impact on health and crime.
- *To stifle the availability of illegal drugs.*
  Interestingly, while this fourth element of the strategy did, as one might expect, include attempts to reduce the drugs trade by reducing supply, the key objective was to reduce access to drugs amongst 5–16-year-olds, thus placing the emphasis on education as much as on enforcement.

A significant feature of this White Paper was the increased emphasis on the use of treatment as a way of achieving its objectives, based on the evidence from a National Treatment Outcome Research Study (see p. 181) that effective and targeted treatment for drug misusing offenders could reduce subsequent offending. This aspect of the White Paper found favour with the adviser to the US White House Office of National Drug Control Policy who commented that,

> Serious drug use can be brought down only through aggressive community-based intervention and treatment programmes. Currently, these programmes lack direction, coherent objectives, and are ineffective in delivering services to younger addicts. The Government's strategy must ensure that community treatment is an integral part of drug policy planning.[3]

As previous initiatives had done, this White Paper stressed the importance of partnership. An innovation was that the seized assets of drug traffickers, previously retained by the Exchequer, would now be used to make extra resources available for work to combat drug misuse. Another initiative by the Labour Government that attracted much attention was the appointment of an Anti-Drugs Co-ordinator (often referred to as the 'drugs tsar'). The first Co-ordinator, Keith Hellawell, a former Chief Constable, took up his appointment in 1998 and issued his first Annual Report and National Plan in 1999 which set targets for, amongst other things, increasing the participation of problem drug misusers, including prisoners, in drug treatment programmes by two-thirds by 2005, and by 100 per cent by 2008 (Hellawell, 1999: 17). Despite such initiatives, the Government came in for criticism from one of the country's leading researchers in the field of drug misuse, who argued that treatment services were under-funded compared with prevention and enforcement.[4]

The Treatment of Drug Misuse

Following the report of a committee chaired by Sir Humphrey Rolleston in 1926, the treatment and control of drug addiction in the United Kingdom was based on what became known as 'the British System'. Rather than aiming at total prohibition, this approach involved the prescribing of a maintenance dose of heroin, and was seen as a means of stabilising the addict while at the same time reducing the risk that addicts would turn to illegal sources. Subsequently the Dangerous Drugs Act 1967 tightened controls on prescribing and introduced Drug Dependency Units (DDUs or 'clinics'). These were the only places where heroin and cocaine could be prescribed, and they became the main centres of treatment, although GPs have continued to play a role in treating addicts, and can prescribe alternatives to heroin such as methadone. The so-called 'British System' came under increasing pressure, however, and the clinics turned more to prescribing methadone as a substitute. Methadone is longer acting than heroin, is taken orally, and is commonly held to avoid some of the worst problems associated with heroin addiction. It can therefore be used to stabilise the addict and offers a basis for gradual withdrawal and rehabilitation. Hough concluded that, 'It thus makes sense to think of methadone maintenance not simply as a treatment which provides a chemical substitute for heroin but also as an effective way of holding clients in treatment whilst other therapeutic processes can take place' (Hough, 1996: 35). However, methadone is less acceptable to many addicts and it has been argued that this makes it less likely that they will present for treatment. Furthermore, it has been argued that methadone also has its dangers (Newcombe, 1996), but the British System has now largely ceased to exist following the closure of the last clinic to prescribe heroin, in Cheshire.[5] Reviewing developments in the treatment of drug misuse during the last thirty years of the twentieth century, Shapiro (1998) commented that 'The political rationale for providing drug treatment has never been because treatment is in itself "a good thing" for drug users. Instead treatment has always been justified by reference to some other policy objective', whether controlling the market in illegal drugs, minimising the public harm that drugs can cause, or preventing crime.

Many drug misusers avoid statutory services, and for several years a number of non-statutory services have worked with people with problems related to drug misuse. These include community-based projects, such as Lifeline in Manchester and the Rockingham Project in Sheffield, which started out as points of contact for drug addicts, and now offer a range of services, such as advice, referral and counselling. There are also residential schemes, including therapeutic communities, such as Phoenix House. (Therapeutic communities were mentioned in Chapter

6, which looked at the work of Grendon Underwood prison). The original therapeutic community for drug addicts was Synanon in California. As with other therapeutic communities, the aim is to transform the whole person, rather than deal just with a particular problem, such as drug abuse. As far as possible, participants are isolated from outside influences for a time, and focus on rebuilding their lives through a thorough reappraisal of themselves, often using intensive group sessions.

The early Synanon and Phoenix House regimes were very strict, with rule breaking being harshly treated. But since the 1970s they have become less autocratic, and have expanded their work to include the families of addicts and have devoted more attention to preparing clients for re-integration into the outside community. The present Phoenix House programme consists of a series of stages. Phase One takes place at the main residential unit and lasts approximately six to eight months. It has three periods. The Induction Period lasts four to six weeks and allows the entrant to break away from their previous lifestyle and adjust to Phoenix concepts and ways of working. Following this the Tribe Period is an introspective period during which the resident develops his or her ability to deal with personal responsibilities and challenges. The Interphase Period is seen as a preparation for the final phase of the programme, known as re-entry. The resident is encouraged to set an example for new entrants and to start moving towards the outside world again. Phase Two is the re-entry phase during which the person moves towards independent accommodation and practical workshops. This period normally lasts for about five to six months.

Despite the existence of such non-statutory drug services, a substantial part of the drug using population have no contact with any service which could help them deal with drug related problems. In April 1994 the Department of Health established a Task Force to review the effectiveness of services for drug misusers. In its final report the Task Force identified two main models of drug misuse:

- **the disease model**, in which drug misuse is seen as a disease of drug dependency, similar to other chronic diseases, with its own natural history and identifiable pattern; and
- **the drug taking career model**, which sees drug misuse in a more social context, with choices about drug taking closely linked to culture and lifestyles.

The report said,

> On our present knowledge it is not possible to establish in general terms whether one type of treatment is more effective than another – treatment must be matched to the client. Purchasers should therefore have access to a full range of well organised, properly monitored services to enable drug

misusers to be offered those which are most appropriate to their particular needs. (Department of Health, 1996: para. 1.6)

Although the Task Force reported in 1996, it commissioned a National Treatment Outcome Research Study (NTORS), 'the largest prospective treatment study of its kind done outside the United States', monitoring the progress of 1,075 addicts, with 54 programmes participating. The NTORS looked at (1) residential rehabilitation, (2) inpatient drug dependence unit treatment, (3) outpatient and community-based methadone treatment, and (4) outpatient methadone maintenance. At the time the Task Force reported only preliminary findings were available, including an assessment of the initial impact of treatment. It was reported that, 'Clients in all four modalities showed substantial improvements in many areas of functioning'. These improvements included reductions in, or abstinence from, heroin, reduced levels of injecting behaviour, reductions in health problems, and reductions in criminal activity. Since the Task Force reported a one-year follow-up of NTORS clients has reported that:

> There were substantial and important improvements in the key outcome behaviours. Clear improvements were found in the use of heroin, cocaine and other drugs. Abstinence rates for illicit opiate use (heroin and non-prescribed methadone) more than doubled. Where clients were using drugs at follow-up, there were improvements both in terms of the quantity and frequency of use. (Department of Health, 1998a: 1)

In addition improvements were found in the physical and psychological health of clients involved in the NTORS, and in crime and related costs. The saving to society in terms of reduction in drug related crime was estimated to be more than £5 million per year, and it was also estimated that for every extra £1 spent on drug misuse treatment, there is a return of more than £3 in cost savings associated with lower levels of victim costs of crime and reduced demands on the criminal justice system. Despite the fact that some variations in treatment effect have emerged from the NTORS, such findings contrast with earlier suggestions that research had failed to demonstrate that medical treatment is successful in achieving long term abstinence, preventing resort to the illegal market, or in reducing criminal activity (Jarvis and Parker, 1990; South, 1994: 416–418).

The Treatment of Drug Misusing Offenders

Because the relationship between drug misuse and offending is a complex one, the treatment of drug misusing offenders has tended to be complicated. In the past this was in part due to the fact that many of the services for drug misusers thought of themselves as health, social or educational services rather than criminal justice agencies, and did not want to have to deal with people under duress as a result of court orders. However, the Criminal Justice Act 1991 introduced provision for the treatment of drug misuse as part of a community sentence. Schedule 1 of the Act amended the Powers of Criminal Courts Act 1973, with paragraph 6 of the Schedule providing for a sentence of probation to be made with a requirement that the offender submit to treatment with a view to the reduction or elimination of dependency on drugs or alcohol. Usually the treatment will be provided by external drug services. But only 1,400 such treatment orders were made in the first 18 months of operation of the Act. Bean (1997) suggested that the reluctance of treatment agencies to take people on the basis of such a sentence was responsible for the low use of this provision.

Studies have assessed the impact of the Criminal Justice Act 1991 provision (Lee and Mainwaring, 1995), and their results suggested that

- the provision was little used and had little impact on the overall volume or type of work done by drug agencies: 12 probation services reported just 61 instances in the 12 months following the Act's implementation, ranging from none in Cambridge to 20 in the Inner London Probation Service;
- the treatment offenders received as a result of the provision was very mixed. In one third of the 61 orders made it was a probation officer who was responsible for taking the lead in directing the treatment rather than a drug worker, and there was a mixture of residential and non-residential treatments;
- in many cases the provision was not being used for people who might otherwise have gone to prison, and it was suggested that 'many probation clients were having a more restrictive order proposed for them than was necessary', in order to appear 'tough';
- even so 'in 57 per cent of cases courts rejected treatment conditions recommended by probation', and it was suggested that recommendations were perceived as not 'credible' because they were 'not punishing enough or too woolly'. Judges and magistrates appeared to prefer the pre-Criminal Justice Act 1991 'condition of residence' provision.

In their study of work done with drug misusing probationers by the Middlesex Area Probation Service, Dorn and Lee reported that probation officers made relatively few formal referrals under the Criminal Justice Act 1991, preferring to keep probation work 'in-house'. Where referrals did occur they tended to be informal, and drug related work under the 1991 Act typically revolved around a standard probation order (Dorn and Lee, 1995: 317). Thus the Act's treatment conditions appeared to have had little impact, but liaison between courts, probation staff and drug agencies relating to the treatment of drug misusing offenders continued and developed, even if this was not within the formal context of the 1991 Act.

Apart from the limited use of the Criminal Justice Act 1991 provisions, more generally drug misusing offenders tend not to have received treatment for their drug use. In 1991 the Inner London Probation Service estimated that over half of the 1,800 drug misusers currently under Probation Service supervision had never had contact with any treatment agencies (Advisory Council on the Misuse of Drugs, 1991: para. 4.8). The situation seemed not to have improved much when, in 1997, a Home Office study of persistent drug misusing offenders reported that a comparatively small proportion of the offenders (17 per cent) were receiving any treatment for their drug misuse when initially convicted. For those that it was possible to contact again a year later, drug treatment was not much more widespread than it had been a year before (23 per cent of those at liberty). It was also found that, regardless of whether offenders initially received custodial or community-based sentences, there was little change in patterns of drug misuse a year later, and neither form of punishment seemed to be especially effective in reducing drug misuse (Home Office, 1997b).

In a study of arrestees referred to earlier (Bennett, 1998), 839 arrestees were interviewed, and about three-quarters of these (622) provided a urine specimen. The urinalysis results showed that 61 per cent tested positive for drugs (apart from alcohol), the most common drug found being cannabis (46 per cent), with just under 20 per cent (18 per cent) testing positive for opiates. Amongst the interviewees just under a half (45 per cent) said they had been dependent on drugs at some time in their lives, and about one-third (30 per cent) said they were currently dependent on one or more drugs at the time of their arrest, indicating that drug dependency was quite common amongst people arrested by the police. However, only 20 per cent of the arrestees said that they had received some form of treatment for drug dependence in the past, while about the same proportion (22 per cent) said that they would like to receive treatment. Interestingly, although a small proportion (2–3 per cent) wanted the treatment to take the form of some kind of regime to maintain or stabilise their drug dependence, a somewhat larger proportion (7–9 per cent) said that they wanted help in coming off drugs. As the author says, 'These findings suggest that there might be an opportunity to provide treatment advice or to make available some kind of treatment programme to arrestees at the point of contact with the criminal justice system' (Bennett, 1998: 60).

This is something that had been happening on a small scale for some years. Following the large increase in drug misuse in the early 1980s some areas, such as Southwark in south London, set up experimental schemes to provide information and referral opportunities for people with drug problems at the point at which they were arrested. Research on some of these schemes found that almost half of a sample of 128 arrestees said that the arrest referral scheme was their first contact with any drug agency, even though most had long criminal histories, with an average of 21 previous convictions (Edmunds et al., 1998). The research also indicated that following contact there was a significant decline in self-reported drug use and a corresponding reduction in expenditure on drugs and the number of crimes committed.

While this is encouraging, the authors of the study urge caution in interpreting the findings of the study too optimistically. A more extensive study examined a range of interventions for drug misusing offenders in London, Brighton, Derby and Salford, including arrest referral schemes, probation referral schemes and work in prisons, and concluded that such treatment services could have a significant impact both on drug taking and on drug related crime (Edmunds et al., 1999). The study examined 2,078 referral and assessment records gathered by criminal justice drug workers and found that there was a fall in the reported use of illicit opiates from 83 per cent of the cases before contact with a drug worker to 55 per cent after contact, and that the average amount spent on drugs each week by offenders fell from £400 to less than £100 within nine months, with corresponding falls in the levels of offending to finance drug use. Research by Newburn and Elliott (1999) has also indicated the importance of locating help with drug problems within youth justice services, although in this study of two projects in Derby and Sandwell it proved impossible to establish whether drug workers' efforts had any impact on the drug use of young offenders. The opening part of this section referred to the early lack of use of provisions introduced by the Criminal Justice Act 1991. Since then there has been an increasing emphasis on linking drug treatment provision to criminal justice interventions, but as the twentieth century closed there was still some way to go in terms of both the provision and delivery of services. One of the researchers involved in the study of the Derby and Sandwell schemes pointed to the fact that 'drug prevention and treatment provision for young offenders remain extremely limited', and also said that there were clear differences of philosophy between those involved in youth justice work and drugs workers (Newburn, 1999).

Probation

Significant proportions of offenders on probation are, or have been, involved in drug misuse. It is probably impossible to obtain a true picture of the extent of drug misuse amongst probationers, if only because in general offenders would prefer that their probation officers did not know about their drug use. Estimates have ranged from 20 per cent of a service's caseload (Advisory Council on the Misuse of Drugs, 1991: para. 2.6 and Inner London Probation Service, 1991), to almost 40 per cent (HM Inspectorate of Probation, 1993b). However, one survey of probationers reported that, when asked about the most commonly used illegal drugs, less than half of the respondents (42 per cent) said that they had not taken any of the drugs within the previous 12 months. Cannabis was the drug most commonly used within the previous 12 months (42 per cent), with 8 per cent of respondents admitting to the use of heroin, cocaine and methadone within the same period (Mair and May, 1997: Table 3.11).

Despite such indications that a substantial number of people on probation misuse drugs, the Probation Service response has been uncertain and uneven. The response has varied not only between the different probation services, but within services, between different field teams and between individual officers (Nee and Sibbitt, 1993). Not only has provision of services for drug misusing offenders been patchy, but there has often been ambivalence about the extent to which a service should attempt to work with drug misusing offenders themselves, and the extent to which it should engage specialist agencies (Dorn and Lee, 1995). In the past, probation services have been more inclined to look to agencies specialising in dealing with problems of drug misuse, and consequently their main role has been to recommend and refer suitable cases for drug agencies to deal with (Nee and Sibbitt, 1993; Briton, 1995). These external services have included community drug teams, NHS Drug Dependency Units, and voluntary sector drop-in services and rehabilitation houses. However, as awareness of a drug using clientele has increased, services have had to make more efforts to address the issues related to drug misuse themselves. Dorn and Lee also identified that the work that probation officers do with clients who use drugs may be either 'drug focused' (i.e. specifically focusing on clients' drug using behaviour), or 'generic probation work' with clients who are drug users. In a survey in the Middlesex Area Probation Service they found that on average a probation officer spent 4.3 hours per week on work related to drugs, of which 1.9 hours was drug focused, compared with 2.4 hours which was generic probation work, with more of the drug focused work occurring at the pre-sentence stage. They suggest that this pre-sentence focus on drugs was probably a consequence of the need to discuss the implications of offenders' drug use for what might happen to them subsequently.

Although there has been an increasing tendency to define the role of the probation officer in terms of the protection of the public, there is still something of a dilemma facing probation officers. While they are expected to be part of the criminal justice system dealing with illegal behaviour, they also have to work with offenders in such a way as to get them to address their offending behaviour and cope with any personal and social problems they may have, including drug dependency. A report of the Advisory Council on the Misuse of Drugs in 1991 urged probation services to adopt harm reduction principles, and recommended that instances of drug misuse by offenders on probation should not automatically lead to breach proceedings (Advisory Council on the Misuse of Drugs, 1991: recommendation 22). But in 1995 the Home Office Probation Service Division and the Association of Chief Officers of Probation issued a circular (PC 45/95), which gave advice on implementing the White Paper, *Tackling Drugs Together*. This emphasised that probationers should be warned about the illegality of continued drug misuse.

In several areas probation services have adopted positive programmes towards work with drug misuse amongst probationers. In West Glamorgan, for example, a Drug and Alcohol Related Offenders Project (DAROP) was developed involving a partnership between the West Glamorgan Probation Service and local drug and alcohol services. This involved the screening and assessment of offenders during pre-sentence reports for possible substance misuse, with the prospect of offering community-based help with substance abuse for offenders, where appropriate. A study of the initial effectiveness of the scheme found indications of proposals in pre-sentence reports that were more relevant for addressing substance misuse, and greater use of sentencing options designed to address substance misuse (Raynor and Honess, 1998). However, it was also noted that to the extent that such schemes are successful in identifying offenders needing help with substance misuse, they can increase the demand for treatment beyond what is available. It was also too early for the study to be able to say whether the treatment had any impact on subsequent substance misuse and offending. Another indication that work with drug using probationers can have positive results has come from Inner London where a survey reported that there had been reductions in their levels of drug use and criminal activity about six months into an order, compared with the four weeks prior to arrest. The probationers also spent much less on drugs following a period on probation, and those subject to probation orders with a condition of treatment were particularly likely to report reductions in the amount spent on illegal drugs. This is indicative, rather than conclusive proof that probation work can have an impact on illegal drug use, and when asked what had been of most help in tackling their drug use, most offenders mentioned factors other than probation. 'However, in doing so, most of these interviewees felt that their probation officer had played a part in securing this help' (Hearnden and Harocopos, 2000).

Another way of dealing with drug misusing offenders in the community began to emerge during the 1990s. This was the introduction of '**drug courts**', which originated in the United States. Offenders are not handed over to probation, but remain under the control of the court itself, and periods may be spent in prison. Drug courts may make use of treatment providers, but decide on treatment and monitor offenders' progress. As the earlier chapter on probation work showed, courts have often held the view that probation and other agencies lack credibility when it comes to controlling offenders. It has been suggested that because the court can exert more authority than other agencies, this perceived lack of 'credibility' is avoided. Individual judges handle cases and can play a mixture of roles. It is claimed that users dealt with in drug courts commit fewer offences and offend less frequently than those dealt with in conventional courts, and that this is not an artefact of the way that defendants are selected. However, it is also reasonable to ask how meaningful the term 'defendant' is if, as the main proponent of the system in the UK has said, 'the judge operates somewhere between a judge, social worker, prosecutor and defender' (Bean, 1995). In such a situation who safeguards due process? Nonetheless, proposals were put forward that there should be similar developments in the United Kingdom (Bean, 1997), and courts specialising in dealing with drug users started in Wakefield and Pontefract in 1998. The process involves screening, assessment, sentencing, treatment and reviews of progress (Thomas, 1999), with the court working in conjunction with a Substance Misuse Treatment Enforcement Programme (STEP). If, following assessment, treatment is deemed to be suitable, then the most likely option is a sentence of probation with a requirement of treatment under Schedule 1A of the Criminal Justice Act 1991. The court holds monthly review hearings to monitor the progress of offenders, which can lead to breach proceedings if progress is not satisfactory.

When in opposition the Labour Party put forward proposals for a drug treatment order. These proposals were enacted in the Crime and Disorder Act 1998, sections 61 to 63 of which provide for a drug treatment and testing order (DTTO). This consists of 'the treatment requirement' (s. 62 (1)) that an offender undergo treatment 'with a view to the reduction or elimination of the offender's dependency on or propensity to misuse drugs', and 'the testing requirement' (s. 62 (4)) that the offender should provide samples 'for the purpose of ascertaining whether he has any drug in his body during the treatment and testing period'. Section 63 of the Act provides for the periodic review of the order 'at intervals of not less than one month'. It has been estimated that such orders could be imposed on some 6,250 offenders per year at a cost of an extra £40 million per annum.[6] The Labour Party's 1997 manifesto said that this would be paid for by bringing remand delays down to the national targets. DTTOs were introduced in three pilot areas

(Croydon, Gloucestershire and Liverpool) for offenders who had committed an offence on or after 1 October 1998. Between that date and 30 June 1999, 78 orders were made in the pilot areas, out of 233 offenders referred for assessment for their suitability for a DTTO: a selection rate of 33 per cent. An early evaluation of the pilots reported that of 688 urine tests on 69 of the offenders just over half (52 per cent) of the tests for opiates were positive and 42 per cent of the tests for cocaine were positive. Despite this, however, offenders reported that there had been substantial reductions in their drug use and offending, and that the average amount they spent on drugs had fallen from £400 per week to £30 per week (Turnbull, 1999).

This section started by noting the preference which many community-based agencies had for dealing with drug misusers on a voluntary basis, arguing that motivation is an important part of any therapy. However, during the 1990s there was an increasing tendency to place more emphasis on coercion, from the provisions of the Criminal Justice Act 1991, through to drug treatment and testing orders and the use of drug courts. This may be justified in part on the basis of the damage that drug misuse can cause, but it has also been reported that coerced treatment is no less effective than voluntary participation in treatment (Hough, 1996). It has also been found that one of the problems that many community-based facilities have had in the past has been the drop-out rate amongst participants. Therefore some form of constraint may be required in order to hold the drug misuser in a programme long enough for treatment to have a chance of making an impact.

Treatment in Prison

It is not easy to estimate the extent of drug use within prisons, but various studies suggest that use is substantial, if not widespread. In a study of 452 recently released prisoners, 55 per cent reported that they had used at least one drug while in custody (Turnbull et al., 1991). As outside prison, the main drug used is cannabis. In a questionnaire survey of 344 male prisoners, 57 per cent reported that they had used cannabis during their current prison sentence, 16 per cent that they had used heroin, 16 per cent LSD and Ecstasy, 15 per cent cocaine, 11 per cent amphetamines and 2 per cent crack. Six per cent reported injecting drugs during their current sentence (Advisory Council on the Misuse of Drugs, 1996). A survey of 1,009 adult male prisoners in 13 prisons in England and Wales during 1994–95 reported that 62 per cent of the men had used cannabis in prison at some time. Forty per cent of the sample had ever used injectable drugs (mainly heroin, amphetamines, cocaine and crack), with 146 (15 per cent) reporting that they had used them within a month of arrival in prison. Twenty-four per cent of prisoners reported using opiates in prison for the first time (Strang et al., 1998).

In the past, treatment in prison for people with drug dependency problems has been limited and inadequate.[7] The Annual Report of the Chief Inspector of Prisons for 1993–94 said, 'The treatment of those prisoners addicted to hard drugs . . . leaves much to be desired' (HM Chief Inspector of Prisons, 1994: 18 para. 2.27). Inspectors did not find any local prison with a regime for drug withdrawal that met the standards applied in NHS drug dependency clinics. But there have been changes as a consequence of growing concern about drug use within prison, as well as the more general concern about drug related crime. The 1995 White Paper *Tackling Drugs Together* made a commitment to improving the availability of effective treatment for drug misusers in prison, but at the same time drug testing was introduced into prisons, and there has been much debate about whether the latter works against the viability of the former.

In April 1995 the Prison Service published a policy document, *Drug Misuse in Prison* (HM Prison Service, 1995), which aimed to reduce both demand for, and supply of drugs in prison, and to address the potential for harm reduction. A key part of this strategy was the introduction of **mandatory drug testing** (MDT), first on a limited basis, and subsequently in all prisons during March 1996. Between February 1995 and February 1996 11,749 prisoners were tested under the programme. Thirty-three per cent tested positive, the majority (2,922 out of 3,860) for cannabis. Various concerns have been expressed about the mandatory drug testing programme. One relates to the reliability of the tests themselves, since it has been reported that 'false positives do occur because tests detect legitimate drugs as well as certain foods (e.g. poppy seeds) and because of human error; it is estimated that the error rate for urinalysis programmes is about 10 per cent, with half of these (5 per cent) being false positives' (Riley, 1995: 108). There have also been indications that, because cannabis remains in the blood longer than opiates, some prisoners may be 'switching' to heroin (Gore et al., 1996). It has been pointed out that testing only detects users – not dealers (Lee, 1996), thus punishing the 'victims' rather than the 'villains'.

Another consideration is the fact that mandatory drug testing is expensive. Apart from the cost of the tests themselves there is the cost of staff time (£4.2 million was made available to cover the costs of drug testing for 1996–97), and the fact that imposition of additional days' imprisonment as a result of disciplinary adjudications is estimated to increase the prison population by around 300 (Home Office, 1996b). The annual cost of holding 300 prisoners in custody is over £7 million, an estimate supported by a study carried out in five prisons (Edgar and O'Donnell, 1998: 32). Furthermore, it has been argued that for the strategy to work, mandatory testing needs to be backed by supportive and treatment services, not just punishment, and that such services are still far from adequate (Hewitt, 1996). The emphasis on such a coercive approach, with its attendant sanctions, may mean that people are less likely to come forward for treatment. Swansea prison introduced its own drug strategy in 1995 just before the introduction of MDT, creating a climate in which, while drugs were not tolerated, drug abuse was tackled as a health problem with prisoners being offered help and assistance. 'The introduction of Mandatory Drug Testing together with the loss of [the programme's Induction Unit due to serious overcrowding and loss of resources] dealt a body blow to our own drug strategy' (Heyes and King, 1996).

An evaluation of mandatory drug testing (Edgar and O'Donnell, 1998) studied a sample of 148 prisoners in five prisons, and provided the opportunity to look at some of the issues that had been raised. Inmates' self-reports showed that heroin and cannabis were the preferred drugs in prison, and 30 prisoners stated that they had tried heroin for the first time while in custody. Of the 111 prisoners who said they had used drugs at some time while in custody, just under half (48 per cent) reported that MDT had not led to any change in their drug use, 27 per cent said they had stopped taking drugs in prison in response to MDT, 15 per cent said they had reduced their consumption, and 6 per cent said their consumption had altered; they were taking less cannabis but continuing to use heroin. Although four prisoners said they had cut down on their cannabis use and tried heroin for the first time in response to MDT, none of these had persisted in their use of heroin, and the authors of the study acknowledged that the extent of a shift from cannabis to heroin was less than had been anticipated (Edgar and O'Donnell, 1998: 20). Nonetheless, there was a belief amongst a majority of the prisoners interviewed (57 per cent) that prisoners were likely to change from cannabis to heroin because of MDT. The study also found that, on the basis of self-reported drug use, 31 per cent of current users in prison evaded detection when tested. The study highlighted concerns that MDT had shifted the emphasis in prisons away from treatment and towards punishment and deterrence, and that MDT was not seen as identifying serious drug users and directing them towards an effective treatment regime:

> The treatment and counselling we found in these five prisons suggest that the distribution of resources to help and support drug misusers is too uneven. Our overall conclusion was that the balance between using MDT as a deterrent and as an avenue for access to treatment had not been achieved and that many of the staff regard this as a failing of the system. (Edgar and O'Donnell, 1998: 37)

The Prison Service's own review of its drugs strategy concluded that the main impact of mandatory drug testing had been on cannabis misuse, but said there was no evidence that prisoners who once used only cannabis were becoming established heroin users: 'Alarmist predictions that MDT would inflict a "health catastrophe" on our prisons have not been fulfilled' (HM Prison Service, 1998a: 7). In addition to random mandatory drug testing the Prison Service also introduced Voluntary Testing Units (VTUs) for prisoners who agree to avoid drugs and to prove it by undergoing regular but random urine testing. Downview prison was the first establishment to introduce a VTU in 1992, and the Prison Service's review noted that as the number of prisoners signed up to voluntary testing grew, the improved behaviour patterns resulting from the drugs strategy produced a fall in the number of adjudications from an average of 60 a month to 10 a month in 1997. By 1997 46 establishments had VTUs, providing around 3,700 places. In May 1998 the Minister responsible for prisons announced a modification to drug testing in prisons. In future the tests would be more carefully targeted on inmates with serious addiction problems. The number of prisoners who must be tested each month would be halved from 10 to 5 per cent of each prison's population, and there would be some differentiation in the way that those caught using drugs in prison were punished, with those caught using cannabis being dealt with less severely than those on drugs such as heroin. At the same time the Prison Service published its business plan for 1998–99, in which key performance indicator number three (KPI 3) was 'to ensure that the rate of positive testing for drugs is lower than 20 per cent'. The rate of positive testing had been 24.4 per cent in 1996–97 and was provisionally estimated at the time to be 20.8 per cent in 1997–98.

Alongside such developments in testing, treatment programmes have been introduced in prisons. A programme run by the Rehabilitation for Addicted Prisoners Trust (APT) at Downview prison impressed the prison inspectors and won an award from the *Guardian* newspaper. It was based on a 12-step approach to abstinence similar to that of Alcoholics Anonymous. Following a study by Player and Martin (1996), the programme was extended to more prisons by the Home Office. However, it appears from the research that the programme only attracted and retained a certain section of the prison population. Those who applied to enter the programme were not representative of the prison population as a whole, but tended to be the more serious and persistent offenders serving medium-term sentences, with long histories of substance abuse, and

Those who were most likely to persevere with the treatment programme were heroin users or alcoholics in their late 20s/early 30s who had experienced a physiological state of dependence and acknowledged their addiction. (Martin, 1996)

Twenty-two establishments were involved in the initial wave of treatment programmes, which included therapeutic community approaches, detoxification units, intensive drug education and counselling services and community linked throughcare. In 1996 funding was increased to £5.1 million and 59 establishments were involved (Tilt, 1997). Despite this, many would argue that there is still an imbalance between control and treatment. In a review of the effectiveness of current drug provision at Winchester prison in 1997, one of the main problems was still found to be that of obtaining access to drug treatment services (McFarlane and Thomson, 1998). Concerns about the Prison Service's ability to deal with drug dependent prisoners was voiced by the All Party Parliamentary Drugs Misuse Group. Although the group was impressed by the Prison Service's efforts at tackling drug misuse, it was in no doubt that, in 1998 at least, provision was far from adequate. The group concluded that,

> there was an overwhelming lack of accessibility to treatment programmes for the majority of prisoners, (para. 3.2.vi)

> Treatment for dependent drug misusers works and we need more treatment programmes throughout the prisons estate. (para. 3.3.ii)

In particular,

> The throughcare and aftercare of drug misusing prisoners is appalling – there is no other way to describe it. (para. 2.1.iv)

The issue of throughcare was subsequently addressed by research that studied prisoners from 17 establishments who received drug treatment while in prison and who were released between October 1998 and January 1999 (Burrows et al., 2000). This found that although half the prisoners concerned were offered help to obtain treatment on release, only 11 per cent had a fixed appointment with a drugs agency; most were given more indirect help, such as the name of a drug service near their home, or were told to contact a probation officer. The study also identified shortcomings in throughcare provision because effective throughcare depends on multi-agency co-operation, but it is not clear which agency has overall responsibility.

The Prison Service's drug strategy was reviewed in May 1998 and it was concluded that 'An ambitious project of expanding drug treatment in prisons has been achieved at a time when population pressures have reached unprecedented levels.' However, 'The monitoring of in-treatment progress and outcomes was generally poor and measures of change were seldom used' (HM Prison Service, 1998a: 2). At the same time the Prison Service published a revised drugs strategy, *Tackling*

Drugs in Prison (1998b), which brought the Prison Service programme in line with the four aims of the Government's strategy announced in *Tackling Drugs to Build a Better Britain* (see p. 177 above). In 1999 the Prison Service launched CARAT (Counselling, Assessment, Referral, Advice and Throughcare) which aims to provide a range of interventions, starting with an initial assessment on a prisoner's entry into custody, and linking prisons with community agencies in order to ensure continuity of care. The Annual Report and National Plan published by the Anti-Drugs Co-ordinator in the same year said that by 2002 CARAT's annual caseload would reach 20,000, with 30 new prison-based rehabilitation programmes, and 5,000 prisoners a year going through treatment programmes (Hellawell, 1999: 17).

In the United States, where historically the drug problem has been greater than in the United Kingdom, more prison-based programmes have been operating for longer, and these have claimed some success 'for offenders who *complete* the programs' (Lipton, 1996: 12; emphasis added). Lipton claimed that, for a series of therapeutic community (TC) based models, 'evaluations show that TCs can produce significant reductions in recidivism among chronic drug-abusing felons and consistency of results over time' (Lipton, 1996: 15). It has been suggested that 'Research from the USA, Sweden and now also the United Kingdom has produced promising results which suggest that well run programmes are worth the investment (Penal Affairs Consortium, 1996: 8). On the other hand, a review of drug treatment in 'boot camps' found that substance abuse education and treatment programmes did not result in the rehabilitation of boot camp participants (Cowles et al., 1995). This may be because of the particular nature of 'boot camps', which place an emphasis on physical activity and discipline rather than rehabilitation, and the researchers recommended the development of the therapeutic community model as the best way forward for these offenders.

Conclusion

During the 1990s policy makers made more attempts than previously to develop a succession of comprehensive strategies to deal with the problems caused by drug misuse. These strategies had several strands, including enforcement, prevention and education, as well as treatment. Since the prevention of a problem is invariably preferred to curing it, treatment will inevitably be but one component of the response to problem drug use. But there has been a growing recognition that the treatment and rehabilitation of those dependent on drugs needs to be an important part of any strategy. The main issue about treatment for drug dependent offenders is therefore only partly about the effectiveness of treatment. It is as much as anything a question of whether treatment is being delivered in a sufficiently well developed manner to be available to all who need it, and about the use of resources available within a hard pressed system.

As far as the effectiveness of treatment itself is concerned, there have been signs of optimism, but as in other areas involving the treatment and rehabilitation of offenders, caution needs to be exercised when looking at the results of any programmes. To start with, a particular treatment may only attract or apply to certain people. The evaluation of the APT programme at Downview prison, for example, showed that only certain types of prisoner applied to join it. Second, people may drop out of a programme, so it must be borne in mind that the effectiveness of any programme is likely to be restricted to those who complete it, who may be different in crucial respects to those who do not. Thus, the effectiveness reported by Lipton applied only to those who completed the programme. Therapeutic communities such as Phoenix House have a similar problem. It is also relevant to consider what criterion of effectiveness is being used. Is it total abstinence from all drugs (including alcohol), or something else? Furthermore, is a study reporting final outcomes, or some interim measure, such as the initial responses to treatment reported by the NTORS? Even if final outcomes are being referred to, it may be important to distinguish between short term effectiveness (staying off drugs for a certain period) and longer term rehabilitation.

In his review of the literature relating to drug misuse and the criminal justice system Hough points to two crucial considerations. The first is that, once the need for treatment is recognised, it is important to get users into treatment as quickly as possible, avoiding long drawn out admission procedures and waiting times. The second is keeping people in treatment for as long as possible, and for three months at a minimum. Hough reported little difference in success between methadone maintenance, therapeutic communities and community-based, drug-free programmes, but did stress that

> treatment should be thought of less as a technology and more as a human process, where a diversity of strategies can all achieve the same effect: shaping and sustaining motivation to change. (Hough, 1996: 35)

Despite reservations, Hough ends his review of the research relating to treatment in a criminal justice context on a positive note, remarking that the research 'leaves little doubt that constructive measures can be taken within the criminal justice system to tackle problem drug use' (Hough, 1996: 48). But a note of caution is necessary, since the indications are that so far there is no *universally* effective programme of treatment and rehabilitation for drug misusing offenders: different types of offender require different types of treatment. Some drug misusers will respond to the highly demanding regimes of a therapeutic community, while others may need more coercion and more incentives. For the foreseeable future, what is needed is a range of programmes and services designed to meet a wide variety of situations. However, research such as that reported by Lipton in the United States, and the National Treatment Outcome Research Study in the United Kingdom, and Hough's review of developments, do suggest that treatment and rehabilitation have a valuable role to play in the response to drug misusing offenders.

Further Reading

For the legal background to the control of drug misuse useful references are the ISDD's *The Misuse of Drugs Act Explained* (ISDD, 1995) and Fortson, *The Law on the Misuse of Drugs* (1992). Developments in drug misuse, and policies to control it, are reviewed by Nigel South in both editions of *The Oxford Handbook of Criminology* (1994 and 1997), and by Geoffrey Pearson (1991). Mike Hough's Drug Prevention Initiative Paper, *Drug Misuse and the Criminal Justice System* (1996), is essential reading for anyone wanting a coherent overview of the literature in this area. A good article on treatment in the context of the Criminal Justice Act 1991 is that by Mike Collison, 'Punishing Drugs: Criminal Justice and Drug Use' (1993). A Special Issue of the *British Journal of Criminology* (1999, **39**, 4) contained articles reflecting on policy and research at the end of the twentieth century.

Questions to Consider

- Is abstinence the only sensible form of harm reduction as far as illegal drugs are concerned ?
- Should treatment for drug dependent offenders be compulsory, or is treatment only likely to be effective if it is undertaken voluntarily?

Notes

1   The sources for this table are Home Office Research Studies Nos 151 (Ramsay and Percy, 1996a, Table 3.1), 172 (Ramsay and Spiller, 1997a, Table 2.1) and 197 (Ramsay and Partridge, 1999, Table 2.1), and the associated Research Findings Nos 33 (Ramsay and Percy, 1996b), 56 (Ramsay and Spiller, 1997b) and 93 (Ramsay et al., 1999).
2   The source for the statistics that follow is *Home Office Statistical Bulletin* 10/98 (Corkery, 1998).
3   Edward H. Jurith, 'It's No Quick Fix', *Guardian*, 13 May 1998.

4   H. Parker, 'What a Waste', *Guardian (Society)*, 26 May 1999, 6.
5   There was a lively debate in the pages of the ISDD's journal *Druglink* between Dr John Marks, who ran the Cheshire clinic, and psychiatrists based in the London clinics who favoured methadone (Marks, 1995; Johns, 1995).
6   *The Times*, 4 December 1997.
7   One of the researchers involved in the study that gained notoriety as a result of its publication by Martinson in 1974 has since said that the lack of adequate treatment for drug dependent prisoners can be partly attributed to the impact of the 'nothing works' doctrine (Lipton, 1996: 14).

PART 4

BEYOND TREATMENT

10

TREATMENT AND SOCIAL POLICY

Treatment in a Wider Context

For most of this book the focus has been, as one might expect, on the individual offender and the treatment agencies that deal with him or her. This last chapter looks beyond these to broader issues affecting the treatment and rehabilitation of offenders and crime management. These issues can be seen in the context of two main areas of policy. First, in relation to criminal justice policy generally and second, in relation to wider social policy concerns. Although both of these policy contexts find a place in this chapter, the main emphasis here is on social policy issues. The focus is more on rehabilitation than on treatment. Two areas of social policy central to successful rehabilitation, housing and employment, are given particular consideration.

These broader policy issues are important for several reasons. The extent and viability of the treatment and rehabilitation of offenders depends on wider criminal justice and social policies. In particular, the priority given to different policy objectives will affect the resources available for treatment and rehabilitation. If, for example, the emphasis is on a punitive response to offenders, and this requires considerable expenditure on prison places, then less money may be available for treatment programmes within and without custodial institutions. Even when individual treatment and rehabilitation efforts work in terms of their own criteria, few would now claim that they are in themselves a sufficient response to offending. In the context of health care, for example, it is not sufficient to rely on good hospitals and treatment services: good health also depends on social and environmental factors. In contrast to the days when the treatment model for dealing with offenders was dominant, a successful approach to the treatment of offenders is clearly not the only answer to crime management. This recognition can be seen in a Home Office review which brought together a range of research findings about the best ways of responding to offending (Nuttall et al., 1998). This review covered community crime prevention and sentencing as well as effective interventions with offenders. Certain implications follow from this. For example, part of the theoretical critique of the old treatment model was based on the fact that, in focusing on the shortcomings of the individual, it neglected the shortcomings of society. More recently this has been expressed in a concern that individual responsibility should be accompanied by social responsibility

(Crime and Social Policy Committee, 1995). This stresses the need to recognise that offending does not take place in a social vacuum. To achieve an integration of individual and social responsibility it is necessary to combat the social exclusion that is experienced by significant sections of society.

It is noticeable that many of the studies of treatment programmes referred to in this book (especially in the earlier chapter about what works) emphasise that they can only be effective if they operate in the context of adequate educational and employment opportunities, and favourable family and community circumstances. This is not surprising, since programmes for offenders are usually of limited duration. Unless treatment of the individual takes place in a wider context, then at the end of a programme participants are likely to remain in, or return to, the same environment in which they committed their offences. The development of individuals takes place over a number of years. Participating in a training programme or treatment facility for a period of time, whether based in an institution or in the community, is likely to influence development only to some extent, and hardly at all if the conditions in which earlier delinquent development took place still exist. For example, in the IMPACT study described in Chapter 2, one third of probationers allocated to specially reduced caseloads were living in hostels or were literally homeless, but probation officers gave help with finding better housing to less than a tenth. As one writer has commented, 'While this finding alone did not account for the unsuccessful outcome of the whole IMPACT experiment, neither can it have helped' (Stewart, 1996: 77).

The response to crime requires that attention be extended beyond how best to deal with individual offenders. Treatment and rehabilitation have a part to play, but crime management is more a case of bringing together various ways of dealing with offending in a co-ordinated strategy. This leads to a consideration of several matters that will be touched on in this chapter:

- programmes which involve economic and social improvements as well as the application of criminal justice and the treatment of individuals;
- how a co-ordinated strategy is to be evolved;
- who needs to be involved in such a strategy;
- what resources are needed, and how they are best deployed, including how much should be devoted to programmes for individual offenders compared with other priorities.

Social Programmes and Policy

It is prudent to explain what is meant by 'social policy' in the present context. It is a term that has the potential to become all embracing, and to raise issues that extend far beyond what can reasonably be discussed in this book. It has long been recognised that offending is associated with various forms of economic and social deprivation, such as poor housing, low income, and lack of job opportunities and, as crime surveys have found, it tends to be most prevalent in certain areas, such as inner city areas and large municipal housing estates. This is not, of course, to suggest that crime and offending are an inevitable or necessary accompaniment to social deprivation or living in a certain area. Crimes are committed by the middle classes and corporations as well as by the less well off, and there are dangers in labelling certain locations and sections of society. Nonetheless, it is appropriate to place as much emphasis on intervention that focuses on people's social and economic circumstances as on treatment of the individual. In terms of people's life opportunities this predominantly (though not exclusively) includes the following:

- education;
- work training;
- employment;
- housing;
- policies to assist growing children;
- combating poverty;
- health;
- recreation and leisure amenities.

These are all matters that need to be addressed at several levels: at the level of individual offenders, at the local level, and at the national level. The first level to consider is that of the needs of the individual. Whatever else may be done about an offender, some attention should be given to the offender's social situation, including his or her accommodation, work training and employment opportunities, and family circumstances. To some extent these may be considered to be matters for the Probation Service to address but, as the reference to the lack of help with housing in the IMPACT study above illustrates, past evidence suggests that this has not always happened. In the days of the old treatment model it was likely that more attention would be devoted to casework with the individual than to the offender's material needs. Following the shift to a non-treatment paradigm referred to in Chapter 5 the situation changed, with the Probation Service giving more attention to the need for jobs and accommodation, but the shortage of suitable options for ex-offenders was often an obstacle to progress. More recently still the

emphasis has moved towards the control of offenders, with more attention being directed towards the protection of the public and addressing
offending behaviour, rather than the problems which give rise to offending. Increasing financial stringency also made it difficult for the
Probation Service to devote enough attention to these matters.

Drakeford and Vanstone (1996) make the case for devoting more
attention to the social circumstances of offenders as a means of addressing their offending, and argue that, 'changes in people's lives can best be
brought about when the circumstances in which they live are also
changed for the better' (Drakeford and Vanstone, 1996: vii). For probation they propose 'a dual strategy for the Service that involves
influencing systems as well as individuals'. Like others, Drakeford and
Vanstone recognise the importance of regarding offenders as moral
agents responsible for their actions, but say that crime cannot be seen as
'the outcome of individuals' reasoned decision making devoid of a
structural context' (Drakeford and Vanstone, 1996: 1). More recently, a
study of the role of social factors in explaining reconviction following a
community sentence found that problems with drugs, employment,
accommodation and finances were related to reconviction, and that
offenders with multiple problems were particularly likely to be reconvicted. This led the researcher to conclude that, 'The results of the study
suggest that probation work with offenders in tackling problems chiefly
with drugs, but also with employment, accommodation and finances,
may play a role in reducing offending' (May, 1999: x). Apart from the
Probation Service, the main providers of social intervention have been
non-statutory organisations such as NACRO, the Apex Trust, MIND
for the mentally disordered, and various agencies working with drug
addicts and alcoholics. The emphasis of such organisations' work has
often been on addressing the basic requirements of somewhere to live,
employment and the skills needed for employment, and combating
inequality and discrimination in justice and social provision, rather than
on treatment *per se*.

Further consideration will be given to local and national levels of
social policy development shortly, but first it may be helpful to look in
a little more detail at the circumstances of individual offenders with
regard to two of the central areas of social policy mentioned earlier:
housing and employment.

Housing

Research over many years has shown that unsatisfactory accommodation and homelessness are related to the development of offending and
contribute to its continuance.[1] A study of a reception centre for homeless
men in south London carried out in the early 1970s said,

It is doubtful if any other group in the community has comparable conviction rates. The many prison sentences must be partly due to the lack of alternative sentences available for homeless criminals. The fact that the men in residence, who had on average spent three months in the centre in the year before their attendance, had spent far less time in prison during that year in spite of longer previous records, suggests that the provision of more adequate accommodation for these men would prevent a certain amount of crime and committal to prison. (Tidmarsh et al., 1972: 15)

The relationship also operates in the opposite direction. A review of research on single homelessness in Britain said: 'There are clear links between homelessness, particularly rough sleeping, and experience of the criminal justice system.' The review pointed out that the factors associated with homelessness are 'well established in the research literature'. In addition to poverty and unemployment and family breakdown they include 'experience of prison or the armed forces; drug or alcohol misuse; school exclusion; and poor mental or physical health', and the events which trigger homelessness include 'leaving prison; and a sharp deterioration in mental health or an increase in alcohol or drug misuse' (Fitzpatrick and Klinker, 2000). Finding satisfactory accommodation is a problem for many groups of offenders, especially ex-prisoners and young people, who for one reason or another have no family home they can go to. A study by NACRO (1977) reported that homeless young offenders were twice as likely to re-offend as those living at home, and in a more recent study Graham and Bowling (1995: 38) found that 46 per cent of young females and 71 per cent of young males who had ever run away from home admitted to offending. In a national survey of the prison population, 12 per cent of convicted prisoners and 16 per cent of remand prisoners said they had no permanent residence just before their imprisonment. Half of the respondents who were near their release date did not expect to return to where they had been living before imprisonment (Walmsley et al., 1992). Of those on probation Stewart says,

> Overall two conclusions emerge from the evidence: that a third of offenders under probation supervision have problems with housing, and that such problems are very important to those who experience them. (Stewart, 1996: 72)

Studies have consistently shown that people are more likely to re-offend if they do not have satisfactory, settled accommodation. Research funded by the Joseph Rowntree Foundation (1996) covering four prisons found that two-thirds of ex-prisoners who had no satisfactory accommodation to go to on release re-offended within 12 months, whereas only a quarter of those with good accommodation did so. Less than half the ex-prisoners in the study were able to return to their previous accommodation after they had been released. Most of those who lost their accommodation while in prison were owner-occupiers whose homes were repossessed. All had been in full time work prior to imprisonment; none had found work since discharge.

There are also indications that housing problems can affect the way offenders are dealt with in the criminal justice process. Having unsettled accommodation is a reason for offenders being considered unsuitable for community service, which may explain why McIvor found that only one in 13 people on community service reported housing problems, much lower than elsewhere in the criminal justice system (McIvor, 1991). Homelessness also renders a defendant more likely to be remanded in custody. Both the Home Office survey of the prison population (Walmsley et al., 1992) and a survey undertaken on behalf of the Association of Chief Officers of Probation (ACOP) found the level of homelessness to be much higher amongst remand prisoners, at 25 per cent, than in the prison population as a whole (Stewart and Stewart, 1993).

Getting people into some form of accommodation has been one of the traditional concerns of both the Probation Service and non-statutory agencies. In the past there was evidence that probation officers were not sufficiently active in addressing the housing needs of their clients (Davies, 1969). But Stewart noted a change in the situation, and commented in the mid-1990s that, 'housing issues are well on the way to becoming a central concern for practitioners in today's Probation Service' (Stewart, 1996: 77). Despite this, the Joseph Rowntree funded study indicated that there was still a long way to go. Housing for ex-offenders has also been a major concern of the voluntary sector, funded by the Home Office through the Probation Accommodation Grant Scheme (PAGS). About 5,500 places are available as a result of this funding. Often resettlement has taken the form of a hostel or short term accommodation in social projects and landlady schemes, but the objective is to settle people into longer term housing. However, according to NACRO there is a shortfall of 20,000 homes for ex-offenders, with at least a third of those released from custody being unable to find a home.[2] Five million pounds had been earmarked for making good this deficit, but this was subsequently suspended by the Home Office. There have also been problems related to the reduction of housing benefit to three months rather than twelve since April 1995, which means that prisoners serving more than 13 weeks are unable to retain their homes, something that particularly affects single mothers. Bell (1998) has also argued that the power given by the Housing Act 1996 for local authorities to exclude certain classes of people from their housing registers has led to an increase in housing exclusion. So the greatest barrier to developing more adequate housing provision for offenders in recent years appears to have been not so much the lack of activity by the Probation Service and others, as Government policies.

An alternative approach to catering for the needs of the homeless has been the development of 'foyers', places which offer temporary social accommodation and cater for a variety of needs, including training and employment opportunities, especially amongst younger people. Although these have been advocated by some as a way of reducing the likelihood of criminal involvement (Graham and Bowling, 1995: xiv), they have also been criticised as being too restrictive for some people,[3] and therefore may not cater for those most prone to get into trouble.

Employment

It is not the purpose of this book to explore the complex relationship between unemployment and crime or to cover the extensive literature that exists concerning this relationship.[4] Here again, however, it has been found that offenders are much more likely than non-offenders to be unemployed, to be particularly susceptible to long term unemployment, and to lack the skills and training that enable them to compete in the job market (Crow et al. 1989; Crow, 1996b). Surveys of Probation Service clients over a period of years have found around 60 to 70 per cent to be unemployed. The Home Office's national survey of the prison population found that a third of prisoners were unemployed prior to their imprisonment, and prior to their release only one sixth had a job to go to. Forty per cent of convicted prisoners felt that having no job was what led them to get into trouble with the police for the first time (Walmsley et al., 1992).

As with homelessness, unemployment can have an effect on how offenders are dealt with, rendering them less likely to be given a fine or suspended sentence of imprisonment, and more likely to be given a community service order, probation or custody (Crow and Simon, 1987). Offenders have found it hard to obtain jobs, and have in the past received only limited assistance from probation officers and others with this. For example, in a study of Probation Service after-care units Silberman and Chapman (1971) found that less than 15 per cent of clients were given direct help with employment problems, and Morris and Beverley (1975) found in a study of parolees that, of those who found work on release, most did so through their own efforts and none with the help of a probation officer. On the basis of interviews with offenders, probation officers, employers and employment officers, the author of another, more recent, study concluded that, 'The findings suggest that ex-offenders seeking work can count on very little help from the criminal justice system and that both employers and ex-offenders are ignorant about the risks and opportunities which exist (Gill, 1997:

337). However, a study of 739 probation cases in 11 different probation services found that, where employment interventions were made, the proportion of offenders who took up employment doubled. Of 262 cases where the offender was unemployed at the start of supervision and there was no employment intervention 20 per cent started a job before supervision ended, whereas of the 218 cases where there was some form of employment intervention, 40 per cent started a job before supervision ended. Despite the fact that employment intervention could be shown to have had some success, the report noted that 'in the majority of cases, no such interventions were made'. It was concluded that more intervention would lead to more job starts: 'Hence the evidence in this research strongly suggests that probation services can increase offender employ-ability' (Bridges, 1998). Another study of two probation schemes in Inner London and Surrey reported that in their first year they were able to find employment for 12 and 25 per cent of their caseloads respec-tively, although there was no indication as to whether this was better than might have been expected if the schemes had not been operating (Sarno et al., 1999). Although these studies suggest that the Probation Service could achieve some progress, another study of the best way to improve employment and training prospects for ex-offenders concluded that provision not only needed to be concerned with the needs of indi-vidual offenders, but had to have a strategic approach to maximising the use of resources for unemployed offenders. Existing provision tended to be fragmented and short term in nature. Services therefore needed to employ holistic approaches to deal with the multiple disadvantages of the group, to integrate them into mainstream provision, and to address the relationship between labour supply and demand in a systematic and integrated manner (Fletcher et al., 1998).

Non-statutory organisations have developed employment and train-ing services for offenders. Schemes such as the Community Programme and Youth Opportunities Programme provided for a wide range of unemployed people during the 1980s. But the emphasis shifted at the end of the decade towards training that favoured those who could be shown to move into employment most easily. This tended to exclude those who needed very basic skills training and made it especially hard for agencies to provide the kind of schemes needed by offenders, who often require special help. In the 1990s the advent of New Deal, a Government initiative intended to move 250,000 young people aged 18–24 off benefit and into work, provided a new opportunity to get ex-offenders into employment. It was estimated that the Probation Service was working with some 100,000 of the New Deal's original target group of 250,000.

The evidence is that, other things being equal, those offenders and ex-prisoners who are without jobs are more likely to re-offend (Crow et al., 1989). If this is the case and if unemployment is linked to a greater probability of committing crime then employment and training programmes for offenders should reduce it. However, despite the fact that there have been a number of programmes for unemployed offenders over the years, it has proved difficult to provide clear and consistent evidence that, in themselves, they reduce offending. Why is this?

There are various possible explanations:

- There has been 'programme failure': the programmes don't work.
- It is the fault of the individuals concerned. In other words, those who commit offences are also no good at getting jobs, for whatever reason. However, studies have taken account of this and suggest that this is not the case.
- Employment and training programmes provide too limited an opportunity to make an impact on the overall situations in which participants find themselves.
- Such programmes cannot provide 'proper', long term jobs, and this is what is really needed to make a difference.
- The programmes themselves may be succeeding, but tend to be of short duration and there are not enough suitable jobs for participants to go on to afterwards.
- The impact of high unemployment extends beyond the unemployed to society as a whole, and so the only real answer is lower unemployment.

None of this means that specialist employment and training programmes for ex-offenders are a waste of resources. But it does mean that they need to be developed within a wider context of job opportunity. Ex-offenders often experience considerable difficulty in obtaining full time, mainstream jobs (NACRO, 1999: 3), but research has shown that, where they do so, there is a good chance that they will become valuable and valued members of the workforce (Apex Trust, 1991), although the author of one study of ex-offenders' employment prospects has commented that, 'obtaining work for ex-offenders may depend as much on eradicating ignorance amongst employers as it does on focusing help on ex-offenders' (Gill, 1997: 337). The indications are that what is needed is a strategy to get ex-offenders into work which has several components. These will often include some special assistance with basic skills prior to more sustained training, intervention to help ex-offenders overcome the bias against them from employers, and the opportunity to prove their abilities. Clearly these are requirements which are easier to sustain in a thriving job market, and there is a need for the kind of economic conditions which can help to overcome the cycle of unemployment and offending which makes it difficult to get a job, which in turn increases the chances of further offending.

The focus here has been on housing and employment because there is every indication that these are the kind of basic assets that can reduce involvement in offending. However, it is possible to extend this. There are indications of a three-way connection between unemployment, drug misuse and crime, and between mental illness, homelessness and a criminal record. By extension it is also possible to see the development of a cycle of deterioration in which unsatisfactory housing or home environment, joblessness and offending, perhaps accompanied by alcohol or drug misuse, reinforce each other, leading for some people to the accumulation of chronic multiple problems. Such vicious cycles may extend beyond a single individual to another generation of young people destined to grow up in circumstances which favour the onset of delinquency (Rutter and Madge, 1976: Ch. 4). This is, admittedly, taking the bleakest view, but there are clear indications that social problems do tend to reinforce each other.

So how does one break such a cycle of deterioration? In many respects schemes designed to get offenders into work, to offer accommodation, education or training may appear to be little different to other programmes intended to 'treat' offenders: they still deal with the individual offender rather than with the underlying social structure. As noted earlier, the programmes that appear to be most successful do address the full range of offenders' needs – social as well as personal – rather than focusing on just one problem. For example, although Phoenix House is primarily a therapeutic community for drug addicts, it includes literacy and job seeking in the programme. But one may ask whether there is really much difference between, say, a cognitive behavioural programme or a therapeutic community on the one hand, and schemes which offer housing or work opportunities on the other, or schemes which attempt to combine remedial treatment with addressing a person's material needs. Such initiatives don't offer structural remedies. So programmes designed to address social needs as well as personal needs are an improvement, but are still not the whole answer. They may, nonetheless, be important components of successful rehabilitation. However, social problems associated with offending need to be addressed at several levels. There are approaches towards offenders and offending that go beyond the individual to address some of the underlying issues that promote and sustain crime and criminality.

A Co-ordinated Approach

There is a need to look beyond treatment programmes and agencies concerned to treat and rehabilitate offenders. This means, amongst other things, that dealing with offenders and offending has to extend beyond specialists concerned purely with criminal justice. Families, schools, training agencies, employers, businesses, and local and central government departments have to be involved. While it may be relatively easy to appreciate this, it is harder to put it into practice. However, a Home Office report has indicated that a range of services involving families, schools, sport and leisure has been developed to reduce criminality among young people (Utting, 1996).

There is also a need to co-ordinate activities to deal with crime and offenders at local, regional and national levels. To some extent this may be found in such things as the Safer Cities initiative of the 1990s. This brought together representatives of many agencies in a city to develop projects and programmes directed towards creating a safer environment. Likewise Drug Action Teams brought together a variety of agencies in a partnership to tackle drug misuse. But such initiatives have had their shortcomings. They may be insufficiently funded to make a real difference, or their resources may be dispersed over too wide an area to have a discernible impact on any one area. There is also a methodological problem in evaluating broadly based initiatives, since it may be difficult to attribute any changes in crime and offending patterns to the initiative itself, let alone to any particular element of an initiative incorporating several different strands of activity. City-wide changes in crime rates may be due to a community safety programme, or to changes in policing practice, or to more general improvements in social provision or the local economy. Nonetheless, there is a strong case for effective treatment programmes operating as part of more broadly based initiatives, rather than working in isolation.

Addressing Social Exclusion and Risk

It is not just a matter of involving non-criminal justice professionals in addressing offending, or situating treatment and rehabilitation programmes within a broader strategy of activity. One social problem can reinforce another, leading to a vicious circle which it is difficult to break. It is necessary to intervene in this cycle at key points, or to address social problems in a holistic manner. Approaches have been developed which are concerned with the interconnectedness of social problems associated with crime and offending. One of the main themes underlying such approaches has been that of combating social exclusion. It has been pointed out that the criminal justice process has tended to be one of exclusion (Braithwaite, 1989; Rutherford, 1998): to denounce offenders and sometimes to remove them from society entirely by placing them in custodial institutions. They then have to be re-integrated, resettled and rehabilitated within society. Not only does society seem to accord a lower priority to re-integration than to rejecting offenders, but other factors also promote exclusion. These include various forms of discrimination, the lack of a job, the lack of access to good quality housing, education, training and health care, and exclusion from financial services (Kempson and Whyley, 1999). A tremendous effort is required to reverse the whole process, to concentrate on inclusion rather than exclusion, and this can only be achieved if it is done in a concerted manner at all levels of society.

An important step was taken in 1997 with the setting up of the Social Exclusion Unit. The Unit defines social exclusion as 'a shorthand label for what can happen when individuals or areas suffer from a combination of linked problems such as unemployment, poor skills, low incomes, poor housing, high crime environments, bad health and family breakdown'. In its first phase (to July 1998), the Unit was asked to concentrate on truancy and school exclusions, rough sleeping and the country's worst estates and produced reports on each of these topics (Social Exclusion Unit, 1998a, 1998b, 1998c). A second phase plan of work announced in July 1998 followed up the earlier reports and took on two new topics: combating the risk of social exclusion for teenage parents, and reducing the number of 16 to 18-year-olds not in education, work or training. The notion of social exclusion developed from the European Union's poverty programme during the late 1980s. However, the approach is not an entirely novel one, and analysts have commented that poverty programmes in the past have met with mixed results, for economic and political reasons.[5] So, although the intentions may be worthy, success cannot be assured.

Related to the idea that social problems interact is the notion of identifying risk factors and protective factors, which makes it possible to target resources at particular areas of concern. Part of the work of probation officers deals with the risk assessment of individuals. Although the intentions are somewhat different, it is also possible to undertake a risk audit of a community. Risk factors usually include poor material conditions, such as bad housing and poverty, high divorce rates, teenage pregnancies, a high incidence of physical and mental health problems, as well as high levels of drug and alcohol abuse and crime. A risk audit is central to the Communities That Care initiative mentioned in Chapter 3, which has been implemented in certain neighbourhoods in the United States and the United Kingdom.

In addressing social exclusion and risk the concern is not solely with crime and criminogenic factors. This is one consideration, but it is based on the understanding that poverty, poor family relationships, poor educational attainment and job prospects, drug misuse and alcoholism and poor neighbourhoods are interrelated. But just because certain individuals or areas have social problems this does not mean that they should automatically be considered bad. The aim is to reverse decline and promote improvements; not to make matters worse by labelling someone or somewhere as crime ridden. Risk audits are based on statistical probability, not inevitability, and a deterministic approach has to be avoided.

Tessa Jowell, as Minister responsible for Public Health, pointed out that, 'Understanding the causes of social exclusion is the first step towards finding solutions.'[6] However, the solutions themselves may take various forms. One option is to identify and address a particular problem which can be seen as fundamental to other concerns, such as homelessness amongst young people, which can be the route to becoming involved in drug use, crime and prostitution (Randall, 1989). Given her role, Tessa Jowell suggested an even more fundamental approach: 'The starting point must be the needs of the child'. In the last few years a great deal of attention has centred on the role of the family and parenting in general, in relation to the development of delinquency in particular. In a substantial review of the literature Rutter, Giller and Hagell (1998) report that parenting is a central and critical risk factor in the development of antisocial behaviour by young people. This includes coercive and hostile parenting, abuse and neglect, and ineffective and poor supervision.

Farrington is amongst those who have focused on childhood development as a key factor in preventing children from becoming offenders, as a result of research that he and others have done over a number of years as part of a longitudinal study of delinquent development. Farrington concludes that the major risk factors for youth crime are low income and poor housing, living in rundown inner city areas, a high degree of impulsiveness and hyperactivity, low intelligence and low school attainment, poor parental supervision and harsh and erratic discipline, as well as parental conflict and broken homes (Farrington, 1996). These risk factors can be reduced by enhancing protective factors involving parents, schools and the community as a whole. Family relationships and parental supervision are also stressed in Graham and Bowling's study of the factors associated with the development of, and desistance from, youth crime, and both Graham and Bowling (1995) and Utting (1996) have drawn attention to the role that can be played by the school in reducing youthful offending. This is beginning to stray away from treatment and rehabilitation into preventive measures, but it emphasises that treatment and rehabilitation need to be seen as part of a broader strategy of investment in people's development.

This brings us back to the way in which strategies designed to inhibit criminogenic factors can be implemented in local areas. Alongside giving more attention to childhood development, another option is to concentrate on certain localities where multiple problems occur. This is the approach of the Communities That Care initiative. It is also a strategy that has been adopted by Government, in developing plans to focus on improving conditions in some of the UK's worst housing estates (Social Exclusion Unit, 1998c). While such an approach has the advantage of targeting resources where they appear to be most needed, there is a danger of directing too much attention to what are assumed to be problem areas, such as certain notorious inner city areas, or housing estates, to the neglect of other areas. Research commissioned by the Joseph Rowntree Foundation found that, while crime is the most widespread source of neighbourhood dissatisfaction,

> householders experiencing the deprivations associated with high levels of dissatisfaction with their neighbourhoods are not only located within the social rented sector – home owners and privately renting households also live in problematic neighbourhoods. Consequently, any area regeneration targeting of the 'worst estates' will miss a significant proportion of households living in what they themselves perceive to be squalid neighbourhoods. (Joseph Rowntree Foundation, 1998: 6)

Resources for Treatment and Rehabilitation

The availability of resources is bound to be a key topic in any discussion of treatment and rehabilitation in the context of wider criminal justice and social policy. This involves both direct and indirect resources. Direct resources are those devoted to treatment and rehabilitation and related programmes. Under the Conservative governments of 1979 to 1997 'law and order' initially fared better than most other budgets. But during the 1990s cash limits and more stringent controls were increasingly applied. Clearly the resources available for the treatment and rehabilitation of offenders will always be constrained, but also of importance is how limited resources are best used: to exact punishment and retribution, to reform and rehabilitate, or to address the kind of problems that are known to be associated with crime and offending. Despite the considerable sums of money spent on criminal justice, most of the money available goes on enforcement and punishment, rather than on prevention, or treatment and rehabilitation, as an audit of criminal justice in Milton Keynes has demonstrated (Shapland et al., 1995).

However, many of the resources needed to rehabilitate offenders depend not just on the amounts devoted to the criminal justice budget and direct funding of treatment programmes, but also on other budgets such as those of health, housing, education, employment training and regeneration. These are the indirect resources needed to fund social programmes of the kind that are likely to reduce offending. The period of Conservative government saw cuts in many of the areas which have a bearing on the incidence of offending. These included,

- changes in eligibility for social security, particularly the removal in 1988 of income benefit from 16–17-year-olds;

- a reduction in the length of time for which housing benefit is available;
- reductions in unemployment benefit and support for the long term unemployed, especially the introduction in 1996 of the job seekers' allowance.

Elliott Currie has drawn attention to the way in which investment in punitive programmes of incarceration restricts investment in the kind of social opportunities that might help to contain crime (Currie, 1996). Equally, it can be argued in reverse that social investment may be one way in which to contain offending. However, it is not just a matter of the restriction or provision of resources. Available resources must be used in the most constructive manner. For many years Government and local authorities adopted policies on the basis of the concerns of individual departments – employment, housing, health, education, and so on – with relatively little linkage between them, apart from the occasional joint circular or liaison group. So, for example, employment policy and criminal justice policy were seen as separate enterprises, with little relationship between the two activities. As a result funding programmes to further policy objectives tended to be distinct from each other. It could even be difficult to get funding for research to investigate relationships between different policy areas. As one commentator noted:

> A much more comprehensive approach is needed, bringing organisations and funding together in strategic partnerships to deliver multi-faceted responses. Urban problems do not break down neatly into compartments according to the boundaries between different government departments – yet initiatives to tackle these problems have in the past been restricted because most funding has come from a single government department for a particular purpose. (Edwards, 1994)

An important change to this pattern began in 1994 with the introduction of the Single Regeneration Budget. This budget brought together programmes sponsored by the Department of the Environment, the Department of Employment (as it was then), the Home Office, the Department of Trade and Industry and the Department of Education, with the aim of tackling needs on a local rather than departmental basis and stimulating the wealth creation needed to improve local areas. This enabled crime and other social problems to be tackled in the context of urban regeneration.

Perhaps the most significant development of recent years has been the recognition that problems need to be addressed as a totality at the highest levels of Government, and in such a way that policy permeates the social system. This has become known as 'joined up' policy making, integrating the work which different Government departments, local authorities and other agencies do in relation to social issues. Whatever the label applied to it, it means that the crime problem is not something to be dealt with by criminal justice agencies alone, and treatment and rehabilitation need to be part of this 'joined up' approach. Whether or not it is effective remains to be seen.

In Conclusion

This leads to a brief consideration of the future of treatment and rehabilitation at the start of the twenty-first century. In many ways the prospects look promising. It was suggested in the Foreword that the old treatment model that dominated the middle of the twentieth century had been replaced by a new approach to treatment that emphasised rights and responsibilities, and the exercising of control over one's actions. By the end of the twentieth century the pessimistic doctrine that 'nothing works' had given way to a policy of determining 'what works', and various forms of intervention directed towards treatment and rehabilitation were back on the agenda.

Another central feature of this resurgent interest in finding interventions that are effective with offenders was that, unlike the old treatment model, it was to take place in the context of other policies to reduce offending, including those directed towards crime prevention in general, and promoting a less criminal society. Part of the problem with the old rehabilitative ideal was that it had tended to be seen as *the* answer, in isolation from other approaches to crime. The more broadly based approach was summarised in the Home Office Research Study, *Reducing Offending* (Nuttall et al., 1998), and saw interventions with individual offenders existing alongside effective policing, community crime prevention initiatives, and effective sentencing. Finally, the prospects for the successful development of effective treatment and rehabilitation were also enhanced by addressing some of the social problems associated with crime and criminality, such as poor employment and housing prospects, and by seeking to combat social exclusion.

So the prospects for interventions to treat and rehabilitate offenders appear to be good. But are they good enough? Are enough resources being devoted to interventions designed to treat and rehabilitate rather than punish and confine, and what if efforts to find 'what works' turn into 'does not work'? Could we be in for a return to an equivalent of 'nothing works'? There are those who already express concern about placing too much emphasis on the principles that are rooted in a cognitive skills approach (Hannah-Moffatt and Shaw, 2000). Furthermore, a progressive approach to dealing with individual offenders could easily be overwhelmed by an instinctive, widespread retributivism, especially if supported by politicians who feel vulnerable. Reasonable, 'evidence-based' policies on crime and justice can be thrown off course by a single incident which, although an isolated example, becomes a focus and point of reference for policy and legislation. One example is the murder of James Bulger in 1993. Reaction to this fed into concerns about the recently introduced Criminal Justice Act 1991, which was subsequently amended. Further examples include the killing of Jonathan Zito, of Megan Kanka, and of Lynn Russell and her daughter, and of Sarah Payne. All of these have understandably caused great public concern, but the reactions have sometimes made it more difficult to pursue efforts directed towards treating, rehabilitating and controlling offenders in the hope of reducing the risks for the future.

Ultimately the prospects for progress towards better treatment and rehabilitation may depend not just on rigorous scientific assessment, important as this may be, but on the will to pursue an inclusive and restorative penal policy, rather than a retributive and exclusionary one. Elsewhere I and others have reviewed different strategies for criminal justice, and have expressed a preference for a policy directed towards restorative justice,

> a philosophy that emphasise reparation, rebuilding and reintegration as holding out the best prospects for a twenty-first century criminal justice system that will not only be better capable of managing crime and offending, but will also be based on the fundamental principles of human rights. (Cavadino, Crow and Dignan, 1999: x)

Such an approach also holds out the best prospects for the development of treatment and rehabilitation.

Further Reading

Beyond Offending Behaviour (1996) by Mark Drakeford and Maurice Vanstone attempts to take the Probation Service beyond addressing the behaviour of individual offenders to looking at the social context in which offending takes place. NACRO has produced two short, but useful, papers summarising the links between housing and offending and lack of employment and offending (*Going Straight Home?* 1998, and *Going Straight to Work,* 1999). Much has been written on the topic of social exclusion in recent years, but in the present context a good starting point is the collection of essays edited by Catherine Jones Finer and Mike Nellis with the title *Crime and Social Exclusion* (1998). The Social Exclusion Unit has a site on the Internet (at http://www.cabinet-office.gov.uk/seu/index.htm) which is well worth visiting in order to keep up to date with the latest details of its work, and for gaining access to its publications.

Questions to Consider

- Would individual treatment and rehabilitation programmes still be needed if more attention was paid to the social causes of crime?
- What resources should be devoted to treating offenders compared with other approaches and priorities?
- What would the ideal programme for dealing with crime look like?

Notes

1   A useful summary of research on the links between homelessness and offending can be found in a paper by NACRO (1998), *Going Straight Home?*
2   *The Times*, 9 September 1996.
3   Kenneth Taylor, 'Big Brother in the Foyer', *Guardian* (*Society*), 14 October 1998.
4   For a consideration of such matters see Crow et. al., 1989; Field, 1990; Crow, 1996b.
5   The Social Exclusion Unit's programme has been likened to the poverty programme that was initiated in the United States during the 1960s. Marris and Rein (1974) wrote about the problems that this programme encountered, and Mark Kleinman in the *Guardian* ('New Deal, Old Barriers', 30 September 1998) has echoed reservations about such programmes.
6   Tessa Jowell, 'Head and Heart of the Matter', *Guardian*, 25 March 1998.

REFERENCES

Ackerley, E., Soothill, K. and Francis, B. (1998), 'When do sex offenders stop offending?', *Research Bulletin*, No. 39, Special Edition, 51–57, Home Office Research and Statistics Directorate. London: Home Office.

Advisory Council on the Misuse of Drugs (1984) *Prevention: Report of the Advisory Council on the Misuse of Drugs.* London: HMSO.

Advisory Council on the Misuse of Drugs (1991) *Drug Misusers and the Criminal Justice System, Part 1: Community Resources and the Probation Service.* London: HMSO.

Advisory Council on the Misuse of Drugs (1996) *Drug Misusers and the Prison System.* London: HMSO.

Advisory Council on the Penal System (1970) *Non-Custodial and Semi-Custodial Penalties: Report of the Advisory Council on the Penal System.* London: HMSO.

Advisory Council on the Treatment of Offenders (1963) *The organisation of after-care.* London: HMSO.

Allen, H. (1987) *Justice Unbalanced: Gender, Psychiatry and Judicial Decisions*, Milton Keynes: Open University Press.

All Party Parliamentary Drugs Misuse Group (1998) *Prisons and Drug Misuse.* London: Houses of Parliament.

American Friends Service Committee (1971) *Struggle for Justice: A Report on Crime and Punishment in America.* New York: Hill & Wang

Andrews, D.A., Zinger, I., Hodge, R.D., Bonta, J., Gendreau, P. and Cullen, F.T. (1990), 'Does Correctional Treatment Work? A Clinically Relevant and Psychologically Informed Meta-Analysis', *Criminology*, **28**, 3, 369–388.

Apex Trust (1991) *The Hidden Workforce.* London: Apex Trust.

Ashworth, A. (1994) *The Criminal Process: An Evaluative Study.* Oxford: Clarendon Press.

Auld, J., Dorn, N. and South, N. (1986) 'Irregular Work; Irregular Pleasures: Heroin in the 1980s', in Matthews, R. and Young J. (eds), *Confronting Crime.* London: Sage.

Balding, J. (1998) *Young People and Illegal Drugs in 1998.* Exeter: Schools Health Education Unit.

Balding, J. (2000) *Young People and Illegal Drugs into 2000.* Exeter: Schools Health Education Unit.

Barclay, G.C. (1995) *Digest 3: Information on the Criminal Justice System in England and Wales.* Home Office Research and Statistics Department. London: Home Office.

Bean, P. (1995) 'Drug Courts USA', *Druglink*, **10**, 3, 13–14.

Bean, P. (1997) 'New Ideas in the Field', *Druglink*, **12**, 2, 12–13.

Beccaria, C. (1963) *On Crimes and Punishments.* Indianapolis: Bobbs-Merrill.

Becker, H.S. (1963) *Outsiders: Studies in the Sociology of Deviance.* Toronto: The Free Press of Glencoe.

Beckett, R., Beech, A., Fisher, D. and Fordham, A. (1994) *Community-Based Treatment for Sex Offenders: An Evaluation of Seven Treatment Programmes.* London: Home Office.

Beech, A., Fisher, D., Beckett, R. and Fordham, A. (1996) 'Treating Sex Offenders in the Community', *Research Bulletin*, No. 38, 21–25. London: Home Office.

Beech, A., Fisher, D. and Beckett, R. (1998a) *STEP 3: An Evaluation of the Prison Sex Offender Treatment Programme, A Report for the Home Office.* London: Home Office.

Beech, A., Fisher, D., Beckett, R. and Scott-Fordham, A. (1998b) *An Evaluation of the Prison Sex Offender Treatment Programme*, Research Findings No. 79, Home Office Research, Development and Statistics Directorate. London: Home Office.

Belfrage, H. (1998) 'A Ten-Year Follow-Up of Criminality in Stockholm Mental Patients: New Evidence for a Relation between Mental Disorder and Crime', *British Journal of Criminology*, **38**, 1, 145–155.

Bell, T. (1998) 'Housing Exclusion', *Safer Society*, **1**, 21–22. London: NACRO.

Belson, W.A. (1968) 'The extent of stealing by London boys and some of its origins', *The Advancement of Science*, **25**, 124, 1–15.

Bennett, T. (1991) 'The Effectiveness of a Police-Initiated Fear-Reducing Strategy', *British Journal of Criminology*, **31**, 1, 1–14.

Bennett, T. (1996) 'What's New in Evaluation Research? A Note on the Pawson and Tilley Article, *British Journal of Criminology*, **36**, 4, 567–573.

Bennett, T. (1998) *Drugs and Crime: The Results of Research on Drug Testing and Interviewing Arrestees*, Research Study No. 183, Home Office Research and Statistics Directorate. London: Home Office.

Birmingham, L., Mason, D. and Grubin, D. (1996) 'Prevalence of Mental Disorder in Remand Prisoners', *British Medical Journal*, **313**, 7071, 1521–1524.

Blumenthal, S. and Wessely, S. (1992) 'National Survey of Current Arrangements for Diversion from Custody in England and Wales', *British Medical Journal*, **305**, 6865, 1322–1325.

Boddis, S. and Mann, R. (1995) 'Groupwork in Prisons', in *'A Good and Useful Life' – Constructive Prison Regimes*. London: Prison Reform Trust.

Bottoms, A.E. (1977) 'Reflections on the Renaissance of Dangerousness', *Howard Journal of Criminal Justice*, **16**, 70–96.

Bottoms, A.E. (1995) *Intensive Community Supervision for Young Offenders: Outcomes, Process and Cost* (with Knapp, A. and Fenyo, A.). Cambridge: Institute of Criminology.

Bottoms, A.E. and McWilliams, W. (1979) 'A Non-Treatment Paradigm for Probation Practice', *British Journal of Social Work*, **9**, 2, 159–202.

Brain, K., Parker, H. and Bottomley, T. (1998) *Evolving Crack Cocaine Careers*, Research Findings No. 85. London: Home Office.

Braithwaite, J. (1989) *Crime, Shame and Reintegration*. Cambridge: Cambridge University Press.

Bridges, A. (1998) *Increasing the Employability of Offenders: An Inquiry into Probation Service Effectiveness*, Probation Studies Unit Report No. 5. Reading: Berkshire Probation Service.

Briggs, D. (1998) *Assessing Men Who Sexually Abuse: a practice guide*. London: Jessica Kingsley.

British Journal of Delinquency (1950) 'Editorial Announcement', *British Journal of Delinquency*, **1**, 1, 1–5.

Briton, C. (1995) 'Mind Your Own Business', *Druglink*, **10**, 1, 16–17.

Broadhead, J. (1998), 'Why do Probation Officers Always Recommend Probation?', *New Law Journal*, **148**, 684–7, 992–993.

Brody, S.R. (1976) *The Effectiveness of Sentencing*, Home Office Research Study No. 35. London: HMSO.

Brooke, D., Taylor, C., Gunn, J and Maden, A. (1996) 'Point Prevalence of Mental Disorder in Unconvicted Male Prisoners in England and Wales', *British Medical Journal*, **313**, 7071, 1524–1527.

Browne, D., Francis, E. and Crow, I. (1993) 'Black People, Mental Health and the Criminal Justice System', in Watson, W. and Grounds, A. (eds), *The Mentally Disordered Offender in an Era of Community Care*. Cambridge: Cambridge University Press.

Brownlee, I.D. (1998) *Community Punishment: a critical introduction*. London: Longman.

Bryant, M., Coker, J., Estlea, B., Himmel, S. and Knapp, T. (1978) 'Sentenced to Social Work', *Probation Journal*, **25**, 4, 110–114.

Buickhuisen, W. and Hoekstra, H.A. (1974) 'Factors Related to Recidivism', *British Journal of Criminology*, **14**, 1, 63–69.

Burnett, R. (1996) *Fitting Supervision to Offenders: Assessment and Allocation Decisions in the Probation Service*, Home Office Research Study No. 153. London: Home Office.

Burney, E. and Pearson, G. (1995) 'Mentally Disordered Offenders: Finding a Focus for Diversion', *The Howard Journal*, **34**, 4, 291–313.

Burrows, J., Clarke, A., Davison, T., Tarling, R. and Webb, S. (2000) *The Nature and Effectiveness of Drugs Throughcare for Released Prisoners*, Research Findings No. 109. Home Office Research, Development and Statistics Directorate. London: Home Office.

Burt, C. (1925) *The Young Delinquent*. London: University of London Press.

Burton, D. (ed.) (2000) *Research Training for Social Scientists: a Handbook for Postgraduate Researchers*. London: Sage.

Butler Committee (1975) *Report of the Committee on Mentally Abnormal Offenders*, Home Office and Department of Health and Social Security, Cmnd 6244. London: HMSO.

Cavadino, M. (1998) 'Death to the Psychopath', *Journal of Forensic Psychiatry*, **9**, 1, 5–8.

Cavadino, M. and Dignan, J. (1997) *The Penal System: An Introduction*, 2nd Edition. London: Sage.

Cavadino, M., Crow, I. and Dignan, J. (1999) *Criminal Justice 2000: Strategies for a New Century*. Winchester: Waterside Press.

Central Drugs Coordination Unit (1995) *Tackling Drugs Together*, Cm 2846. London: HMSO.

Central Drugs Coordination Unit (1998) *Tackling Drugs to Build a Better Britain: The Government's 10-year Strategy for Tackling Drug Misuse*, Cm 3945. London: The Stationery Office.

Chartered Institute of Housing (1998) *Rehousing Sex Offenders – a summary of the legal and operational issues.* Coventry: Chartered Institute of Housing.

Cloward, R.A. and Ohlin, L.E. (1960) *Delinquency and Opportunity: A Theory of Delinquent Gangs.* New York: The Free Press.

Coker, J. (1984) 'Sentenced to Social Work?: The Revival of Choice', *Probation Journal*, **31**, 4, 123–125.

Collison, M. (1993) 'Punishing Drugs: Criminal Justice and Drug Use', *British Journal of Criminology*, **33**, 3, 382–399.

Connell, J.P. and Kubisch, A.C. (1997) *Applying a Theory of Change Approach to the Evaluation of Comprehensive Community Initiatives*, Aspen, CO: Aspen Institute Roundtable on Comprehensive Community Initiatives for Children and Families.

Cook, T.D. and Campbell, D.T. (1979) *Quasi-Experimentation.* Chicago: Rand-McNally.

Corkery, J.M. (1997) *Statistics of Drug Addicts Notified to the Home Office, United Kingdom, 1996*, Home Office Statistical Bulletin Issue 22/97. London: Home Office Research and Statistics Directorate.

Corkery, J.M. (1998) *Statistics of Drug Seizures and Offenders Dealt With, United Kingdom, 1996*, Home Office Statistical Bulletin, Issue 10/98. London: Home Office Research and Statistics Directorate.

Corkery, J.M. (2000) *Drug Seizures and Offender Statistics, United Kingdom, 1998*, Home Office Statistical Bulletin Issue 3/00, Research, Development and Statistics Directorate. London: Home Office .

Cowan, D. Gilroy, R., Pantazis, C. and Bevan, M. (1999) *Housing Sex Offenders: an Examination of Current Practice.* London: Chartered Institute of Housing / Joseph Rowntree Foundation.

Cowles, E.L., Castellano, T.C. and Gransky, L.A. (1995) *'Boot Camp' Drug Treatment and Aftercare Interventions: an Evaluation Review.* National Institute of Justice Research Brief, at http://www.ncjrs.org/txtfiles/btcamp.txt

Coyle, A. (1992) 'The Responsible Prisoner: Rehabilitation Revisited', *The Howard Journal*, **31**, 1, 1–7.

Crime and Social Policy Committee (1995) *Crime and Social Policy.* London: NACRO.

Criminal Justice Consultative Council (1997) 'Mentally Disordered Offenders in Custody', *CJCC Newsletter*, 7. London: Criminal Justice Consultative Council.

Crow, I. (1991) *Community-Based Drug Misuse Prevention: Report on the Work of NACRO's Drug Misuse Prevention Unit, 1988–1990.* University of Sheffield: Centre for Criminological and Legal Research.

Crow, I. (1996a) *Approaches to Youth Crime: a Study of the Views of Magistrates, Justices' Clerks and Social Workers.* University of Sheffield: Centre for Criminological and Legal Research.

Crow, I. (1996b) 'Employment, Training and Offending', in Drakeford, M. and Vanstone, M. (eds.) *Beyond Offending Behaviour.* Aldershot: Arena.

Crow, I. (1998) *The Sheffield Victim-Offender Mediation Project: Interim Research Report.* Sheffield: Centre for Criminological and Legal Research.

Crow, I. (ed.) (1982) *The Handsworth Alternatives Scheme: a Report on the Pilot Period.* London: NACRO.

Crow, I. and Simon, F. (1987) *Unemployment and Magistrates' Courts.* London: NACRO.

Crow, I., Richardson, P., Riddington, C. and Simon, F. (1989) *Unemployment, Crime and Offenders.* London: Routledge.

Crow, I., Cavadino, M., Dignan, J., Johnston, V. and Walker, M. (1996) *Changing Criminal Justice: The Impact of the Criminal Justice Act 1991 in Four Areas of the North of England.* University of Sheffield: Centre for Criminological and Legal Research.

Cullen, J.E. (1981) *The Prediction and Treatment of Self-Injury by Female Young Offenders*, Directorate of Psychological Services Report, Series 1, No. 17. London: Prison Service.

Cullen, E. (1994) 'Grendon: The Therapeutic Prison That Works', *Journal of Therapeutic Communities*, **15**, 4, 301–310.

Cullen, E. (1998) *Grendon and Future Therapeutic Communities in Prison.* London: Prison Reform Trust.

Cullen, F.T. and Applegate, B.K. (eds) (1997) *Offender Rehabilitation.* Dartmouth: Ashgate.

Currie, E. (1996) *Is America Really Winning the War on Crime and Should Britain Follow Its Example?* NACRO 30th Anniversary Lecture. London: NACRO.

Davies, M. (1969) *Probationers in Their Social Environment: A Study of Male Probationers aged 17–20*, Home Office Research Study No.2. London: Home Office.

Department of Health / Home Office (1992), *Review of Health and Social Services for Mentally Disordered Offenders and Others Requiring Similar Services*, Cm 2088. London: HMSO.

Department of Health (1996) *The Task Force to Review Services for Drug Misusers: Report of an Independent Review of Drug Treatment Services in England.* London: Department of Health.

Department of Health (1998a) *NTORS at One Year: the National Treatment Outcome Research Study*, London: Department of Health.

Department of Health (1998b) *Modernising Mental Health Services: Safe, Sound and Supportive*. London: Department of Health.

Department of Health (1999a) *Reform of the Mental Health Act 1983: Proposals for Consultation*. London: Department of Health.

Department of Health (1999b) *The Future Organisation of Prison Health Care*. London: Department of Health.

Department of Health/Home Office (1999) *Managing Dangerous People with Severe Personality Disorder: Proposals for Policy Development*. London: Department of Health/Home Office.

Ditchfield, J. and Marshall, P. (1990) 'A Review of Recent Literature Evaluating Treatments for Sex Offenders in Prison', *Prison Service Journal*, **81**, 24–28.

Doctor, R.M. and Polakow, R.L. (1973) 'A Behavior Modification Program for Adult Probationers'. Paper presented at the Annual Meeting of the American Psychological Association.

Dorn, N. and South, N. (1987) *A Land Fit for Heroin*. London: Macmillan.

Dorn, N. and Lee, M. (1995) 'Mapping Probation Practice with Drug Using Offenders', *The Howard Journal*, **34**, 4, 314–325.

Drakeford, M. and Vanstone, M. (eds) (1996) *Beyond Offending Behaviour*. Aldershot: Arena.

Duff, P. (1997) 'Diversion from Prosecution into Psychiatric Care: Who Controls the Gates?', *British Journal of Criminology*, **37**, 1, 15–34.

Edgar, K. and O'Donnell, I. (1998), *Mandatory Drug Testing in Prisons: The Relationship between MDT and the Level and Nature of Drug Misuse*, Research Study No. 89, Home Office Research and Statistics Directorate. London: Home Office.

Edmunds, M., May, T., Hearnden, I. and Hough, M. (1998) *Arrest Referral: Emerging Lessons from Research*, Drugs Prevention Initiative Paper 23. London: Home Office.

Edmunds, M., Hough, M., Turnbull, P.J. and May, T. (1999) *Doing Justice to Treatment: Referring Offenders to Drug Services*, Drugs Prevention Advisory Service, Paper 2. London: Home Office.

Edwards, H. (1994) 'New Opportunities for Tackling Crime', *NACRO News*, 13. London: NACRO.

Epps, K. (1996) 'Sex Offenders', in Hollin, C.R. (ed.), *Working with Offenders*. Chichester: John Wiley & Sons.

Everitt, A. and Hardiker, P. (1996) *Evaluating for Good Practice*. Basingstoke and London: Macmillan.

Eysenck, H.J. (1978) 'An Exercise in Mega-Silliness', *American Psychologist*, **33**, 517.

Farrall, S., Bannister, J., Ditton, J. and Gilchrist, E. (1997) 'Questioning the Measurement of the "Fear of Crime": Findings from a Major Methodological Study', *British Journal of Criminology*, **37**, 4, 658–679.

Farrington, D.P. (1992) 'Trends in English Juvenile Delinquency and Their Explanation', *International Journal of Comparative and Applied Criminal Justice*, **16**, 2, 151–163.

Farrington, D.P. (1996) *Understanding and Preventing Youth Crime*. York: York Publishing Services.

Farrington, D.P. (1997) 'Evaluating a Community Crime Prevention Program', *Evaluation*, **3**, 2, 157–173.

Farrington, D.P. (1998) 'Evaluating "Communities That Care": Realistic Scientific Considerations', *Evaluation*, **4**, 2, 204–210.

Farrington, D.P. and Morris, A. M.(1983) 'Sex, Sentencing and Reconviction', *British Journal of Criminology*, **23**, 3, 229–248.

Fattah, E.A. (1997) *Criminology: Past, Present and Future, A Critical Overview*. London: Macmillan.

Fazey, C. (1988) *Heroin Addiction, Crime and the Effect of Medical Treatment*, Report to the Home Office. London: Home Office.

Feaver, N. and Smith, D. (1994) 'Editorial Introduction', *British Journal of Social Work*, **24**, 4, 379–386.

Field, S. (1990) *Trends in Crime and Their Interpretation: A Study of Recorded Crime in Post-War England and Wales*, Home Office Research Study No. 119. London: HMSO.

Finer, C.J. and Nellis, M. (eds) (1998) *Crime and Social Exclusion*. Oxford: Blackwell.

Finkelhor, D. (1984) *Child Sexual Abuse*. New York: Free Press.

Fisher, D. and Mair, G. (1998) *A Review of Classification Systems for Sex Offenders*, Research Findings No. 78, Home Office Research and Statistics Directorate. London: Home Office.

Fisk, K. (1998) 'Arkwright: Cotton King or Spin Doctor', *History Today*, **48**, 3, 25–30.

Fitzpatrick, S. and Klinker, S. (2000) *Research on Single Homelessness in Britain*. York: Joseph Rowntree Foundation.

Fletcher, D.R., Woodhill, D. and Herrington, A. (1998) *Building Bridges into Employment and Training for Ex-Offenders*. York: York Publishing Services.

Folkard, M.S., Smith, D.E. and Smith, D.D. (1976) *Intensive Matched Probation and After-Care Treatment, Vol. II*, Home Office Research Study No. 36. London: HMSO.

Fortson, R. (1992) *The Law on the Misuse of Drugs*. London: Sweet & Maxwell.

Foucault, M. (1977), *Discipline and Punish: The Birth of the Prison*. London: Penguin.

Fowles, A. J. (1993) 'The Mentally Abnormal Offender in the Era of Community Care', in Watson, W. and Grounds, A. (eds.), *The Mentally Disordered Offender in an Era of Community Care*. Cambridge: Cambridge University Press.

Furby, L., Weinrott, M.R. and Blackshaw, L. (1989) 'Sex Offender Recidivism: A Review', *Psychological Bulletin*, **105**, 1, 3–30.

Garland, D. (1985) *Punishment and Welfare*. Aldershot: Gower.

Garland, D. (1988) 'British Criminology before 1935', *British Journal of Criminology*, **28**, 2, 1–17.

Garland, D. (1996) 'The Limits of the Sovereign State: Strategies of Crime Control in Contemporary Society', *British Journal of Criminology*, **36**, 4, 445–471.

Garland, D. (1997) 'Of Crimes and Criminals: The Development of Criminology in Britain', in Maguire, M., Morgan, R. and Reiner, R. (eds), *The Oxford Handbook of Criminology, Second Edition*. Oxford: Clarendon Press.

Garrett, C.J. (1985) 'Effects of Residential Treatment on Adjudicated Delinquents: A Meta-Analysis', *Journal of Research in Crime and Delinquency*, **22**, 4, 287–308.

Genders, E. and Player, E. (1995) *Grendon: A Study of a Therapeutic Community*. Oxford: Clarendon Press.

Gendreau, P. and Ross, R.R. (1979) 'Effective Correctional Treatment: Bibliotherapy for Cynics', *Crime and Delinquency*, **25**, 463–489.

Gill, M. (1997) 'Employing Ex-Offenders: A Risk or an Opportunity?', *The Howard Journal*, **36**, 4, 337–351.

Glass, G.V., McGaw, B. and Smith, M.L. (1981) *Meta-Analysis in Social Research*. London: Sage.

Glover, E. (1955) 'Prognosis or Prediction: a Psychiatric Examination of the Concept of "Recidivism"', *British Journal of Delinquency*, **6**, 2, 116–125.

Goldberg, D., Benjamin, S. and Creed, F. (1987) *Psychiatry in Medical Practice*. London: Routledge.

Gore, S. M., Bird, A. G. and Ross, A. J. (1996) 'Prison Rights: Mandatory Drug Tests and Performance Indicators', *British Medical Journal*, **312**, 7043, 1411–1413.

Goring, C. (1913) *The English Convict: A Statistical Study*. London: HMSO.

Graham, J. and Bowling, B. (1995) *Young People and Crime*, Home Office Research Study No. 145, Home Office Research and Statistics Department. London: Home Office.

Grounds, A. (1991) 'The Mentally Disordered Offender in the Criminal Process: Some Research and Policy Questions', in Herbst, K. and Gunn, J. (eds), *The Mentally Disordered Offender*. London: Butterworth-Heinemann, in association with the Mental Health Foundation.

Grubin, D. (1998) *Sex Offending against Children: Understanding the Risk*, Police Research Series Paper 99, Research, Development and Statistics Directorate. London: Home Office.

Grubin, D. and Thornton, D. (1994) 'A National Programme for the Assessment and Treatment of Sex Offenders in the English Prison System', *Criminal Justice and Behaviour*, **21**, 1, 55–71.

Gudjonsson, G.H., Clare, I., Rutter, S. and Pearse, J. (1993) *Persons at Risk During Interviews in Police Custody: The Identification of Vulnerabilities*, Research Study No. 12, Royal Commission on Criminal Justice. London: HMSO.

Gunn, J. and Robertson, G. (1987) 'A Ten Year Follow-Up of Men Discharged from Grendon Prison', *British Journal of Psychiatry*, **151**, 674–678.

Gunn, J., Maden, A. and Swinton, M. (1991) *Mentally Disordered Prisoners*. London: Home Office.

Hamlyn, B. (2000) *Women Prisoners: A Survey of their Work and Training Experiences in Custody and on Release*, Research Findings No. 122, Home Office Research, Development and Statistics Directorate. London: Home Office.

Hannah-Moffatt, K. and Shaw, M. (2000) 'Thinking about Cognitive Skills? Think Again!' *Criminal Justice Matters*, 39, 8–9.

Harris, R. (1992) *Crime, Criminal Justice and the Probation Service*. London: Routledge.

Hearnden, I. and Harocopos, A. (2000) *Problem Drug Use and Probation in London*, Research Findings No. 112, Home Office Research, Development and Statistics Directorate. London: Home Office.

Hebenton, B. and Thomas, T. (1996) '"Tracking" Sex Offenders', *The Howard Journal*, **35**, 2, 97–112.

Hebenton, B. and Thomas, T. (1997) *Keeping Track? Observations on Sex Offender Registers in the US*, Police Research Group, Crime Detection and Prevention Series, Paper 83. London: Home Office.

Hedderman, C. (1991) 'Custody Decisions for Property Offenders in the Crown Court', *The Howard Journal*, **30**, 3, 207–217.

Hedderman, C. (1993) *Panel Assessment Schemes for Mentally Disordered Offenders*, Research and Planning Unit Paper 76. London: Home Office.

Hedderman, C. (1998) 'A Critical Assessment of Probation Research', *Research Bulletin* No. 39, 1–8, Home Office Research and Statistics Directorate. London: Home Office.

Hedderman, C. and Gelsthorpe, L. (1997) *Understanding the Sentencing of Women*, Home Office Research Study No. 170. London: Home Office.

Hedderman, C. and Hough, M. (1994) *Does the Criminal Justice System Treat Men and Women Differently?* Research Findings No. 10, Home Office Research and Statistics Department. London: Home Office.

Hedderman, C. and Sugg, D. (1996) *Does Treating Sex Offenders Reduce Reoffending?* Research Findings No. 45, Home Office Research and Statistics Directorate. London: Home Office.

Hedderman, C. and Sugg, D. (1997) 'The Influence of Cognitive Approaches: A Survey of Probation Programmes', in *Changing Offenders' Attitudes and Behaviour: What Works?*, Part II, Home Office Research Study No. 171. London: Home Office.

Hedderman, C., Ellis, T. and Sugg, D. (1999) *Increasing Confidence in Community Sentences: The Results of Two Demonstration Projects*, Home Office Research Study No. 194, Research, Development and Statistics Directorate. London: Home Office.

Heidensohn, F. (1989) *Crime and Society*. Basingstoke: Macmillan.

Heidensohn, F. (1996) *Women and Crime, Second Edition*. Basingstoke and London: Macmillan.

Hellawell, K. (1999) *United Kingdom Anti-Drugs Co-ordinator's First Annual Report and National Plan*. London: Cabinet Office.

Hewitt, A. (1996) 'Drug Testing in Prisons', *Druglink*, **11**, 3, 16–18.

Heyes, J. and King, G. (1996) 'Care and Control', *Druglink*, **11**, 5, 8–10.

HM Chief Inspector of Prisons (1994) *Report of Her Majesty's Chief Inspector of Prisons, 1993–1994*, House of Commons Paper 688. London: HMSO.

HM Chief Inspector of Prisons (1997) *Report of an Inspection of HMP Grendon and Springhill*. London: Home Office.

HM Chief Inspector of Prisons (1998) *Report of Her Majesty's Chief Inspector of Prisons, 1996–97*. London: HMSO.

HM Inspectorate of Probation (1991) *The Work of the Probation Service With Sex Offenders*, Report of thematic inspection. London: Home Office.

HM Inspectorate of Probation (1993a) *The Criminal Justice Act 1991 Inspection*. London: Home Office.

HM Inspectorate of Probation (1993b) *Offenders Who Misuse Drugs: the Probation Service Response*. London: Home Office.

HM Inspectorate of Probation (1995) *Annual Report*. London: Home Office.

HM Inspectorate of Probation (1998) *Exercising Constant Vigilance: The Role of the Probation Service in Protecting the Public from Sex Offenders: Report of a Thematic Inspection*. London: Home Office.

HM Prison Service (1991) *Treatment Programmes for Sex Offenders in Custody: a Strategy*. London: HM Prison Service.

HM Prison Service (1993) *National Framework for the Throughcare of Offenders in Custody to the Completion of Supervision in the Community*. London: HM Prison Service.

HM Prison Service (1995) *Drug misuse in prison*. London: HM Prison Service.

HM Prison Service (1997) *Audit of Prison Service Resources*. London: HM Prison Service.

HM Prison Service (1998a) *The Review of the Prison Service Drug Strategy: 'Drug Misuse in Prison'*. London: HM Prison Service.

HM Prison Service (1998b) *Tackling Drugs in Prison: The Prison Service Drug Strategy*. London: HM Prison Service.

HM Prison Service (1998c) *HM Prison Service Business Plan 1998–1999*. London: HM Prison Service.

HM Prison Service (1999) *Corporate Plan 1999–2000 to 2001–2002*. London: HM Prison Service.

HMSO (1998) *Tackling Drugs to Build a Better Britain: The Government's 10-Year Strategy for Tackling Drug Misuse*, Cm 3945. London: HMSO.

Hobson, J. and Shine, J. (1998) 'The Measurement of Psychopathy in a UK Prison Population Referred for Long-Term Psychotherapy', *British Journal of Criminology*, **38**, 3, 504–515.

Hollin, C.R. (1991) 'Rehabilitation with Offenders – Still Not Working', Proceedings of the *What Works* Conference. Greater Manchester and Hereford and Worcester Probation Services, 18–19, April 1991.

Hollin, C.R. (1996a) 'Young Offenders', in Hollin, C. R. (ed.), *Working with Offenders: Psychological Practice in Offender Rehabilitation*. Chichester: John Wiley & Sons.

Hollin, C.R. (1996b) *Psychology and Crime: An Introduction to Criminological Psychology*. London: Routledge.

Hollin, C.R. and Howells, K. (1996) *Clinical Approaches to Working with Young Offenders*. Chichester: John Wiley and Sons.

Home Office (1959) *Penal Practice in a Changing Society: Aspects of Future Development*, Cmnd 645. London: HMSO.

Home Office (1964) 'Children and Young Persons Act 1963: Parts I and II', *Home Office Circular 22/64*. London: Home Office.

Home Office (1965) *The Child, the Family and the Young Offender*, Cm 2742. London: HMSO.

Home Office (1971) *The Sentence of the Court: A Handbook for Courts on the Treatment of Offenders*. London: HMSO.

Home Office (1988) *Punishment, Custody and the Community*, Cm 424. London: HMSO.

Home Office (1990a) *Supervision & Punishment in the Community: A Framework for Action*, Cm 966. London: HMSO.

Home Office (1990b) *Partnership in Dealing with Offenders in the Community*. London: Home Office.

Home Office (1990c) *Circular 66/90: Provisions for Mentally Disordered Offenders*. London: Home Office.

Home Office (1991) *A General Guide to the Criminal Justice Act 1991*, London: Home Office.

Home Office (undated, probably 1991) *Organising Supervision and Punishment in the Community: A Decision Document*. London: Home Office.

Home Office (1995a) *National Standards for the Supervision of Offenders in the Community*. London: Home Office.

Home Office (1995b) *Strengthening Punishment in the Community: A Consultation Document*, Cm 2780. London: HMSO.

Home Office (1995c) *Circular 12/95: Mentally Disordered Offenders: Inter-Agency Working*, London:

Home Office (1995d) *The Supervision of Restricted Patients in the Community*, Research and Statistics Department, Research Findings No. 19. London: Home Office.

Home Office (1995e) *National Standards for the Supervision of Offenders in the Community*. London: Home Office.

Home Office (1996a) *Protecting the Public: The Government's Strategy on Crime in England and Wales*, Cm 3190. London: HMSO.

Home Office (1996b) *Projections of Long Term Trends in the Prison Population to 2004*, Home Office Statistical Bulletin 4/96. London: Home Office.

Home Office (1996c) *The Probation Service*. London: Home Office.

Home Office (1997a) *Challenging the Myth of Escalating Drug Misuse*, Home Office Press Release, 231/97. London: Home Office.

Home Office (1997b) *Persistent Drug Misusing Offenders*, Research and Statistics Directorate, Research Findings No. 50. London: Home Office.

Home Office (1997c) *Summary Probation Statistics, England and Wales, 1996*, Home Office Statistical Bulletin, Issue 13/97, Research and Statistics Directorate. London: Home Office.

Home Office (1998a) *Criminal Statistics, England and Wales, 1997*, Cm 4162. London: HMSO.

Home Office (1998b) *Summary Probation Statistics, England and Wales, 1997*, Issue 12/98, Home Office Research and Statistics Directorate. London: Home Office.

Home Office (1998c) *Prisons – Probation Review, Final Report*. London: Home Office.

Home Office (1998d) *Exercising Constant Vigilance: The Role of the Probation Service in Protecting the Public from Sex Offenders*, Report of HM Inspectorate of Probation. London: Home Office.

Home Office (1998e) *Joining Forces to Protect the Public: a consultation paper*, London: Home Office.

Home Office (1999) *Statistics on Women and the Criminal Justice System: A Home Office Publication under Section 95 of the Criminal Justice Act 1991*. London: Home Office.

Horkheimer, M. and Adorno, T. W. (1973) *Dialectic of Enlightenment*. London: Allen Lane.

Hough, M. (1996) *Drug Misuse and the Criminal Justice System: a Review of the Literature*, Drug Prevention Initiative, Paper 15. London: Home Office.

House of Commons (2000) *Provision of NHS Mental Health Services*, Health Select Committee – Fourth Report. London: House of Commons.

Howells, K. and Hollin, C.R. (eds) (1989) *Clinical Approaches to Violence*, Chichester: John Wiley and Sons.

Hullin, R. (1978) 'The Effect of Two Randomly Allocated Court Procedures on Truancy', *British Journal of Criminology*, **18**, 3, 232–244.

Hullin, R. (1985) 'The Leeds Truancy Project', *Justice of the Peace*, **149**, 31, 488-491.

Ignatieff, M. (1978) *A Just Measure of Pain: The Penitentiary in the Industrial Revolution, 1750–1850*. London: Macmillan.

Inner London Probation Service (1991) *Demonstration Unit: Drug and Alcohol Survey*. London: ILPS.

Institute for the Study and Treatment of Delinquency (1994) 'Serious Young Offenders: Treatment, Security and Future Prospects', Conference Report, *Criminal Justice Matters*, No. 18. London: Institute for the Study and Treatment of Delinquency.

Institute for the Study and Treatment of Delinquency (1995) 'Does Punishment Work?', Conference Report, *Criminal Justice Matters*, No. 22. London: Institute for the Study and Treatment of Delinquency.

Institute for the Study and Treatment of Delinquency (1996) 'What Works with Young Prisoners?', Conference Report, *Criminal Justice Matters*, No. 23. London: Institute for the Study and Treatment of Delinquency.

Institute for the Study of Drug Dependence (1995) *The Misuse of Drugs Act Explained*. London: ISDD.

Izzo, R.L. and Ross, R.R. (1990) 'Meta-Analysis of Rehabilitation Programs for Juvenile Delinquents', *Criminal Justice and Behaviour*, **17**, 1, 134–142.

James, D.V. and Hamilton, L.W. (1991) 'The Clerkenwell Scheme: Assessing Efficacy and Cost of a Psychiatric Liaison Service to a Magistrates' Court', *British Medical Journal*, **303**, 282–285.

Jarvis, G. and Parker, H. (1990) 'Can Medical Treatment Reduce Crime amongst Young Heroin Users?', *Home Office Research Bulletin*, 28, 29–32.

Johns, A. (1995) 'Is There Really a London Connection?', *Druglink*, **10**, 5, 14.

Johnson, S. and Taylor, R. (2000a) *Statistics of Mentally Disordered Offenders in England and Wales 1998*, Home Office Statistical Bulletin, Issue 7/00. London: Home Office.

Johnson, S. and Taylor, R. (2000b) *Statistics of Mentally Disordered Offenders in England and Wales, 1999*, Home Office Statistical Bulletin in, 21/00. London: Home Office.

Johnstone, G. (1996) *Medical Concepts and Penal Policy*. London: Cavendish Publishing.

Jones, R. (1988) *Mental Health Act Manual, Second Edition*. London: Sweet & Maxwell.

Joseph, P.L.A. and Potter, M. (1993) 'Diversion from Custody I: Psychiatric Assessment at the Magistrates' Court', *British Journal of Psychiatry*, **162**, 325–330.

Joseph Rowntree Foundation (1996) *The Housing Needs of Ex-Prisoners*, Findings: Housing Research No. 178. York: Joseph Rowntree Foundation.

Joseph Rowntree Foundation (1998) *Patterns of Neighbourhood Dissatisfaction in England*, Findings. York: Joseph Rowntree Foundation.

Kempson, E. and Whyley, C. (1999) *Kept Out or Opted Out? Understanding and Combating Financial Exclusion*. York: Joseph Rowntree Foundation and Policy Press.

Kemshall, H. (1996) Review of 'What Works: Reducing Reoffending. Guidelines from Research and Practice', *British Journal of Criminology*, **36**, 4, 594–595.

Kent, G. (2000) 'Ethical Principles', in Burton, D. (ed.), *Research Training for Social Scientists: A Handbook for Postgraduate Researchers*. London: Sage.

Kershaw, C. (1997) *Reconvictions of Those Commencing Community Penalties in 1993, England and Wales*, Home Office Statistical Bulletin 6/97. London: Government Statistical Service.

Kershaw, C. (1998) 'Interpreting Reconviction Rates', *The Use and Impact of Community Supervision*, Research Bulletin No. 39, special edition, 9–16, Home Office Research and Statistics Directorate. London: Home Office.

Kershaw, C. and Renshaw, G. (1997) *Reconvictions of Prisoners Discharged from Prison in 1993, England and Wales*, Home Office Statistical Bulletin 5/97. London: Government Statistical Service.

Kershaw, C. and Renshaw, G. (1998) *Statistics of Mentally Disordered Offenders in England and Wales 1997*, Home Office Statistical Bulletin 19/98. London: Home Office.

Kershaw, C., Dowdeswell, P. and Goodman, J. (1997) *Restricted Patients – Reconvictions and Recalls by the End of 1995: England and Wales*. Home Office Statistical Bulletin 1/97. London Home Office.

Kershaw, C., Goodman, J. and White, S. (1999a) *Reconvictions of Offenders Sentenced or Discharged from Prison in 1995, England and Wales*, Home Office Statistical Bulletin 19/99. London: Home Office.

Kershaw, C., Goodman, J. and White, S. (1999b) *Reconviction of Offenders Sentenced or Released from Prison in 1995*, Research Findings No. 101, Home Office Research, Development and Statistics Directorate. London: Home Office.

King, J.F.S. (1964) *The Probation Service, 2nd Edition*. London: Butterworths.

King, R. and Morgan, R. (1980) *The Future of the Prison System*. Aldershot: Gower.

Knight, B. J., Osborn, S. G. and West, D. J. (1977) 'Early Marriage and Criminal Tendency in Males', *British Journal of Criminology*, **17**, 4, 348–360.

Knott, C. (1995) 'The STOP Programme: Reasoning and Rehabilitation in a British Setting', in McGuire, J. (ed.), *What Works: Reducing Reoffending – Guidelines from Research and Practice*. Chichester: John Wiley & Sons. Chapter 5.

Kuhn, T. S. (1970) *The Structure of Scientific Revolutions*. Chicago and London: University of Chicago Press.

Laing, J.M. (1999a) 'Diversion of Mentally Disordered Offenders: Victim and Offender Perspectives', *Criminal Law Review*, 805–819.

Laing, J.M. (1999b) *Care or Custody? Mentally Disordered Offenders in the Criminal Justice System*. Oxford: Oxford University Press.

Laing, R.D. (1965) *The Divided Self*. Harmondsworth: Penguin.

Learmont, J. (1995) *Review of Prison Service Security in England and Wales and the Escape from Parkhurst Prison on Tuesday, 3rd January 1995*, Cm 3020. London: HMSO.

Lee, M., (1996) 'Proof Positive', *Druglink*, **11**, 3, 4.

Lee, M. and Mainwaring, S. (1995) 'No Big Deal: Court-Ordered Treatment in Practice', *Druglink*, **10**, 1, 14–15.

Leitner, M., Shapland, J. and Wiles, P. (1993) *Drug Usage and Drugs Prevention*. London: HMSO.

Lindqvist, P. and Allebeck, P. (1990) 'Schizophrenia and Crime: A Longitudinal Follow-up of 644 Schizophrenics in Stockholm', *British Journal of Psychiatry*, **157**, 345–350.

Lindqvist, P. and Allebeck, P. (1999) 'Research Note: Criminality among Stockholm Mental Patients', *British Journal of Criminology*, **39**, 3, 450–451.

Lipsey, M.W. (1992) 'The Effect of Treatment on Juvenile Delinquents: Results from Meta-Analysis', in Lösel, F., Bender, D. and Bliesner, T. (eds.), *Psychology and Law: International Perspectives*. Berlin: Walter de Gruyter.

Lipton, D.S. (1995), *The Effectiveness of Treatment for Drug Abusers under Criminal Justice Supervision*, National Institute of Justice, Research Report. Washington D.C.: US Department of Justice.

Lipton, D.S. (1996) 'Prison-Based Therapeutic Communities: Their Success with Drug Abusing Offenders', *National Institute of Justice Journal*, 12–20, February. Washington D.C.: US Department of Justice.

Lloyd, C., Mair, G. and Hough, M. (1994) *Explaining Reconviction Rates: A Critical Analysis*, Home Office Research Study No. 136. London: HMSO.

Lombroso, C. and Ferrero, W. (1895) *The Female Offender*. London: T. Fisher Unwin.

Lösel, F. (1993) 'The effectiveness of treatment in institutional and community settings', *Criminal Behaviour and Mental Health*, **3**, 416–437.

Mackay, R.D. and Machin, D. (1998) *Transfers from Prison to Hospital – the Operation of Section 48 of the Mental Health Act 1983*. London: Home Office.

Maguire, M., Morgan, R. and Reiner, R. (1994) *The Oxford Handbook of Criminology*. Oxford: Clarendon Press.

Maguire, M., Morgan, R. and Reiner, R. (1997) *The Oxford Handbook of Criminology, Second Edition*. Oxford: Clarendon Press.

Maguire, M., Raynor, P., Vanstone, M. and Kynch, J. (1998) *Voluntary After-Care*, Research Findings No. 73, Home Office Research and Statistics Directorate. London: Home Office.

Mair, G. (ed.) (1997a) *Evaluating the Effectiveness of Community Penalties*. Aldershot: Avebury.

Mair, G. (1997b) 'Community Penalties and the Probation Service' in Maguire, M., Morgan, R. and Reiner, R. (eds) *The Oxford Handbook of Criminology, Second Edition*. Oxford: Clarendon Press.

Mair, G. and Copas, J. (1996) 'Nothing Works and What Works – Meta-Analysis?'. Unpublished paper received from first author, School of Law, Social Work and Social Policy, Liverpool, John Moores University.

Mair, G. and May, T. (1997) *Offenders on Probation*, Home Office Research Study No. 167. London: Home Office.

Mair, G., Lloyd, C. and Hough, M. (1997) 'The Limitations of Reconviction Rates', in Mair, G. (ed.), *Evaluating the Effectiveness of Community Penalties*. Aldershot: Avebury.

Mannheim, H. and Wilkins, L.T. (1955) *Prediction Methods in Relation to Borstal Training*, Studies in the Causes of Delinquency and the Treatment of Offenders No. 1. London: HMSO.

Marks, J. (1995) 'Who Killed the British System?', *Druglink*, **10**, 4, 15.

Marris, P. and Rein, M. (1974) *Dilemmas of Social Reform*. London: Pelican.

Marshall, P. (1994) 'Reconviction of Imprisoned Sexual Offenders', *Research Bulletin*, No. 36, Home Office Research and Statistics Department. London: Home Office.

Marshall, P. (1997a) *The Prevalence of Convictions for Sexual Offending*, Research Findings No. 55, Home Office Research and Statistics Directorate. London: Home Office.

Marshall, P. (1997b) *A Reconviction Study of HMP Grendon Therapeutic Community*, Research Findings No. 53, Home Office Research and Statistics Directorate. London: Home Office.

Marshall, T. and Merry, S. (1990) *Crime and Accountability: Victim Offender Mediation in Practice*. London: Home Office.

Marshall, W.L. and Barbaree, H. E. (1990) 'An Integrated Theory of the Etiology of Sexual Offending', in Marshall, W., Laws, D. and Barbaree, H., *Handbook of Sexual Assault*. London: Plenum Press.

Marshall, W. L. and Pithers, W. D. (1994) 'A Reconsideration of Treatment Outcome with Sex Offenders', *Criminal Justice and Behaviour*, **21**, 1, 10–27.

Martin, C. (1996) 'Coming Clean: Drugs Research in a Prison Setting', *Criminal Justice Matters*, No. 24, 22–23. London: Institute for the Study and Treatment of Delinquency.

Martinson, R. (1974) 'What Works? Questions and Answers about Prison Reform,' *The Public Interest*, **35**, 22–54.

Martinson, R. (1979) 'New Findings, New Views: A Note of Caution regarding Sentencing Reform', *Hofstra Law Review*, **7**, 2, 243–258.

Matza, D. (1969) *Becoming Deviant*. Englewood Cliffs, NJ: Prentice-Hall.

May Committee (1979) *Report of the Committee of Inquiry into the United Kingdom Prison Services*, Cmnd 7673. London: HMSO.

May, C. (1999) *Explaining Reconviction following a Community Sentence: the Role of Social Factors*, Home Office Research Study 192. London: Home Office.

May, T. (1994) 'Probation and Community Sanctions', in Maguire, M., Morgan, R. and Reiner, R. (eds.), *The Oxford Handbook of Criminology*. Oxford: Clarendon Press.

McConville, S. (1998) 'An Historic Folly?', *Criminal Justice Matters*, No. 30, 4–5. London: Institute for the Study and Treatment of Delinquency.

McFarlane, M.A. and Thomson, A. (1998) 'Asking Around: Changing a Service from the Inside – on the Inside', *Druglink*, **13**, 2, 18–20.

McGuire, J. (1991) 'Things To Do To Make Your Programme Work', Proceedings of the *What Works* Conference. Greater Manchester and Hereford and Worcester Probation Services, 18–19 April 1991.

McGuire, J. (ed) (1995) *What Works: Reducing Reoffending – Guidelines from Research and Practice*. Chichester: John Wiley & Sons.

McGuire, J. and Priestley, P. (1995) 'Reviewing "What Works": Past, Present and Future', in McGuire, J. (ed), *What Works: Reducing Reoffending – Guidelines from Research and Practice*. Chichester: John Wiley & Sons.

McGurk, B.J., Thornton, D.M. and Williams, M. (1987) *Applying Psychology to Imprisonment*, London: HMSO.

McIvor, G. (1990) *Sanctions for Serious or Persistent Offenders: A Review of the Literature*. University of Stirling, Social Work Research Centre.

McIvor, G. (1991) 'Social Work Intervention in Community Service', *British Journal of Social Work*. **21**, 591–609.

McWilliams, W. (1983) 'The Mission to the English Police Courts, 1876-1936', *The Howard Journal*, **22**, 129–147.

McWilliams, W. (1985) 'The Mission Transformed: Professionalism of Probation between the Wars', *The Howard Journal*, **24**, 4, 257–274.

McWilliams, W. (1986) 'The English Probation System and the Diagnostic Ideal', *The Howard Journal*, **25**, 4, 241–260.

McWilliams, W. (1987) 'Probation, Pragmatism and Policy', *The Howard Journal*, **26**, 2, 97–121.

Melossi, D. and Pavarini, M. (1981) *The Prison and the Factory: Origins of the Penitentiary System*. London: Macmillan.

Mental Health Act Commission (1991) *Fourth Biennial Report, 1989–91*. London: HMSO.

Mental Health Foundation (1990) *Mental Illness: The Fundamental Facts*. London: Mental Health Foundation.

Miller, P. and Plant, M. (1996) 'Drinking, Smoking and Illicit Drug Use among 15 and 16 year olds in the United Kingdom', *British Medical Journal*, **313**, 394–397.

Morgan, R. (1994) 'Imprisonment', in Maguire, M., Morgan, R. and Reiner, R. (eds), *The Oxford Handbook of Criminology*. Oxford: Clarendon Press.

Morgan, R. (1997) 'Imprisonment: Current Concerns and a Brief History since 1945', in Maguire, M., Morgan, R. and Reiner, R. (eds.), *The Oxford Handbook of Criminology, Second Edition*. Oxford: Clarendon Press.

MORI (1998) *Re-Branding the Probation Service*, Research Study Conducted for Association of Chief Officers of Probation. London: Association of Chief Officers of Probation.

Morris, P. and Beverley, F. (1975) *On Licence: A Study of Parole*. Chichester: John Wiley and Sons.

Mott, J. (1989) 'Reducing Heroin-related Crime', *Research Bulletin*, No. 26, 30–33. London: Home Office Research and Planning Unit.

Moxon, D. (1988) *Sentencing Practice in the Crown Court*, Home Office Research Study No. 103. London: HMSO.

Moxon, D. (1998) 'The Role of Sentencing Policy', in Nuttall, C., Goldblatt, P. and Lewis, C. (eds), *Reducing Offending: an Assessment of Research Evidence on Ways of Dealing with Offending Behaviour*, Home Office Research Study No. 187. London: Home Office.

NACRO (1977) *Homelessness and Offending*. London: NACRO.

NACRO (1989) *The Real Alternative: Strategies to Promote Community Based Penalties*. London: NACRO.

NACRO (1996) *Criminal Justice Digest*, No. 88. London: NACRO.

NACRO (1998) *Going Straight Home?* London: NACRO.

NACRO (1999) *Going Straight to Work*. London: NACRO.

National Local Authority Forum on Drug Misuse (1988) *Slaying the Dragon: The Role of Local Authorities in Tackling Drug Misuse*, London: Association of Metropolitan Authorities.

National Victim Center (1996) 'Community Notification of the Release of Sex Offenders', at Web site http://www.nvc.org/hdir/community.htm.

Nee, C. and Sibbitt, R., (1993) *The Probation Response to Drug Misuse*, Home Office Research and Planning Unit Paper No. 78. London: Home Office.

Newburn, T. (1995) *Crime and Criminal Justice Policy*. London and New York: Longman.

Newburn, T. (1997) 'Youth, Crime and Justice', in Maguire, M., Morgan, R. and Reiner, R. (eds.), *The Oxford Handbook of Criminology, 2nd Edition*. Oxford: Clarendon Press.

Newburn, T. (1999) 'Drug Prevention and Youth Justice: Issues of Philosophy, Practice and Policy', *British Journal of Criminology*, **39**, 4, 609–624.

Newburn, T. and Elliott, J. (1999) *Risks and Responses: Drug Prevention and Youth Justice*, Drug Prevention Advisory Service Paper No. 3. London: Home Office.

Newburn, T. and Shiner, M. (1997) 'E for Error: Wrong Tune, Wrong Label', *Guardian*, 20 August.

Newcombe, R. (1996) 'Live and Let Die: Is Methadone More Likely to Kill You Than Heroin?' *Druglink*, **11**, 1, 9–12.

Newman, O. (1973) *Defensible Space: People and Design in the Violent City*. London: Architectural Press.

Newton, M. (1971) 'Reconviction after Treatment at Grendon', *Chief Psychologist's Report, Series B*, No. 1. London: Office of the Chief Psychologist, Prison Department, Home Office.

Nichols, G. and Taylor, P. (1996) *West Yorkshire Sports Counselling: Final Evaluation Report*. Sheffield: University of Sheffield Leisure Management Unit.

Nuttall, C., Goldblatt, P. and Lewis, C. (1998) *Reducing Offending: an Assessment of Research Evidence on Ways of Dealing with Offending Behaviour*, Research Study No. 187, Home Office Research and Statistics Directorate. London: Home Office.

Palmer, C. and Hart, M. (1996) *A PACE in the Right Direction?* Sheffield: University of Sheffield Institute for the Study of the Legal Profession.

Palmer, J. W. (1977) *Constitutional Rights of Prisoners, Second Edition*. Cincinnati: Anderson.

Palmer, T. (1975) 'Martinson Revisited', *Journal of Research in Crime and Delinquency*, **12**, 133–152.

Pantazis, C. and Gordon, D. (1997) 'Television Licence Evasion and the Criminalisation of Female Poverty', *The Howard Journal*, **36**, 2, 170–186.

Parker, H., (1995) *Drugs Futures: Changing Patterns of Drug Use Amongst English Youth*, ISDD Research Monograph No. 7. London: ISDD.

Parker, H., Aldridge, J. and Measham, F. (1998) *Illegal Leisure: The Normalisation of Adolescent Recreational Drug Use*. London: Routledge.

Parker, J., Pool, Y., Rawle, R. and Gay, M. (1988) 'Monitoring Problem Drug-Use in Bristol', *British Journal of Psychiatry*, **152**, 214–221.

Paterson, A. (1951) *Patterson on Prisons*. London: Frederick Muller Ltd.

Patten, J. (1991) 'Making the Punishment Fit the Frame', *Guardian*, 20 February.

Pawson, R. and Tilley, N. (1994) 'What Works in Evaluation Research?' *British Journal of Criminology*, **34**, 3, 291–306.

Pawson, R. and Tilley, N. (1996) 'What's Crucial in Evaluation Research: A Reply to Bennett', *British Journal of Criminology*, **36**, 4, 574–578.

Pawson, R. and Tilley, N. (1997) *Realistic Evaluation*. London: Sage.

Pawson, R. and Tilley, N. (1998a) 'Caring Communities, Paradigm Polemics, Design Debates', *Evaluation*, **4**, 1, 73–90.

Pawson, R. and Tilley, N. (1998b) 'Cook-Book Methods and Disastrous Recipes: A Rejoinder to Farrington', *Evaluation*, **4**, 2, 211–213.

Pearson, B. (1990) 'How Normal is Normal?' *Druglink*, **5**, 2, 8–9.

Pearson, G. (1987) *The New Heroin Users*. Oxford: Blackwell.

Pearson, G. (1991) 'Drug Control Policies in Britain', in Tonry, M. and Morris, N. (eds), *Crime and Justice: A Review of Research*, **14**, 167–227. Chicago: University of Chicago Press.

Pearson, R. (1976) 'Women Defendants in Magistrates' Courts', *British Journal of Law and Society*, **3**, 265–273.

Pease, K. and Wolfson, J. (1979) 'Incapacitation Studies: A Review and Commentary', *The Howard Journal*, **18**, 160–167.

Pease, K., Billingham, S. and Earnshaw, I. (1977) *Community Service Assessed in 1976*, Home Office Research Study No. 39. London: HMSO.

Peay, J. (1997) 'Mentally Disordered Offenders', in Maguire, M., Morgan, R. and Reiner, R. (eds), *The Oxford Handbook of Criminology. Second Edition*. Oxford: Clarendon Press.

Penal Affairs Consortium (1996) *Drugs on the Inside*. London: Penal Affairs Consortium.

Penal Affairs Consortium (1998) *An Unsuitable Place for Treatment: Diverting Mentally Disordered Offenders from Custody*. London: Penal Affairs Consortium.

Penal Affairs Consortium (1999) *The Prison System: Regime and Population Trends*. London: Penal Affairs Consortium.

Perkins, D.E. (1987) 'A Psychological Treatment Programme for Sex Offenders', in McGurk, B.J., Thornton, D.M. and Williams, M. (eds), *Applying Psychology to Imprisonment*. London: HMSO.

Phillpotts, G.J.O. and Lancucki, L.B. (1979) *Previous Convictions, Sentence and Reconviction*, Home Office Research Study No. 53. London: HMSO.

Pitts, J. (1992) 'The end of an era', *Howard Journal of Criminal Justice*, **31**, 133–149.

Plant, M. and Miller, P. (2000) 'Drug Use Has Declined among Teenagers in United Kingdom', *British Medical Journal*, **320**, 1536–1537.

Player, E. and Martin, C.A. (1996) *Preliminary Evaluation of the ADT Drug Treatment Programme at HMP Downview*, Research Findings No. 31, Home Office Research and Statistics Department. London: Home Office.

Popper, K.R. (1968) *The Logic of Scientific Discovery*. London: Hutchinson.

Power, H. (1999) 'The Crime and Disorder Act 1998: (1) Sex Offenders, Privacy and the Police', *Criminal Law Review*, 3–16.

Prentky, R. (1995) 'A Rationale for the Treatment of Sex Offenders: *Pro Bono Publico*', in McGuire, J. (ed.), *What Works: Reducing Reoffending: Guidelines from Research and Practice*. Chichester: John Wiley & Sons

Prins, H. (1993) 'Offender-Patients: The People Nobody Owns', in Watson, W. and Grounds, A. (eds.), *The Mentally Disordered Offender in an Era of Community Care*. Cambridge: Cambridge University Press.

Prins, H. (1995) *Offenders, Deviants or Patients? Second Edition*. London and New York: Routledge.

Ramsay, M. and Partridge, S. (1999) *Drug Misuse Declared in 1998: Results from the British Crime Survey*, Home Office Research Study No. 197. London: Home Office.

Ramsay, M. and Percy, A. (1996a) *Drug Misuse Declared: Results of the 1994 British Crime Survey*, Home Office Research Study No. 151. London: Home Office.

Ramsay, M. and Percy, A. (1996b) *Drug Misuse Declared: Results of the 1994 British Crime Survey*, Research Findings No. 33. London: Home Office.

Ramsay, M. and Spiller, J. (1997a) *Drug Misuse Declared in 1996: Latest Results from the British Crime Survey*, Home Office Research Study No. 172. London: Home Office.

Ramsay, M. and Spiller, J. (1997b) *Drug Misuse Declared in 1996: Key Results from the British Crime Survey*, Research Findings No. 56. London: Home Office.

Ramsay, M., Partridge, S. and Byron, C. (1999) *Drug Misuse Declared in 1998: Key Results from the British Crime Survey*, Research Findings No. 93. London: Home Office.

Randall, G. (1989) *Homeless and Hungry – a Sign of the Times*. London: Shelter.

Raynor, P. and Honess, T. (1998) *Drug and Alcohol Related Offenders Project: an Evaluation of the West Glamorgan Partnership*, Home Office Drugs Prevention Initiative Paper No. 14. London: Home Office.

Raynor, P. and Vanstone, M. (1994) *Straight Thinking on Probation: Third Interim Report*. Bridgend: Mid-Glamorgan Probation Service.

Reed, J. (1992) *Review of Health and Social Services for Mentally Disordered Offenders and Others Requiring Similar Services: Final Summary Report*, Department of Health and Home Office, Cm 2088. London: HMSO.

Reed, J. and Lyne, M. (2000) 'Inpatient Care of Mentally Ill People in Prison: Results of a Year's Programme of Semistructured Inspections', *British Medical Journal*, **320**, 1031–1034.

Richardson, C. (1997) 'Treating Sex Offenders in a Custodial Setting', *Criminal Justice Matters*, No. 28, London: ISTD.

Richardson, G. (1993) *Law, Process and Custody: Prisoners and Patients*. London: Weidenfeld and Nicolson.

Riley, D. (1995) 'Drug Testing in Prisons', *International Journal of Drug Policy*, 6, 2, 106–111.

Robertson, G., Pearson, R. and Gibb, R. (1993) *Entry of Mentally Disordered People to the Criminal Justice System* (Interim report to the Home Office Research and Planning Unit, unpublished).

Robertson, G., Pearson, R. and Gibb, R. (1995) *The Mentally Disordered and the Police*, Research Findings No. 21, Home Office Research and Statistics Department, London: Home Office.

Rock, P. (1996) *Reconstructing a Women's Prison: The Holloway Redevelopment Project, 1968–88*. Oxford: Clarendon Press.

Rock, P. (1988) *A History of British Criminology*. Oxford: Clarendon Press.

Rogers, A. and Faulkner, A. (1987) *A Place of Safety*. London: MIND.

Rosenthal, R. (1991) *Meta-Analytic Procedures for Social Research*. London: Sage.

Ross, R.R. (1991) 'Reasoning and Rehabilitation of Offenders', Proceedings of the *What Works* Conference. Greater Manchester and Hereford and Worcester Probation Services, 18–19, April 1991.

Ross, R.R. and Fabiano, E.A. (1985) *Time to Think: A Cognitive Model of Delinquency Prevention and Offender Rehabilitation*, Johnson City, TN: Institute of Social Sciences and Arts.

Rotman, E. (1986) 'Do Criminal Offenders Have a Constitutional Right to Rehabilitation?', *Journal of Criminal Law and Criminology*, 77, 4, 1023–1068.

Royal College of Psychiatrists (1996), *Report of the Confidential Inquiry into Homicides and Suicides by Mentally Ill People*. London: Royal College of Psychiatrists.

Russell, B. (1925) 'Moral Rules', in *What I Believe*. London: Kegan Paul, Trubner & Co. Chapter 3, pp. 60–62.

Rutherford, A. (1992) *Growing out of Crime: The New Era*. Winchester: Waterside Press.

Rutherford, A. (1998) 'Criminal Policy and the Eliminative Ideal', in Finer, C. J. and Nellis, M. (eds.), *Crime and Social Exclusion*. Oxford: Blackwell.

Rutter, M. and Madge, N. (1976) *Cycles of Disadvantage*. London: Heinemann.

Rutter, M., Giller, H. and Hagell, A. (1998) *Antisocial Behaviour by Young People*. Cambridge: Cambridge University Press.

Sampson, A. (1994a) 'The Future for Sex Offenders in Prison', in Player, E. and Jenkins, M. (eds), *Prisons after Woolf: Reform through Riot*. London: Routledge. Chapter 11.

Sampson, A. (1994b) *Acts of Abuse: Sex Offenders and the Criminal Justice System*. London: Routledge.

Sarno, C., Hough, M., Nee, C. and Herrington, V. (1999) *Probation Employment Schemes in Inner London and Surrey – An Evaluation*, Research Findings No. 89, Home Office Research, Development and Statistics Directorate. London: Home Office.

Shapiro, H. (1998) 'From Clinic to Community: The Changing Face of Treatment', *Druglink*, 13, 6, 8–11.

Shapland, J. (1991) 'Where Do We Put Them? Coping with Mentally Disordered Offenders'. Paper presented to the British Criminology Conference, York. 24–27 July, 1991.

Shapland, J., Hibbert, J., I'Anson, J., Sorsby, A. and Wild, R. (1995) *Milton Keynes: Criminal Justice Audit*. Sheffield: University of Sheffield Institute for the Study of the Legal Profession.

Shapland, J., Willmore, J. and Duff, P. (1985) *Victims in the Criminal Justice System*, Cambridge Studies in Criminology, 53. Aldershot: Gower.

Shaw, S. (1980) *Paying the Penalty: An Analysis of the Cost of Penal Sanctions*. London: NACRO.

Sheldon, B. (1995) *Cognitive Behavioural Therapy: Research, Practice and Philosophy*. London and New York: Routledge.

Sherman, L.W., Gottfredson, D.C., MacKenzie, D.L., Eck, J., Reuter, P. and Bushway, S.D. (1998) *Preventing Crime: What Works, What Doesn't, What's Promising*, Research in Brief, National Institute of Justice. Washington: US Department of Justice.

Shinnar, S. and Shinnar, R. (1975) 'The Effects of the Criminal Justice System on the Control of Crime: a Quantitative Approach', *Law and Society Review*, 9, 581–611.

Silberman, M. and Chapman, B. (1971) 'After-Care Units in London, Liverpool and Manchester', in *Explorations in After-Care*, Home Office Research Unit Study No. 9. London: HMSO.

Simon, F. (1999) *Prisoners' Work and Vocational Training*. London and New York: Routledge.

Social Exclusion Unit (1998a) *Truancy and School Exclusion – Report by the Social Exclusion Unit*. London: Social Exclusion Unit.

Social Exclusion Unit (1998b) *Rough Sleeping – Report by the Social Exclusion Unit*, Cm 4008. London: Social Exclusion Unit.

Social Exclusion Unit (1998c) *Bringing Britain Together: A National Strategy for Neighbourhood Renewal*, Cm 4045. London: Social Exclusion Unit.

South, N. (1994) 'Drugs: Control, Crime and Criminological Studies', in Maguire, M., Morgan, R. and Reiner, R. (eds.), *The Oxford Handbook of Criminology*. Oxford: Clarendon Press.

South, N. (1997) 'Drugs: Use, Crime and Control', in Maguire, M., Morgan, R. and Reiner, R. (eds.), *The Oxford Handbook of Criminology, Second Edition*, Oxford: Clarendon Press.

Spencer, A.P. (1999) *Working with Sex Offenders in Prisons and through Release to the Community*. London and Philadelphia: Jessica Kingsley.

Staite, C., Martin, N., Bingham, M. and Daly, R. (1994) *Diversion from Custody for Mentally Disordered Offenders: a Practical Guide*. Aldershot: Arena.

Stanley, S. and Baginsky, M. (1984) *Alternatives to Prison: An Examination of Non-Custodial Sentencing of Offenders*. London: Peter Owen.

Steadman, H.J. and Cocozza, J.J. (1974) *Careers of the Criminally Insane: Excessive Social Control of Deviance*. Lexington: D.C. Heath.

Steadman, H.J., Monahan, J., Duffee, B., Hartstone, E. and Robbins, P.C. (1984) 'The Impact of State Hospital De-Institutionalization on United States Prison Populations, 1968-78', *Journal of Criminal Law and Criminology*, **75**, 474–490.

Stewart, G. (1996) 'Housing', in Drakeford, M. and Vanstone, M. (eds.), *Beyond Offending Behaviour*. Aldershot: Arena.

Stewart, G. and Stewart, J. (1993) *Social Circumstances of Younger Offenders under Probation Supervision*. London: Association of Chief Officers of Probation.

Stimson, G. (1989) 'AIDS and HIV: The Challenge for British Drug Services'. The Fourth James Oakey Memorial Lecture, Institute of Psychiatry, 25 May. Reprinted in Stimson, G. and Strang, J. (1990), *AIDS and Drug Misuse*. London: Routledge.

Strang, J., Heuston, J., Gossop, M., Green, J. and Maden, T. (1998) *HIV/AIDS Risk Behaviour among Adult Male Prisoners*, Research Findings No. 82, Home Office Research, Development and Statistics Directorate. London: Home Office.

Sugg, D. (1998) *Motor Projects in England and Wales*, Research Findings No. 81, Home Office Research, Development and Statistics Directorate. London: Home Office.

Sutherland, E.H. (1947) *Principles of Criminology, 4th Edition*. Philadelphia, PA: Lippincott.

Tarling, R. (1979) 'The "Incapacitation" Effects of Imprisonment', *Home Office Research Bulletin*, No. 7, 6–8.

Tarling, R. (1993) *Analysing Offending: Data, Models and Interpretations*. London: HMSO.

Taylor, I., Walton, P. and Young, J. (1973) *The New Criminology: For a Social Theory of Deviance*. London: Routledge & Kegan Paul.

Taylor, I., Walton, P. and Young, J. (1975) *Critical Criminology*. London: Routledge & Kegan Paul.

Taylor, P.J. and Gunn, J. (1999) 'Homicides by People with Mental Illness: Myth and Reality', *British Journal of Psychiatry*, **174**, 9–14.

Thomas, T. (1999) 'Drug Testing and Treatment Orders', *New Law Journal*, **149**, 6895, 1015–1016.

Thomas, T. (2000) *Sex Crime: Sex Offending and Society*. Cullompton, Devon: Willan Publishing.

Thornton, D. (1987) 'Treatment Effects on Recidivism: a Reappraisal of the "Nothing Works" Doctrine', in McGurk, B. J., Thornton, D. M. and Williams, M., *Applying Psychology to Imprisonment*. London: HMSO.

Tidmarsh, D., Wood, S. and Wing, J.K. (1972) *Camberwell Reception Centre: Summary of the Research Finding and Recommendations*. London: Institute of Psychiatry.

Tilley, N. (1993) 'Crime Prevention and the Safer Cities Story', *The Howard Journal*, **32**, 1, 40–57.

Tilt, R. (1997) 'Prison Service Drugs Strategy', *Criminal Justice Consultative Council Newsletter*, Issue 7, 1–3, Criminal Justice Consultative Council.

Turnbull, P.J. (1999) *Drug Treatment and Testing Orders – Interim Evaluation*. Research Findings No. 106, Research, Development and Statistics Directorate. London: Home Office.

Turnbull, P.J., Dolan, G.V. and Stimpson, G.V. (1991) *Prisons, HIV and AIDS: Risks and Experiences in Custodial Care*. London: AVERT.

Utting, D. (1996) *Reducing Criminality among Young People: a Sample of Relevant Programmes in the United Kingdom*. Home Office Research Study No. 161. London: Home Office.

Van Dine, S., Dinitz, S. and Conrad, J.P. (1977) 'The Incapacitation of the Dangerous Offender: a Statistical Experiment', *Journal of Research in Crime and Delinquency*, **14**, 1, 22–34.

Vennard, J. and Hedderman, C. (1998) 'Effective Interventions with Offenders', in Nuttall, C., Goldblatt, P. and Lewis, C. (eds), *Reducing Offending: An Assessment of Research Evidence on Ways of Dealing with Offending Behaviour*, Home Office Research Study No. 187. London: Home Office.

Vennard, J., Hedderman, C. and Sugg, D. (1997) *Changing Offenders' Attitudes and Behaviour: What Works?*, Home Office Research Study No. 171, Home Office Research and Statistics Directorate. London: Home Office.

von Hirsch, A. (1976), *Doing Justice: the Choice of Punishments*, Report of the Committee for the Study of Incarceration. New York: Hill and Wang.

Walker, C. and Wall, D. (1997) 'Imprisoning the Poor: Television Licence Evaders and the Criminal Justice System', *Criminal Law Review*, 173–186.

Walker, M.A. (1994) 'Are Men Discriminated Against in the Criminal Justice System?', *Radical Statistics*, 57, 43–50.

Walker, N. (1987) *Crime and Criminology: A Critical Introduction*. Oxford: Oxford University Press.

Walmsley, R., Howard, L. and White, S. (1992) *The National Prison Survey 1991: Main Findings*. Home Office Research Study No. 128. London: HMSO.

Watkins, B. and Bentovim, A. (1992) 'The Sexual Abuse of Male Children and Adolescents: a Review of Current Research', *Journal of Child Psychology and Psychiatry*, **33**, 197–248.

Watson, L. (1996) *Victims of Violent Crime Recorded by the Police, England and Wales, 1990–94*, Home Office Statistical Findings, 1/96. London: Home Office.

West, D.J. (1996) 'Sexual Molesters', in Walker, N. (ed.), *Dangerous People*. London: Blackstone Press.

West, D.J. and Farrington, D.P. (1977) *The Delinquent Way of Life*. London: Heinemann.

Whitehead, J.T. and Lab, S.P. (1989) 'A Meta-Analysis of Juvenile Correctional Treatment', *Journal of Research in Crime and Delinquency*, **26**, 3, 276–295.

Whitfield, D. (1998) *Introduction to the Probation Service, Second Edition*. Winchester: Waterside Press.

Windlesham, D. (1993) *Responses to Crime, Volume 2: Penal Policy in the Making*. Oxford: Clarendon Press.

Wolf, F.M. (1986) *Meta-Analysis: Quantitative Methods for Research Synthesis*. London: Sage Publications.

Woodcock, J. (1994) *The Escape from Whitemoor Prison on Friday 9th September 1994 (The Woodcock Enquiry)*, Cm 2741. London: HMSO.

Woolf, Lord Justice and Tumim, S. (1991) *Prison Disturbances April 1990: Report of an Inquiry by the Rt Hon. Lord Justice Woolf (Parts I and II) and His Honour Judge Stephen Tumim (Part III)*, Cm 1456. London: HMSO.

Worral, A. (1997) *Punishment in the Community: The Future of Criminal Justice*. London and New York: Longman.

Zimring, F.E. and Hawkins, G. (1995) *Incapacitation: Penal Confinement and the Restraint of Crime*. Oxford: Oxford University Press.

Zito Trust (1997) *Community Care Homicides since 1990*. London: The Zito Trust.

Zito Trust (1998) *Medication, Non-Compliance and Mentally Disordered Offenders: The Role of Non-Compliance in Homicide by People with Mental Illness and Proposals for Future Policy*. London: The Zito Trust.

INDEX

CPSIA information can be obtained
at www.ICGtesting.com
Printed in the USA
JSHW042132120221
11841JS00003B/17